BETWEEN PHILOSOPHY AND HISTORY

BETWEEN PHILOSOPHY AND HISTORY

The Resurrection of
Speculative Philosophy of
History Within the
Analytic Tradition

BY HASKELL FAIN

PRINCETON UNIVERSITY PRESS
PRINCETON, NEW JERSEY
1970

Copyright © 1970 by Princeton University Press

ALL RIGHTS RESERVED

L.C. Card: 70-90946

ISBN: 0-691-07158-6

Chapter XV, "History as Science," appeared in
History and Theory, vol. IX, no. 2 (May 1970).

This book has been composed in Linotype Granjon

Printed in the United States of America by

Princeton University Press, Princeton, New Jersey

For Carl Bögholt, Philosopher

Se moquer de la philosophie,
c'est vraiment philosopher.

PASCAL, *Pensées*

Preface

History has been either unfairly treated or ignored by most philosophers in the Anglo-American tradition. This book grew out of an attempt, in some lectures delivered at Oxford during Hilary term in 1967, to see where the trouble lay. I did not begin with profound anxieties about the lack of contact between philosophy and history. Nor did I share Collingwood's conviction that "the chief business of twentieth-century philosophy is to reckon with twentieth-century history." It was rather that, having taught for many years a course on the philosophy of history, I had become increasingly annoyed at my inability to reconcile the innocent pleasures of reading history with the all too bleak and professional prospects presented by topics of current interest in Anglo-American analytical philosophy of history. Then, too, there were the secret delights of reading speculative philosophers of history, delights shared by most of my students. Yet everything in recent Anglo-American philosophy sternly interdicted those pleasures. The standard course of lectures on the philosophy of history begins with the temptation of Hegel and ends with the redemption of Hempel. (Was it possible to write a book on philosophy of history without examining the covering law model of historical explanation? I almost succeeded until a failure of nerve weakened my resolve and induced me to add an epilogue.)

Philosophy of history, even on its analytical side, can consist of something more than leftovers from philosophy of science. I tried in this book to transplant the heart of speculative philosophy of history into an analytical body. This radical operation necessitated a lengthy preamble. The chief obstacle to gaining a proper appreciation of speculative philosophy of history, so far as the analytical tradition is concerned, is the common prejudice that professional philosophers have no business getting involved with history—that historical interpretation is what historians do, as philosophical analysis is what philosophers do. But what, then, do historians of philosophy do? Even the coolest of analytical philosophers have, on occasion, been perplexed by this question. A careful consideration of it, in fact, provides for philosophers an excellent point of departure into the speculative no-man's land; Hegel fashioned his speculative philosophy of history, in part, with an eye toward providing a suitable framework for constructing an adequate history of philosophy.

The first eleven chapters explore various points of contact between history and philosophy and prepare the ground for acceptance of the proposition that there is nothing amiss in philosophers becoming involved with history. In writing those chapters, I had to navigate between Crocean whirlpools and the rocks of Ayer. The remaining chapters deal directly with the problem of justifying speculative philosophy of history as a genre. Readers impatient to discover how I propose to honor the promise contained in the subtitle—to resurrect speculative philosophy of history within the analytic tradition—may begin with Chapter XII and work their way backward and forward until the book becomes intelligible. That, in fact, is the procedure I followed in writing it.

It is impossible to list all the friends, colleagues, and students who, in one form or another, provided the criticism and encouragement necessary for the writing of this book. Some of them, I expect, would be astonished to discover that they had made any contribution, however remote, to the philosophy of history. I wish, in particular, to thank H. R. Harré and T. Waldman for their patient readings of earlier versions of portions of the manuscript. I also must express my appreciation to J. R. Weinberg, J. Tussman, P. Ziff, W. Kaufmann, I. Soll, J. Temkin, T. Kearns, I. Brawer, P. Brown, J. Cheney, and T. Reynolds.

My greatest debt I owe to my otherwise gentle wife, whose

keen editorial eye and passion for clarity savaged those infelicities of expression which abounded in earlier drafts. I should further like to acknowledge my gratitude to the University of Wisconsin Research Committee, which provided financial support for one semester and two summers.

Contents

xi

BETWEEN PHILOSOPHY AND HISTORY

CHAPTER I

Introduction: Some Anglo-Saxon Philosophical Attitudes

THIS IS A BOOK about philosophy written for historians as well as philosophers. Its particular focus is the philosophy of history. It is not a manual of the philosophy of history; the object is not to systematize or summarize those topics and issues that have most concerned professional philosophers. Professional philosophers tend to treat the philosophy of history as if it were a province of philosophy firmly under their control, whereas it is, in fact, border country. Those philosophers who write about the philosophy of history usually assume their audience to have an insider's knowledge of philosophy as well as the patience to examine adaptations of philosophical arguments, themselves somewhat threadbare from the use they have received elsewhere, to the subject matter of history. Certain conceptual difficulties allegedly facing the historian are exposed while philosophy itself somehow remains intact—this despite the fact that Anglo-American philosophy is just beginning to recover from a series of searching, yet simultaneously paralyzing, reexaminations by philosophers themselves.

In the last three or four decades, the two most influential schools of Anglo-American philosophy, logical positivism and the "ordinary language" movement, have given the discipline a different and tart flavor by bringing into question the value of philosophy itself. Not that this inquest has dampened philosophical reflection and analysis. Quite the contrary. Just as the spiritual withdrawal counseled by Stoic doctrine seemed to spur Roman Stoics to greater involvement in the practical affairs of the Empire, so nihilism in philosophy appears to breed more philosophizing. Philosophical nihilism, however, has affected decidedly the attitudes of contemporary philosophers toward their subject, and this change of perspective has naturally carried over into the philosophy of history, so much so that it is impossible for historians to assess recent philosophical discussions of history without some knowledge of the history of contemporary philosophy. True, the messianic impulse which fathered each of the two schools—the programmatic zeal to undertake a total revision of traditional philosophical practices—has largely dissipated. An Anglo-American philosopher today can call himself a metaphysician and almost keep a straight face. Nonetheless, even the new Anglo-American attitudes carry echoes of philosophical *Hassliebe*. The basis for the love-hate relationship between philosophers and philosophy needs airing.

The credo of the logical positivist, as stated by A. J. Ayer in his *Language, Truth and Logic* (1936), was that "the philosopher is not in a position to furnish speculative truths, which would, as it were, compete with the hypotheses of science, nor yet to pass *a priori* judgements upon the validity of scientific theories. . . . [Rather,] his function is to clarify the propositions of science by exhibiting their logical relationships, and by defining the symbols which occur in them."[1] In abandoning traditional metaphysics, the positivists fell upon science as providing the only possible way through which real-

---

[1] *Language, Truth and Logic* (New York: Dover Publications, n.d.), pp. 31-32.

"In other words, the propositions of philosophy are not factual, but linguistic in character—that is, they do not describe the behavior of physical, or even mental, objects; they express definitions, or the formal consequences of definitions. Accordingly, we may say that philosophy is a department of logic. For we shall see that the characteristic mark of a purely logical enquiry is that it is concerned with the formal consequences of our definitions and not with questions of empirical fact." *Ibid.*, p. 57.

ity could be confronted and understood. Curiously, their idea of science seemed to rest upon an unquestioned use of the old Comtean hierarchy—physics before biology, biology before psychology, and so on—although they for the most part ignored Comte. The net effect of relying upon this taxonomy was that the concepts and modes of explanation and aims of the most "advanced" sciences tended to provide the models for inquiries of lesser rank. The logical positivists were timorous and respectful with regard to the "hard" or physical sciences; they became much more bold and assertive when "clarifying" the propositions of the "softer" sciences, often playing the role of a credentials committee. Had physics remained deterministic, the positivists would, no doubt, have been completely impatient with the statistical modes of explanation employed in the social sciences. Statistical accounts would have been regarded solely as temporary and theoretically replaceable substitutes for causal explanations. Even as it was, in essays presumably written for social scientists, the positivists put greater effort into explicating the nature of causal than into clarifying statistical explanation. History, insofar as it emerged into separate focus at all, was at best considered the softest of the soft sciences, blending imperceptibly into sociology. At that end of the scale the spirit of Comte reigned unchallenged. Any distinct characteristics deserving of serious notice, it sometimes seemed, stemmed from the circumstance that statements about the past are not subject to direct verification. Some positivists, in an effort to preserve the scientific status of history (which for them meant its intellectual respectability), went so far as to suggest that statements about the past are really disguised statements about documents and artifacts. Except for this minority view, history was held to be simply sociology *cum* documents, incapable of raising intellectual problems worthy of special attention.

The ordinary language school of philosophy, which grew out of and gradually eclipsed logical positivism, has also been tinged with skepticism toward philosophy. Skepticism toward philosophy, though, is quite the reverse of philosophical skepticism. Skepticism, provided it is of the right kind and is introduced on the proper occasion, is the animus of philosophy. A philosophical or skeptical question differs profoundly from an ordinary question. The point of a well-placed philosophical question, I want to argue, is to provoke reflection about concepts, concepts whose normal applications may be so familiar that they would escape notice entirely were it not for the skeptic's barbs. The official ordinary language attitude toward philosophical questions is quite different from this: an important tenet of the movement has been that the sting of some, many, or all philosophical questions (depending upon how radical an ordinary language philosopher one is) can be withdrawn by a refusal to depart from the ordinary employment of questions in practical deliberation and positive inquiry. "A philosophical question is not solved," wrote Friedrich Waismann in the mid-1950's, "it *dis*solves. And in what does the 'dissolving' consist? In making the meaning of the words used in putting the question so clear to ourselves that we are released from the spell it cast on us. . . . [It] therefore *was* a confusion about the use of language. . . . It is here that philosophy and grammar meet."[2]

The ordinary language philosopher views history in a far more cordial manner than did the positivist. Indeed, his inclination is to protect the autonomy of history by defending the historian's right to continue using his concepts and modes of explanation as he has traditionally employed them. Ludwig Wittgenstein's dictum that "ordinary language is in order as it is" has been transmuted into the general opinion that ordinary history is all right. When the philosopher (here read "logical positivist") attempts to apply the rules and standards of other disciplines to the writing of history, the historian who

[2] "How I See Philosophy," in *Logical Positivism*, ed. A. J. Ayer (Glencoe, Ill.: The Free Press, 1959), p. 354.

listens will develop "mental cramps," which is the ordinary language jargon for "having a philosophical problem." To the positivist claim that causal explanation in history must be the same as that found in the sciences—in particular, that causal explanation cannot be achieved without explicit mention of general laws—the ordinary language retort is that the positivist account creates *philosophical* difficulties for the historian. Although the historian is unable to come up with general laws of history, he often attempts to explain historical events causally. Hence, the historian faces a dilemma if the positivist analysis of causal explanation (as well as of science) is correct: either he must cease being a historian and become a scientist, or he must surrender his traditional right and vested interest in explaining historical events.

If historians took this dilemma seriously, the writing of history would undergo radical change. But why, one might ask, is this dilemma a philosophical one? Because, according to the ordinary language philosopher, it need never have arisen if philosophers, wrongheaded philosophers, had not attempted to arrive at a general formula for the use of the word "cause." "The man who is philosophically puzzled," said Wittgenstein in *The Blue Book*, "sees a law in the way a word is used, and, trying to apply this law consistently, comes up against cases where it leads to paradoxical results. . . . Philosophy, as we use the word, is a fight against the fascination which forms of expression exert upon us."[3]

[3] "The man who is philosophically puzzled sees a law in the way a word is used, and, trying to apply this law consistently, comes up against cases where it leads to paradoxical results. Very often the way the discussion of such a puzzle runs is this: First the question is asked 'What is time?' This question makes it appear that what we want is a definition. We mistakenly think that a definition is what will remove the trouble (as in certain states of indigestion we feel a kind of hunger which cannot be removed by eating). The question is then answered by a wrong definition; say: 'Time is the motion of the celestial bodies.' The next step is to see that this definition is unsatis-

The moral, as it is understood by some who were influenced by Wittgenstein, is that there is no single rule of language adequate to cover all the uses of the term "cause," though the positivist makes it appear as if there is. Careful examination of the diverse applications of the great variety of causal expressions found in ordinary language (plain English, to be precise), such as "impel," "influence," "occasion," "originate," "bring on," "produce," and so on, will reveal that there is not one concept of causation but a family of them and that some of the concepts can be applied successfully without a knowledge of general laws. By sticking to these, the historian can carry on, quite untroubled by philosophical *Angst*. How ironic that the positivist account of causal explanation, itself designed to eliminate metaphysical wool-gathering, should be attacked by the ordinary language philosopher in part on the ground that it raises, rather than settles, philosophical problems!

I have written this book in the hope of communicating an insider's perspective on contemporary Anglo-American philosophy. Before a historian can assess adequately what contemporary philosophers say about history, he must have some notion of what philosophers think about philosophy and philosophizing. It is frequently difficult to discern what a philosopher believes to be *philosophically* at stake when he writes about the study of history. Quite often a problem that

---

factory. But this only means that we don't use the word 'time' synonymously with 'motion of the celestial bodies.' However in saying that the first definition is wrong, we are now tempted to think that we must replace it by a different one, the correct one.

"Compare with this the case of the definition of number. Here the explanation that a number is the same thing as a numeral satisfies that first craving for a definition. And it is very difficult not to ask: 'Well, if it isn't the numeral, *what is* it?'

"Philosophy, as we use the word, is a fight against the fascination which forms of expression exert upon us." Ludwig Wittgenstein, *The Blue Book*, in *Philosophy in the 20th Century*, ed. William Barrett and Henry David Aiken (New York: Random House, 1962), i, 733.

perplexes the historian is used by the philosopher as an occasion to enter the lists against other philosophers. The particular battle may appear to be about the reliability of historical evidence, the nature of historical explanation, or the status of value judgments in history, but the real war is taking place off stage.

Despite recent gropings for an *entente cordiale* between philosophy and history, the interest of the ordinary language philosopher in history differs markedly from that traditionally shown by philosophers on the Continent. It is not unfair to characterize most Anglo-American philosophy from the eighteenth century on as profoundly ahistorical in temperament. There is little fascination with how things change in time or with the effect of broader historical change on moral, intellectual, or philosophical outlook. There are exceptions, of course. One is found in some recent work in the philosophy of science which exhibits a far deeper awareness of the history of science than hitherto. Nevertheless, few modern philosophers in England and America have contributed challenging historical perspectives, even in the history of philosophy. One easily gets the erroneous impression that the impetus for the history of philosophy comes solely from within, that it proceeds sealed off from the stormy winds of broader intellectual controversy. I believe a more apt conception is that philosophy moves in the calm centers of great historical hurricanes.

The divergence between history and philosophy in England and America is perhaps best personified by David Hume, a philosopher and a historian but not both at once. His principal ideas in philosophy did not stem from his concern with history; rather, when he turned to history, he had already completed his philosophical system. In his essay *Of the Study of History*, Hume eulogized history with the following words: "history is not only a valuable part of knowledge, but opens the door to many other parts, and affords materials to most of the sciences. . . . A man acquainted with history may, in some respect, be said to have lived from the beginning of the world, and to have been making continual additions to his stock of knowledge. . . ."[4] Here we find the historian given the role of quartermaster, stocking materials for the serious scientific campaigns of the future. The conception is familiar enough. More revealing is Hume's "addition theory of knowledge," if I may call it that—the view that changing theories and ideas result in an addition to, but not an alteration of, mankind's conception of what knowledge itself is. Knowledge, like Human Nature, is judged everywhere the same, though methods for arriving at it change.

Only two major English-speaking philosophers, in recent times, produced philosophies imbued, albeit in different ways, with a sense for history: John Dewey and R. G. Collingwood. Although the fact is not often noticed, much of Dewey's philosophical insight had its source in certain speculations about history. Consider, for example, his thesis concerning the divorce between practical and theoretical inquiry in ancient Greece, with its consequences not only for Greek philosophy but also for Western philosophy which grew from it. But Dewey is not much read any longer by Anglo-American philosophers, and Collingwood, though he has come into

---

[4] "I must add, that history is not only a valuable part of knowledge, but opens the door to many other parts, and affords materials to most of the sciences. And indeed, if we consider the shortness of human life, and our limited knowledge, even of what passes in our own time, we must be sensible that we should be forever children in understanding, were it not for this invention, which extends our experience to all past ages, and to the most distant nations; making them contribute as much to our improvement in wisdom, as if they had actually lain under our observation. A man acquainted with history may, in some respect, be said to have lived from the beginning of the world, and to have been making continual additions to his stock of knowledge in every century." David Hume, "Of the Study of History," *The Philosophical Works of David Hume*, ed. T. H. Greene and T. H. Grosse (London: Longmans, Green & Co., 1898), iv, 390.

fashion again, belongs to the Continental tradition. His historicist leanings, in particular, are viewed with alarm.

Even idealism, a philosophy translated from the original Berkeleian English into Hegelian German and then back again into English by Bradley and Bosanquet, remained disengaged in England and America from the enthusiasm for history displayed so markedly by the German master. Notwithstanding Bradley's first published work, *The Presuppositions of Critical History*, which was, as its title suggests, an essay in the philosophy of history, his more mature reflections were as little affected by thoughts about historical process as were Parmenides' about cosmic flux. "History," Bosanquet declared in his Gifford lectures of 1911-12, "is a hybrid form of experience, incapable of any considerable degree of 'being or trueness.' The doubtful story of successive events cannot amalgamate with the complete interpretation of the social mind, of art, or of religion. . . . Social morality, Art, Philosophy, and Religion take us far beyond the spatio-temporal externality of history. . . ."[5]

It is understandable that those philosophers on the Continent whose theories were molded by a preoccupation with historical process, by some embracing vision of how and why ideas and ideals change in time, have claimed the greater share of attention by historians. Still, to most philosophers in England and America who have attained their majority within the last thirty years, thinkers such as Hegel, Dilthey, Bergson, and Croce appear opaque in fundamental ways. When one attempts to penetrate Hegel, one comes up against a bureaucracy of the intellect in which one can wander forever from department to department. If many philosophers in England and America can be justly accused of neglecting history, many philosophers on the Continent can be charged with philo-

[5] *The Principle of Individuality and Value* (London: Macmillan & Co., 1912), pp. 78-80.

sophical negligence, with relying too heavily on ancient prerogatives and perennial questions.

It is time for English-speaking philosophers and historians to become seriously involved with one another's work. The process has already begun with the appearance of the journal *History and Theory*, as well as with the recent publication of a surprising number of books in the philosophy of history. It is my aim in this book to explore some of the possibilities for a new *rapprochement*.

CHAPTER II

The Alienation of Philosophy from History

C ONTEMPORARY Anglo-American philosophical thinking about history has been dominated by two powerful stereotypes, one reinforcing the other. The first presents a sharp division between philosophy and history, and thus it acts as a weir to separate philosophy and history into different intellectual currents, almost to the point of isolating philosophy from the flow of its own history. Every philosopher, of course, prefers to think of himself as an absolute beginner, of philosophers before him as clashing by night. Part of the charm of doing philosophy is that a search for fundamentals seems to justify a license to ignore whatever one wishes—even the entire history of philosophy. Small wonder that many philosophers should choose to forget the past! The second stereotype further channels philosophical thought about history. It depicts two streams: one leads to a brackish swamp called "speculative philosophy of history," the other to the clear lake of "analytical philosophy of history." I chose as a title for this book the phrase "between philosophy and history" not simply because I was weary of the repetitious use of the preposition "of," so often resorted to as a way of linking philosophy with other disciplines, but also because I wanted to call attention to the possibility that there might exist common ground between philosophy and history.

In the first part of this book, I sketch a theory of philosophy and of philosophical thinking that brings out some of the connections between philosophy and history. The project requires numerous digressions and creaking shifts of gears—

jumps from the history of philosophy to the philosophy of history and back again. The dialectical power-plays of Benedetto Croce notwithstanding, parts of philosophy and parts of history remain stubbornly disengaged from each other; the philosophy of history is not the same thing as the history of philosophy. Yet reality so commonly proves symmetrical that perhaps a complete synthesis of philosophy with history occurs at a higher level of abstraction, and one's slogan should be: the philosophy of the history of philosophy is the history of the philosophy of history. Other permutations are also possible. Still, one need not proclaim the complete identity of philosophy with history at any level in order to acknowledge that acquaintance with the history of philosophy can be useful for attaining a general picture of what contemporary philosophers are up to when they concern themselves with history. A less elaborate mode of presentation, an attempt to formulate some precise definitions of "philosophy" and "history" so as to reveal at once the relationships between them, would be naive. Such Cartesian entertainments are no longer credible.

The second half of the book is focused, sometimes directly but more often indirectly, on the second stereotype that holds there to be a sharp division between reputable and disreputable philosophy of history. Viewed through this distorted lens, the philosophy of history is seen to be trying to live down a delinquent youth, the period when a philosopher of history played the role of a *weltgeschichtliche* prophet on horseback whose demonic vision of historical truth conferred upon him the right to trample on the petty, fact-gathering morality of the workaday historian. That was heady stuff, and tempting too, before the days of philosophical prohibition. Nowadays philosophers dismiss the reprobate as a historian who has gone off the rails. It is assumed (and here the first stereotype comes into play) that philosophy is one thing and history another; therefore, should a philosopher become interested in the meaning of history, or whatever curious notions speculative philosophers of history are supposed to become exercised about, he is immediately stamped as a species of historian. After all, who but a historian could be directly concerned with history?

Traditional divisions of labor can harden to the point of making it seem necessary to define history as only that which professional historians do and philosophy as only that which professional philosophers do. Admittedly, professional philosophers and professional historians have had relatively little to do with each other. Yet are there any theoretical reasons to justify present-day tables of academic organizations? I shall examine some arguments supporting the view that philosophy and history have no common border; and I shall also cast an eye on the rival contention, advanced earlier by some idealists, that philosophy and history not only share common ground but are, in fact, identical pursuits.

Consider, as a preliminary example, a thesis that seems tailored to function as a *theoretical* basis for distinguishing between philosophy and history. I referred earlier to the once widely held opinion that the philosopher's task consists solely in examining the logical relations between the propositions of science (and of history, it should be added) and in defining "the symbols" which occur in them. Stated bluntly, this view assumed that the philosopher is supposed to think about the *language* of the historian, unlike the historian, who is supposed to think about history. Not the history of England, but the *Cambridge History of England*, was held to be the province of the philosopher.

Now if this thesis were sound—if, that is, the study of the language of the historian, whatever that might ultimately involve, were a completely different enterprise from the study of the rise and fall of empires, the decline of the gold standard, and the assassination of Kennedy and if, further, it proved possible to justify the claim that the proper object of philosophical attention is language—then it would appear that philosophy and history, or philosophy and any other empirical inquiry, could have nothing essentially to do with one another. The logical positivists, in fact, launched a pincer attack in order to support both contentions. They attempted to rationalize the entanglement of philosophy with problems of language by arguing that typical philosophical problems throughout history arose solely because philosophers had played fast and loose with grammar. All philosophical questions, they tried to show, were more or less on the order of "In what place is time?" The other prong of the attack was positive. If traditional philosophical problems were "linguistic" in origin, then the modern philosopher, recognizing this truth, should undertake a thorough study of language in order to pinpoint the mistakes made by those who used (or rather misused) their language for such illicit activities as doing philosophy.

It was all very well to insist that philosophers in general should study language and that philosophers of history in particular should study the language of historians. Something further was needed, however, to show that an involvement with the language of physicists is different from an involvement with physics, that a concern for the language of historians is completely different from a concern with history. Don't words, after all, themselves have histories? England has a history, but so does "England," a history echoing that of England. (Surely the word "England" now has resonances unheard when the holy lamb of God was on England's pleasant pastures seen.) But if words have histories, then something had to be said about how a philosophical interest in them differs from a historical interest. A theory was required that discriminates the ahistorical features of a language and focuses philosophical attention upon those and only those features.

The logical positivists, in fact, had just such a theory at the center of their philosophical position. Many believed, particularly during positivism's salad days, that Russell and Whitehead's *Principia Mathematica* (which had as its expressed purpose the demonstration that mathematics is, in an important sense, a part of logic) contained the logical skeleton for any language, a logical syntax suitable for expressing symbolically every statement of natural languages as diverse as Swahili and French. On this view of language, the all too visible differences between Swahili and French could be put down as mere differences in the interpretations given to the symbols of *Principia Mathematica.* Whatever else one thinks of this brave but simplistic theory, one must recognize that it does present an ahistorical conception of language. It presupposes that the logical syntax of a language is not subject to historical change, for, according to the theory, all languages must have the same logical syntax. Since, from the logical syntax point of view, there are no differences between the cognitive features of different languages, the theory does not furnish any principles of "linguistic individuation," or ways of distinguishing one language from another. And if it offers no criteria for distinguishing between *different* languages, then it certainly does not provide any help in characterizing historical changes within the *same* language. (What is it that makes both a sentence of fourteenth-century French and a sentence of modern French part of the same language?) It must be remembered that the theory was not designed with such historical purposes in mind, so that anyone who accepts it uncritically will tend to regard language as essentially like logic—as something fixed and permanent, from which all historical impurities have been washed away.

The ordinary language attack on logical positivism was concentrated on the positivist theory of language. It was averred that very few of the features of any given natural language were derivable through suitable interpretations of formulae that could be formed in the language of *Principia Mathematica.* Although the positivists themselves were interested only in what they called the "cognitive features" of any language— features expressible by sentences in the present indicative, in effect—they were accused of emphasizing unduly the "statement-making" function of language and of ignoring its many other uses, as in the begging of boons or in the conferring of knighthoods. Inasmuch as the positivists claimed to be hunting for a cognitive map of language—one that would expose the workings of the languages of science and mathematics—the ordinary language philosophers could draw blood only by showing that certain cognitive features of language were not explicated by the overall positivist analysis. Obviously, the ordinary language general critique was not exactly fair. Nonetheless, it was therapeutic, for many of the positivists probably did believe deep down that only the statement-making function of language could be philosophically important. They thought that, when not making assertions, one can only make noise or remain silent. Consequently, their understanding of such traditional fields of philosophy as ethics and esthetics was often philosophically shallow.

More to the point, the positivist conception of philosophy was itself fatal. The reason was not simply that the positivists espoused a particular theory of language that happened to have some serious omissions (for all its shortcomings, the theory did have philosophical depth). Nor was it that, as an outsider style of criticism has it, positivism was "linguistically oriented." Rather, the trouble with positivism was its presupposition that, if one were concerned with words, one could escape being involved with the world—that, in particular, it was possible to analyze in a *significant* way the language of the historian without becoming involved with history.

It is appropriate, then, to start by examining critically the first stereotype—the attitude that philosophy and history are conceptually independent of each other—before looking for common ground between them. I shall begin with a brief historical sketch of some of the incidents that led to the development of the first stereotype. I shall, however, be concerned with a generalized version of the stereotype: namely, that philosophy and any empirical "positive inquiry," like physics or history, necessarily have different subject matters. In what follows, I shall use the general term "science" to stand for any such positive inquiry. I hope that, by my adoption of the general term, I shall not be taken to be begging the question of whether science and history are distinct kinds of inquiry. My own view, which I press in Chapter XV, is that the usual debate on the topic turns on faulty characterizations of both science and history. Just consider, *en passant*, whether one should call the geologist who attempts the narration of a history of the earth a "scientist" or "historian."

THE RISE of science has played an absolutely fundamental role in determining the direction of modern philosophy from the seventeenth century on. Yet prior to the seventeenth century there was no sharp distinction between philosophy and science to be drawn. Even René Descartes (1596-1650), the father of modern philosophy, did not suppose there to be any important difference between science and philosophy. And he had no reason to think so because mathematics, then considered the very exemplar of science, was his *métier*. His *philosophical* masterpiece, the *Meditations*, had the stated aim of providing a firm foundation for the *sciences*.[1] Descartes remarked in his *Discourse on Method* that it was "those long chains of reasoning, simple and easy as they are, of which geometricians make use in order to arrive at the most difficult demonstrations" which gave him the idea that "all those things which fall under the cognizance of man might very likely be mutually related in the same fashion. . . ."[2]

Philosophy, for Descartes, was the search for the first principles of science. Because Euclid's *Elements* was at that time

[1] "Meditation I," *The Philosophical Works of Descartes*, tr. Elizabeth S. Haldane and G.R.T. Ross (New York: Dover Publications, 1955), I, 144.
[2] "Discourse on Method," *ibid.*, p. 92.

deemed by all to be the paradigm of what it meant to be a science, it was only natural that Descartes should have looked to geometry, considering the first principles of any science to be its axioms, postulates, and definitions. One need not balk at accepting a definition which portrays philosophy as a search for first principles. Any definition constructed along these lines is, in a general way, as correct as it is innocuous. The Cartesian interpretation of this definition of philosophy is not so innocent, however. If the first principles of a science are held to be its axioms, postulates, and definitions, presumably joined to the propositions of that science by means of deductive connection, then one has presupposed axiomatizability as an ideal for all science. Need a body of truths, in order to be identified as science, be axiomatizable? Gödel showed, in the early thirties, that even branches of mathematics are not, in principle, completely axiomatizable. True, the Cartesian view has the merit of presenting the relationship between philosophy and science in a relatively straightforward fashion. The task of the philosopher, on that view, is to axiomatize science, no more and no less; Descartes saw the philosopher as standing in much the same relationship to the scientist as did Euclid, say, to Pythagoras. Many, perhaps most, of the theorems proved by Euclid had been discovered by earlier mathematicians. Euclid's particular genius lay in demonstrating that these results could be put together in one deductive system. In like manner, according to Descartes, the philosopher must attempt to show that "all those things which fall under the cognizance of man might very likely be mutually related in the same fashion."

Suppose axiomatizability were a realizable ideal for any science. Would there *then* be any reason for not accepting the Cartesian integration of philosophy and science? Yes, for there are still logical difficulties with Cartesianism. The first principles of a science, Descartes would say, contain not only those propositions from which all others are deducible but also those which, in some sense, are supposed to be better known than the others. Consider Euclidean geometry, for example. Most people believe, as did Euclid and Descartes, that the axioms and postulates of Euclidean geometry are more certain, intuitively speaking, than those propositions deducible from them. Everyone "knows" that if equals are added to equals the results are equal, that the shortest distance between two points on a plane is a straight line, and so on. Yet some of the theorems of Euclidean geometry can be surprising; one can be in doubt about them until they are shown to be deducible from the axioms and postulates about which one is not in doubt. One searches for the first principles of a science, Descartes thought, because one wishes to guarantee the certainty of the whole edifice built upon them. Now it is a property of the deducibility relationship that, if B is deducible from A and A is true, then so must B be true also. Does the same hold for certainty? If a proposition A is certified as reasonably certain and B is deducible from A, is proposition B equally certain? Let us examine this presupposition of Cartesianism.

Everyone will grant that certainty admits of degrees. A proposition A can be ranked, theoretically, as being either more certain, or less certain, or equally certain vis-à-vis any other proposition B. Suppose one is given two propositions B and A such that B is deducible from A but A is not deducible from B. Suppose, further, that A and B are not equally certain. Then we may ask, is A more certain than B or is B more certain than A? If one accepts uncritically the Cartesian picture of geometry, the reasoning will proceed as follows: if A is a postulate or axiom, then, since B is deducible from A, B is a theorem; and since theorems are less certain than axioms and postulates, A is more certain than B. The plausibility of this analysis provides a good deal of the philosophical motivation behind Cartesianism. On the Cartesian view, the quest for certainty, for philosophical first principles, is equated with the quest for axioms and postulates, for a set of propositions from which all others can be derived. Yet, despite the apparent soundness of the preceding analysis, it is fundamentally mistaken. For it is not true that, if B is deducible from A and the two propositions are not equally certain, then A must be more certain than B. Just the opposite holds, in fact. So the quest for certainty cannot be equated with the quest for axioms and postulates. There is something basically wrong with the Cartesian program.

Imagine a horse race between Rumpelmeyer and Rumpelstiltskin. Obviously, the proposition that one or the other horse wins is deducible from the proposition that Rumpelmeyer wins. It is also manifest that the proposition that Rumpelmeyer wins is less certain than the proposition that either Rumpelmeyer or Rumpelstiltskin wins; anyone would relish betting that one or the other horse wins, were someone so foolish as to offer the contrary bet.

Here, then, is a case in which a proposition B—either Rumpelmeyer or Rumpelstiltskin wins—is deducible from a proposition A—Rumpelmeyer wins—even though proposition A is less certain than proposition B. The quest for philosophical first principles cannot be equated with the quest for axioms and postulates, for a set of propositions from which all others can be derived. The Cartesian program for integrating philosophy with science would probably have been abandoned eventually even if Euclidean geometry had remained the exemplar of science. In fact, however, Cartesianism did not lose its philosophical hold because of internal stresses and strains or as a result of philosophical criticism, but because of certain unanticipated developments in the history of thought: namely, the replacement of geometry by physics as the exemplar of science. Moreover, it was the latter, more than anything else, that was responsible for dislocating philosophy from science.

Although modern physics was developed by scientists of different nationalities, it was reserved for philosophers in England to be the first to recognize its philosophical importance. The rationalist paradigm of science, Euclidean geometry, was dethroned and replaced by physics. And though certain features of Euclidean geometry continued to be accepted as criteria of knowledge—axiomatizability, for example—the geometrical model itself was set aside.

Whereas the rationalists had contended that "the true method of discovery is to form thoughts from some given definition,"[3] the English empiricists held it to be systematic thinking about what is experienced by the senses. This new "true method of discovery" required close attention to observational details, as well as the use of refined experiments to wrench from nature secrets hidden from the eye. For such work a group of specialists had to be trained in a very special way. It was, in fact, the rise of empirical science that threatened philosophy, because it created a division of conceptual labor that had not really existed before. As long as mathematics could be considered the exemplar, there was no particular difficulty, no alienation of philosophy from positive inquiry. Descartes, Spinoza, and Leibnitz moved easily between philosophy and mathematics. In their own minds, philosophy itself was a kind of applied mathematics.

If the study of nature, of physics, was a task for specialists, what was left for a philosopher to do? John Locke (1632-1704), whose philosophy was touched by the spirit of the new science, proposed an answer. Knowledge of the universe, he reasoned, is in part a function of the constitution of the "human understanding." He hoped that the philosopher, by examining systematically the nature of mind and thought, could arrive at some picture of the measuring instrument, even if he were to be excluded from the more exciting task of investigating what is measured by the instrument. Both cautious

[3] Baruch de Spinoza, "On the Improvement of the Understanding," *The Chief Works of Benedict de Spinoza*, tr. R. H. Elwes (New York: Dover Publications, 1951), II, 34-35.

and modest about what he thought could be attained, Locke was very much in the position of a man who argues that, although astronomy is a science really worth pursuing for its own sake, there is also a subsidiary need for the investigation of telescopes. "The commonwealth of learning," Locke wrote, "is not at this time without master-builders, whose mighty designs, in advancing the sciences, will leave lasting monuments to the admiration of posterity: but every one must not hope to be a Boyle or a Sydenham...."[4]

George Berkeley (1685-1753), Locke's important successor in the empirical tradition, was more arrogant about the claims of philosophy. With a number of very ingenious arguments, he quite convinced himself that there is no good reason for believing that what is observed by the senses is a physical world, a world of matter in motion with an existence independent of the mind that perceives it, a world that produces in the mind the various sensations that it experiences. Quite the contrary, Berkeley argued; supposing the independent existence of a physical reality created great conceptual confusion. It was as if the investigator of telescopes concluded that there is no reason for assuming the independent existence of stars which project images upon the lenses of telescopes, astronomy becoming, on this new conception, nothing but the study of the succession of images on telescope lenses. Berkeley steadfastly maintained that his arguments did not tell against the possibility of empirical science; the true method of discovery could still be held to be the systematic thinking about what is observed by the senses. The sciences of nature remained intact, though their import was somewhat different from what was usually taken for granted by scientists themselves.

"You will say," wrote Berkeley in Section 50 of his *Principles of Human Knowledge*,

[4] *An Essay Concerning the Human Understanding*, ed. A. C. Fraser (Oxford: Clarendon Press, 1894), I, 14.

there have been a great many things explained by matter and motion: take away these, and you destroy the whole corpuscular philosophy, and undermine those mechanical principles which have been applied with so much success to account for the phenomena. In short, whatever advances have been made, either by ancient or modern philosophers, in the study of Nature, do all proceed on the supposition, that corporeal substance or matter doth really exist. To this I answer, that there is not any one phenomenon explained on that supposition, which may not as well be explained without it, as might easily be made appear by an induction of particulars. To explain the phenomena, is all one as to shew, why upon such and such occasions we are affected with such and such ideas. But how matter should operate on a spirit, or produce any idea in it, is what no philosopher will pretend to explain. It is therefore evident, there can be no use of matter in natural philosophy.[5]

David Hume (1711-76) carried Berkeley's line of argument to a more skeptical conclusion. He accepted Berkeley's view that any explanation of phenomena amounts to nothing more than "to show, why upon such and such occasions we are affected with such and such ideas." But, he contended, scientists can never be in a position to know why, on such and such occasions, such and such ideas occur. All the scientist can do is to state what he believes by means of universal laws of nature that are supposed to admit of no exceptions. Yet if we were to ask ourselves what reason we have for believing that such laws of nature are true and thus hold for all occasions and ideas past, present, and future, we would discover that the only evidence consists of a number of instances in which the laws were borne out in the past. Surely it is fallacious, Hume reasoned, to argue that because a law was never contravened in

---

[5] *The Works of George Berkeley, Bishop of Cloyne*, ed. A. A. Luce and T. E. Jessop (Thomas Nelson & Sons, 1949), vol. II, sect. 50.

the past (and even this we cannot know for certain since we are not familiar with all past cases) we have the right to assume that the law will hold for all future occurrences. Why, then, do physicists believe that Newton's inverse square law is true when there is no sound reason for believing in the truth of any law of nature? The physicists' belief that the inverse square law is true must be accounted for in some way. Such beliefs, Hume concluded, could be explained by supposing some sort of psychological conditioning to be at work.

The physicist is in the same position as a dog, in a Pavlovian experiment, who is trained to expect food when a bell rings. The conditioning process depends upon repetition. For some "mysterious reason" (Hume's own words) the mind connects ideas that have been presented to it in regular succession. A dog in Pavlov's laboratory who happened to have a scientific turn of mind would soon think he had discovered a law of nature: whenever bells ring, food appears. We all know, however, that the dog would be making a grave mistake, and we also know why he would make it. In similar fashion Nature, the Great Psychologist, conditioned Newton, a very intelligent animal, to formulate the inverse square law. In Hume's view, such formulations were nothing but projections of certain mental habits and expectations that could have no more validity than the surmises of canine scientists in Pavlovian laboratories.

Empiricism, a philosophy that Locke had thought would be able to justify the confrontation of reality with the methods of empirical science, was led into the *cul de sac* of Humean skepticism. What began as an ancillary investigation of the mind with the hope of consolidating the knowledge-claims of the new sciences soon became the instrument for undermining them. It was as if the philosopher had taken revenge on the scientist for having been displaced by him.

Physicists, of course, did not take Hume's conclusions seriously, if only because they were unaware of them. Nor did

Hume think it really possible to take them seriously when engaged in everyday business. No consideration of abstract philosophical arguments can get a person to doubt for long that bread nourishes, fire is hot, and so on. And a good thing it is, too, that such skepticism is in practice impossible to maintain, Hume felt, for otherwise man would perish. Philosophical nourishment, apparently, is not conducive to long life, and Hume did not have a high opinion of philosophy. Believing is one thing; having good or sound reasons for believing is something else again. Hume's point was that there are no sound reasons for believing in the truth of any so-called law of nature.

Ever since Hume, a favorite occupation of philosophers has been to try to refute his position. Immanuel Kant (1724-1804) was one of the first to make the attempt. However, Hume is really unbeatable if one accepts the problem in the terms in which he formulated it. Kant realized that a radical critique of such empiricist concepts as experience, sensation, idea, and the like was necessary if one were not to be impaled by Hume's skeptical thrust. He recognized that one will be led inevitably to a skeptical conclusion regarding the possibility of empirical knowledge if one accepts the empiricist picture of the mind as a passive receptor, receiving ideas coming to it through the senses (yet active enough now and then to perform one or two simple inductions from those ideas). This was a misleading picture, Kant thought. Even when one is aimlessly staring at clouds in the sky, the mind, unknown to itself, is actively at work organizing one's sensations into the patterns that are ultimately characterizable by the physicist's laws of nature. In addition, Kant contended, if one could know in advance the principles by which the mind organizes experience—and Kant believed there had to be such principles—one could also know *a priori* the patterns by which nature *must* reveal itself to the mind. One could thus be in a position to anticipate nature.

27

Of course, something is wrong with this conclusion; still, it is important to note that Kant's solution to Hume's problem contained, as an integral part, an interesting conception of philosophy and a defense of philosophizing. Moreover, such definition and defense were necessary to combat the philosophical malaise that was part of the price of Hume's brilliant use of philosophy against itself. On Kant's interpretation, the search for first principles became the search for the principles by which the mind rationalizes experience; and as it was also Kant's view that there must be such principles if a scientific knowledge of nature is to be possible at all, philosophy was again put into a more direct contact with science—at least in theory.

Although Kant had a vastly more ambitious program for philosophy than Locke, he was in many ways a similarly modest and cautious philosopher, having the greatest respect for the achievements of the sciences of his day. And though he thought it possible for philosophy to guarantee, as it were, the validity of science, Kant maintained that there are certain limits to what can be made intelligible to the mind by the mind. The mind cannot become directly aware of itself, or of that which ultimately "produces" sensations from "outside" the mind. Insofar as the empirical study of nature, as Kant conceived it, remained safely within these limits, it was possible to underwrite the validity of science through the elucidation of the organizing principles of the mind, principles that could be known *a priori* by philosophical probing.

For G.W.F. Hegel (1770-1831) and the idealists who followed him, Kant's solution to the problem set by Hume was intolerable to the extent that it required the postulation of two "unknowables"—that which ultimately produces sensations and that which ultimately receives them. Like Berkeley, Hegel believed that there can be nothing "outside" the mind, and so, in his view, that which produces sensations and that which accepts them must both be minds. In fact, Hegel suggested that that which produces ideas must be identical with that which receives them in such a way that the universe exhibits a perfect reflexivity, consisting essentially of only one mind which both generates and entertains the same ideas. That, at least as far as Hegel was concerned, killed two Kantian unknowables with one philosopher's stone. Yet Kant had also claimed that the mind can never be directly aware of itself but only of ideas, suitably transformed and made digestible, of course, in accordance with its own dietary principles. How, then, can a mind know itself?

This problem had certainly baffled Berkeley, who hedged, as philosophers often do, by introducing a bit of technical vocabulary. Even though we can have no idea of the mind, Berkeley averred, we can yet get "a notion" of it. This was hardly a satisfactory resolution of the issue. Nor was Hume's suggestion that the mind does not exist, being nothing but a bundle of ideas:

> For my part, when I enter most intimately into what I call *myself*, I always stumble on some particular perception or other, of heat or cold, light or shade, love or hatred, pain or pleasure. I never can catch *myself* at any time without a perception, and never can observe any thing but the perception. When my perceptions are remov'd for any time, as by sound sleep; so long am I insensible of *myself*, and may truly be said not to exist.[6]

Hume confessed in an addendum to his *Treatise* that he could not really accept his own solution; he had again posed a problem so cleverly that, as with most of the puzzles he brought to light, there did not seem to be any solution.

Hegel certainly recognized the difficulty; his entire philosophy can be viewed as an attempt to overcome it. He took the Delphic injunction to "know thyself" quite literally and

[6] *A Treatise of Human Nature*, ed. L. A. Selby-Bigge (Oxford: Clarendon Press, 1888), p. 252.

projected the entire history of the world on it. Because one cannot become aware of oneself by a simple mental act of inspection, the mind has to play on itself an elaborate series of ploys and tricks in order to catch itself out. Hegel decided that, for the mind to find out what it is, it must first find out what it isn't. By performing enough dialectical about-faces, Hegel hoped, it might be possible for the mind finally to catch sight of itself. Mental development takes time, however—even the mental development of Ubiquitous Mind. Thus Hegel found himself involved with history, and especially with the history of philosophy because he thought the history of philosophy revealed most clearly the struggles of Ubiquitous Mind to know itself.

The attainment of self-awareness was, for Hegel, one way of expressing the main theme of the history of mankind. There were other ways as well: the warring of statesmen, no less than the quarreling of philosophers, expressed the thrashings and coilings of Ubiquitous Mind upon itself. Ordinary history (that is, political history) Hegel took to be the history of philosophical thought incarnate, and the correct philosophy of history was to be found by studying the history of philosophy.

What, then, did Hegel take to be the relationship between science and philosophy? The question is not an easy one to answer. Hegel began his lectures on the philosophy of history by saying that "the only Thought which Philosophy brings with it to the contemplation of History, is the simple conception of *Reason*; that Reason is the Sovereign of the World; that the history of the world, therefore, presents us with a rational process."[7] Clearly, Hegel was claiming to have access

[7] *Lectures on the Philosophy of History*, tr. J. Sibree (New York: Dover Publications, 1956), p. 9 (Hoffmeister, p. 28). Hegel developed his thoughts on the philosophy of history in the course of five sets of lectures he delivered during the years between 1822-23 and 1830-31. His own lecture notes contained many additions, changes, emenda-

to a very important insight about history, one gained through philosophical reflection. Yet—and this is a point often overlooked by Hegel's critics—Hegel did not assert that only by philosophical reflection can one have access to it. The historian might equally have concluded that history presents us with a rational process by making "an inference from the history of the World, that its development has been a rational process; that the history in question has constituted the rational necessary course of the World-Spirit—that Spirit whose nature is always one and the same, but which unfolds this its one nature in the phenomena of the World's existence."[8] Hegel cautioned, "We must proceed historically—empirically."[9] Hegel's general thesis was that there has to be a point of convergence between the study of philosophy and other realms of inquiry because the most basic fact about the universe—that it is organized by a rational spirit—only philosophers armed with a dialectical logic can *demonstrate*.

It is one of those ironies of history that, although there should have been, on Hegelian principles, the closest possible

---

tions, and marginalia; various editions of the lectures have appeared since Hegel's death, but there is only one major English edition—the Sibree translation of the original Gans-Hegel edition. The most authoritative text of Hegel's introductory section, in which Hegel outlines and summarizes the philosophical substance of his lectures, appears in the Johannes Hoffmeister edition: *Die Vernunft in der Geschichte* (Hamburg: Felix Meiner Verlag, 1955). Whenever I cite from the introductory section of the Sibree translation, I also give the reference to the Hoffmeister edition.

[8] "It is only an inference from the history of the World, that its development has been a rational process; that the history in question has constituted the rational necessary course of the World-Spirit— that Spirit whose nature is always one and the same, but which unfolds this its one nature in the phenomena of the World's existence. This must, as before stated, present itself as the ultimate *result* of History. But we have to take the latter as it is. We must proceed historically—empirically." *Ibid.*, p. 10 (Hoffmeister, p. 30).

[9] *Ibid.*

integration of philosophy with science, idealist philosophers instead lost almost all contact with science during the eighty odd years of the philosophical hegemony of Hegelianism. Perhaps it was, in part, the intellectual arrogance displayed by many of them that prompted their academic colleagues to ignore them. In any case, their claim to possess the dialectic, a special philosophical method for penetrating into a reality not accessible to ordinary thought, led eventually to their downfall. Despite the abundance of confidence men among them, the idealists could no longer get their checks accepted by professional philosophers, although the length of time taken to call their bluff was astonishing.

For Anglo-American philosophers, the collapse of idealism involved more than just a rejection of a particular philosophical system. It brought about a contempt for philosophy as a whole. Philosophers had associated philosophy with one particular system for too long; to reject the system meant, at the emotional level, to reject philosophy. At first, many sought to ally themselves with scientists and mathematicians in their efforts to ventilate and dispel the idealist miasma. It was thought for a time that, if philosophy were to have any value at all, it too would have to develop itself into a science. Some looked upon philosophy as potentially a more general kind of science than, say, physics or biology. Others set to work in those areas of philosophy that had certain obvious affinities with science. Mathematical logic, for example, received intense cultivation by philosophers before it became a legitimate part of the standard mathematics curriculum in the United States and England. When Whitehead and Russell published three of the four projected volumes of *Principia Mathematica* between 1910 and 1913, many philosophers regarded the work as a vindication of philosophy—it was technical; it was knowledge; it was mathematics; it was philosophy.

But *was* it philosophy? Not too many asked this question at the time, except for idealist émigrés who spoke in what already

was a strange tongue and who refused to learn the philosophical Newspeak of the day—"P.M.ese," as it was called. If anyone required convincing, it could always be argued that, inasmuch as logic was, traditionally, part of philosophy and *Principia Mathematica* a treatise on logic, *ergo.* . . . Of course, this
argument can be carried further. Had Whitehead and Russell succeeded in their objective of showing how mathematics
could be developed as a branch of logic (and few at the time
doubted that this could be done), then mathematics would,
by similar reasoning, also be a part of philosophy. What an
inadvertent variety of Cartesianism that would have turned
out to be! And though no one could accept the conclusion of
the argument when stated in this way, many Anglo-American philosophers did—and some still do—subscribe to something like it. Philosophical self-respect apparently demands
deeper and deeper forays into mathematics proper.

I certainly do not wish to suggest that there is anything improper about philosophers working in history or mathematics.
In fact, I think that only by philosophers becoming mathematicians or historians—and historians or mathematicians becoming philosophers—are ideal commonwealths of learning
founded. Yet it is wrong for philosophers to seek their personal
salvations in some particular positive inquiry. (Some philosophers have even attempted to turn philosophy into mathematics by the simple device of transforming philosophy
students into mathematicians.)

It is true that philosophers since Plato have had an off-again,
on-again love affair with mathematics, but philosophy has
just as much an affinity with any positive inquiry as with
mathematics. In the nineteenth century it was history's turn
to be wooed, at least by German philosophers. And the favorite
among many Anglo-American philosophers, just now, is
linguistics. I shall propose the thesis that any positive inquiry
has a philosophical and a nonphilosophical part. The academic
divisions of labor in universities tend to separate the two:

when philosophers are to be found in philosophy departments, there is a disposition to say that philosophy should only be done by philosophers in philosophy departments. This has had a divisive effect upon philosophy. On the one hand, it has made philosophers continually hunt for the proper subject matter of their discipline; on the other, it has encouraged the view that philosophical problems do not arise naturally in any positive inquiry.

Consider the misleading but widely accepted picture of the various specialized sciences growing out of philosophy and then pursuing their positive courses unencumbered by excess philosophical baggage. Comte, who first made the idea popular, tried to give this alleged development the inevitability of a process governed by a law of nature, his so-called law of three stages. Intellectual progress, he proclaimed, depends on the "positive" sciences emerging from their metaphysical or philosophical cocoons. According to Comte, in the development of a discipline there comes a stage when all problems are scientific and no problems are philosophical. Many people still subscribe to some version of Comte's view, although the thesis is quite absurd when stated baldly, as absurd as the idea that the growth of human progress is governed by a law of three stages or, indeed, any other law.

CHAPTER III

Philosophy as the Search for Criteria of Intelligibility

I HAVE PRESENTED, as a story-line, a theme of philosophical alienation, a theme that could easily support the weight of a serious history of philosophy. Historical prefaces will seem natural to historians, although some may object to the presentation of an untried story-line in lieu of actual history. Since I am concerned, however, with what other writers have termed (in a rather high-flown way) "the historical understanding," story-lines will do as well as histories. The particular story-line chosen by a historian reveals *his* understanding (if not *the* historical understanding) of what has gone on in history. The intelligibility of history, as usually studied, is in large measure a function of those story-lines that historians employ in the narration of history. I shall touch on these matters in the latter portion of this book. In any case, although historians no doubt find historical approaches congenial routes by which to draw near any topic, many Anglo-American philosophers will bristle at their use in connection with philosophy. A recent history of contemporary British philosophy, for example, begins with the disclaimer that "the history of philosophy, though certainly it is not just history, is not just philosophy either, and hence is for the most part only indirectly or incidentally relevant to the course of philosophy itself."[1]

In one of its forms, the ahistorical position presents itself thus: What a philosopher believes is not as important as the

[1] G. J. Warnock, *English Philosophy Since 1900* (London: Oxford University Press, 1958), p. vii.

35

arguments he uses to defend his beliefs. Philosophy is the study of the uses of argument. Is it important that, as a matter of historical fact, Anselm in the eleventh century advanced an ontological argument to prove the existence of God and that Kant, writing at the end of the eighteenth century, tried to defend with certain arguments the validity of scientific laws of nature? If Anselm's argument was sound in the eleventh century, it is just as sound today, and the same holds for any philosopher's arguments.

. What, then, are we to make of the history of philosophy? What would it look like in outline to someone who advocates the position just indicated? The following, though a caricature, is not far off: Philosopher X sets out to prove proposition p by means of argument a. Philosopher Y tries to refute philosopher X either by establishing that one of the premises in argument a is false, or by demonstrating that proposition p is false, or by showing that argument a is invalid. Whatever he does, philosopher Y must also provide an argument in support of what he says about philosopher X's argument. But then along comes philosopher Z, who tries to show that philosopher Y's argument is unsound by means of still another argument, and so on. Fortunately, a history of philosophy written along these lines would be as unintelligible in substance as it is tedious in form. Interestingly enough, it not only misses the mark as a characterization of what goes into producing an adequate history of philosophy but also gives a misleading picture of what it is to do philosophy in *any* century, including this one.

Certainly, philosophers make much use of argument (just as they argue much about use). And the schema has this in its favor: it imposes a certain elenctic flavor on the history of philosophy. It would be even more misleading to suppose that the history of philosophy reveals a basic pattern of cumulative growth, a design in which each philosopher puts the propositions proved by his predecessor to work in proving a few more propositions of his own. Such a schema possibly fits the history of science, at least from a positivistic point of view. (Karl Popper and his followers, who prefer a more eristic model, have bitterly attacked this conception of the history of science, but it has quite a few proponents nonetheless.) But whichever model one prefers, and for whatever reasons, it should be recognized that one is here concerned with questions about the structure of the history of science or of philosophy; in my view, these make up the substance of speculative philosophy of history. There is such a thing as speculative philosophy of the history of science; it is often called, more simply, "philosophy of science." This is in anticipation, however.[2]

What is wrong with characterizing the history of philosophy by means of the model given above? Isn't it true that philosophers philosophize by presenting arguments, and don't other philosophers attack those arguments? And doesn't the history of philosophy contain the record of who attacked whom and why? One obvious deficiency of the model is that it fails to indicate what philosophical arguments are about. One has no way of understanding why there have been certain propositions which philosophers, at a particular time, have thought worthy of proving or disproving; and even the most casual glance at the history of philosophy reveals that the center of philosophical attention has often shifted with time. Moreover, the changing winds of doctrine are not generated by the logical force of philosophical argumentation alone. Aquinas, for example, disputed a premise of Anselm's argument for the existence of God, and Anselm and Aquinas were both vitally concerned to discover a proof for the existence of God. Yet one doesn't get from the Anselmian grasp of the problem to the Thomistic one through a series of arguments and counterarguments. The rediscovery of Aristotle is more important in accounting for the difference in approach than any criticism Aquinas directed against Anselm.

[2] Relevant discussion occurs in Chaps. XII, XV, and XVI.

Nevertheless, it will be pointed out, philosophers do proceed by argumentation, and though their interests vary with time, they seem to employ canons of argumentation to which they appeal and without which the doing of philosophy itself would be impossible. It is this atemporal feature of philosophy, we are led to believe, that makes it possible for Karl Popper to debate with Plato, though the former does not have Plato's command of Greek, and for Bertrand Russell to debate with Anselm, though the latter did not have Russell's command of mathematical logic. If an argument was valid or invalid in Greek antiquity or the Middle Ages, it is still valid or invalid today. The history of philosophy is the study of philosophical arguments, it will be said, and whether all arguments ever thought up by philosophers were produced less than five minutes ago is irrelevant to understanding them. It is a conceptual accident, as it were, that the history of philosophy extends beyond the last five minutes. That some of the arguments were advanced over two thousand years ago in another culture with different problems is not philosophically interesting. On this view, the history of philosophy is the critique of philosophical arguments that, as a matter of curious fact, were presented in other times and other places. Accordingly, there is no difference between doing philosophy and doing the history of philosophy, not because the history of philosophy is important but because philosophy has no important history.

This attitude, in fact, is one of the linchpins of Anglo-American philosophical ahistoricism. It would be futile to attempt to remove it directly, for a whole conception of philosophy is at stake, and there are no knockdown arguments or final solutions here. When reading Plato's *Republic* intelligently, one cannot help thinking in terms of right and wrong, valid and invalid—even true and false. Philosophical understanding must include assessing and judging. At such moments the Vietnam war becomes as remote as the Peloponnesian, and one will only be annoyed and confused by thoughts of historical parallels. Does it matter that Athenian democracy provoked a war and was defeated by Spartan totalitarianism, that Plato's ideas about the nature of justice were "molded" (what a slippery concept that is!) by that war, as our responses when we read Plato now are molded by parallel events in Vietnam? And yet any philosopher who has lived long enough to change his philosophical opinions once or twice knows in his bones, though he may profess the contrary, that logical considerations alone are not decisive. An argument that once seemed utterly compelling suddenly loses logical force. One sees new difficulties, counterexamples. It is not the counterexample itself that deflates; it is the very belief that counterexamples to one's philosophical convictions are possible. Somehow one always manages to find counterexamples when one is ready to believe it possible to do so. Certitude in philosophy is not solely a matter of the formal validity of argument; it is a function also of a crucial deployment of the key concepts occurring in the argumentation. What, then, are we to say of the use by one philosopher of such terms as "valid," "invalid," "right," "wrong" in evaluating the position of another philosopher? It is at least *possible* that the criteria for the intelligible application of the concepts expressed by these terms change in response to the changing historical situation. Accordingly, one of the most interesting problems in the philosophy of history is posed by a penetrating consideration of the history of philosophy, and this is as it should be. All these remarks are somewhat pointless, however, until one understands the conception of philosophy that lies back of them.

I SHALL START by providing an interpretation of that venerable definition of philosophy as the search for first principles. I must introduce some jargon, though, in order to convey in a short formula my own interpretation of the expression "first principles," and so I shall have to give a somewhat prolix account of the meanings of terms in the formula I plan to employ. What I believe to be the general nature of the relationship between philosophy and any positive inquiry, in particular history, should gradually become apparent through my exegesis and defense of the formula.

Philosophy, in the *primary* sense, is the search for, as well as the formulation and critique of, first principles, and by "first principles" I mean *criteria that must be fulfilled for the intelligible application of concepts* or, for short, *criteria of intelligibility*. Any positive inquiry, be it mathematics or history, is characterizable in terms of a certain set of concepts it employs; the philosophy of mathematics, accordingly, consists in the formulation and critique of the criteria of intelligibility of mathematical concepts, and the philosophy of history consists in the formulation and critique of the criteria of intelligibility of historical concepts. A number of examples will serve as a preliminary way of showing what is meant by the cumbersome expression "criteria that must be fulfilled for the intelligible application of concepts" or the shorter "criteria of intelligibility." Consider, to begin with, the concept of history itself. In attempting to come to grips with it, one might ask what is at first sight a curious, but is nonetheless a basic, question: what sorts of things can have histories? And paired with this question is one just as curious: what sorts of things cannot have histories? Do such questions have any bearing upon the study of history?

Leopold von Ranke, who avowed in the Preface to his *Histories of the Latin and Germanic Nations from 1494-1514* that he did not aspire to any higher end in writing that particular history than to show what actually happened,[3] also claimed that "the final goal—not yet attained—[of historical inquiry] always remains the conception and composition of

---

[3] Preface to *Histories of the Latin and Germanic Nations from 1494-1514*, reprinted in part in *The Varieties of History*, ed. Fritz Stern (New York: Meridian Books, 1956), p. 57.

a history of mankind."[4] Now to say that the final goal of historical inquiry lies in the attempt to compose a history of mankind can be taken as a pleasant conceit, something impressive for historians to utter on formal occasions yet something that need not commit one to anything at all. Looked at one way, the phrase is on a par with such bromides as the contention that the final goal of physics is the attainment of an understanding of nature. Despite its easy rhetoric, however, Ranke's declaration has been taken seriously by a number of philosophically-minded historians and historically-minded philosophers. Ranke himself was one of that number. So was Oswald Spengler, who began his *Decline of the West* by attacking the very idea that it was possible to write a history of mankind. "Mankind, however," he alleged, "has no aim, no idea, no plan, any more than the family of butterflies or orchids. 'Mankind' is a zoological expression, or an empty word."[5] In place of a single history of mankind, Spengler proposed to bring forth a series of histories, each a story of the birth, growth, decline, and death of an entity that Spengler called a *Kultur*.

I see, in place of that empty figment of *one* linear history which can only be kept up by shutting one's eyes to the overwhelming multitude of the facts, the drama of *a number* of mighty Cultures, each springing with primitive strength from the soil of a mother-region . . . ; each stamping its material, its mankind, in its *own* image; each having *its own* idea, *its own* passions, *its own* life, will and feeling, *its own* death. . . . I see world-history as a picture of endless formations and transformations, of the marvellous waxing and waning of organic forms. The professional historian, on the contrary, sees it as a sort of tapeworm industriously adding on to itself one epoch after another.[6]

[4] *Ibid.* p., 61.
[5] *The Decline of the West* (New York: Alfred A. Knopf, 1926), I, 21.
[6] *Ibid.*, pp. 21-22.

We ought not to allow Spengler's Wagnerian fanfares to deafen us to his philosophic melodies. He laid down (without much argument, it is true, but then Spengler was no more a professional philosopher than a professional historian) several criteria for the intelligible application of the concept of history. One criterion was negative: there cannot be, Spengler claimed, intelligible histories written about abstractions such as mankind because the concept of history cannot be intelligibly applied to abstractions. Spengler seems to have been suggesting as well a number of positive criteria for the intelligible application of the concept of history. One of them appears to be: the concept of history, or of having a history, can be applied only to concrete objects that can undergo change; if it really makes sense to think of sitting down to write a history of X, then X must be a concrete thing that undergoes change. Mankind, he argued, is not a concrete thing that is subject to change. It is therefore absurd to suppose that a history of mankind can be written. The Rankean goal is a will-o'-the-wisp. *Also sprach Spengler.*

Suppose you were asked to write a history of the number π. You might try to discover when it first occurred to someone that there was such a number, what various attempts were made to determine its decimal value to some n^{th} place, what role the concept of π played in the development of mathematics, and so on. Would you in this manner be gathering materials that would enable you to write a history of the number π? You might, perhaps, be embarked on writing a history of what mathematicians have said about the number π, but it is difficult to imagine that π itself has a history. Similarly, one can undertake writing a history of man's conception of God, but this is not the same as writing a history of God, who, if He exists, can have no history—according to at least one variety of orthodox theology.

A history of the number π cannot be written, one might say, because numbers do not exist concretely. Likewise, one cannot write a history of Moby Dick, a character in fiction and a whale besides. One can write histories only of collections of real things, and it is always possible to write such histories. The situation, however, is not quite so simple. Is it possible to write a history of two people chosen at random—Abraham Lincoln, say, and your cousin Harry? One could, of course, write two biographies—one of Lincoln and one of Harry—and put them together in a book, but this could hardly be called a history of Lincoln and Harry.

Because my purpose at this point is to explain what it is to do philosophy, rather than philosophy of history proper, I shall not now pursue this curious topic. Yet I hope everyone will at least agree that the issues just broached *sound* queer enough to be philosophical, even though no defense has yet been offered to show that such issues *are* philosophical—in fact, are basic to the philosophy of history. And it should be pointed out that, although questions concerning what sorts of things one can or cannot write histories about are of utmost importance for the philosophy of history, they are hardly ever discussed by analytical philosophers who do philosophy of history. Perhaps the reason is that such issues surface only when one is dealing with the narration of history, a matter of major concern in speculative philosophy of history but not in analytical philosophy of history as commonly conceived.

I submit, then, that, when one begins to worry about what sorts of things can or cannot have histories, a philosophical issue emerges. This is so because one is thinking about criteria that might govern the intelligible application of the concept of history. Spengler maintained that abstractions can have no histories. Marx claimed that ideas can have no histories. Collingwood contended that one can write history only of human actions done in the past. In each instance, a philosopher attempted to lay down the criteria that allegedly govern the intelligible application of the concept of history. Once one understands the criteria a philosopher employs, then many of his later moves make sense. Spengler, for example, talked about cultures as if they were literally entities. At first sight, this way of speaking seems most peculiar. It would be futile, however, to try to prove or disprove the existences of such entities. It is more important to discover the criteria of intelligibility Spengler used that led him to treat cultures as entities. Spengler evidently believed that, if it makes sense to undertake writing a history of X, then X must be an entity that undergoes change. Moreover, he certainly thought it intelligible to write histories of cultures, or else he wouldn't have tried to write them. Instead of denying that cultures are entities, one should tackle the general problem by asking whether it is in fact possible to write a history of something without presupposing that the object of the history is an entity of some type that undergoes change. Can there be histories of events, of properties, of classes, of relations, of numbers, of concepts, of ideas? Can one write a history of a flash of lightning, of the property of being red, of the class of objects on my desk, of the relation of brotherhood, of the number π, of the concept of history itself? Is it even *intelligible* to think of writing a history of a property or of a number? What are the criteria for the intelligible application of the concept of history?

Let us now turn to another example, this one from mathematics, of what I call a "criterion of intelligibility." One of the criteria that must be fulfilled for the intelligible application of the concept of numerical division is that no divisor have the property of being identical with the number zero. Imagine that there is some number z such that the number four, say, divided by zero, is identical with z. Since any number x divided by any number y is identical with some number z if and only if x is identical with the product of y and z and since, moreover, any number multiplied by zero equals zero, we could deduce at once that the number four is identical with the number zero—a manifest absurdity. Mathematicians guard themselves by saying that any expression of the form $x \div y$ is *undefined* when $y = 0$. In my own jargon, the application of the concept of the division of one number by a second number is unintelligible wherever the second number is zero. Hence, one criterion of intelligibility that must be fulfilled in applying the concept of division to two numbers is that the divisor have the property of not being the same as the number zero.

One could say, more loosely, that the *concept* of four divided by zero is unintelligible, but this statement, taken literally, commits one inadvertently to the view that there are two sorts of concepts: intelligible and unintelligible. A more innocuous way of making the point is to say that the *expression* "four divided by zero" is meaningless. Since the application of the concept of division of one number by another is unintelligible for all cases where the latter is zero, the assertion that $4 \div 0 = 3$ is unintelligible. On the other hand, the assertion $4 \div 2 = 3$, though surely false, is at least intelligible. Unintelligible assertions are neither true nor false; it is absurd to apply the concepts of truth and falsehood to them, just as it seems—on the surface, at any rate—senseless to apply the concepts of truth and falsehood to questions or commands. Suppose you ask, being parched, for the shortest route to the nearest tavern, and the funny-looking stranger replies that he must first know whether your question is true or false! The situation, perhaps, precludes philosophical dalliance; in such desperate circumstances you may grasp at any interpretation. Is he asking, for example, whether your question is sincere? On a more leisurely occasion, however, you may begin to reflect on whether it makes sense to apply the concepts of truth and falsehood to questions, and such reflections about criteria of intelligibility are philosophical in nature.

It is not always easy to decide whether one should label an assertion "false" rather than "unintelligible." Suppose a Pakistani tells you that he has had surds for breakfast. You gently correct his English by pointing out that the word he wants is "curds." To your astonishment, he retorts that, although he often breakfasts on curds, he now and again prefers surds. Indeed, he adds, that very morning he ate the square root of the number two, though he admits shyly that it was a most irrational thing to eat. What should be your response? Is what he has just said absurd or only false? Is he mad or a liar? If the expression "P ate the square root of 2" is meaningful, then you would argue that the Pakistani certainly did *not* eat the square root of the number two, an assertion on a par with the claim of having drunk the Indian Ocean. It can't be *done*! On the other hand, if you believe the expression "P ate the square root of 2" to be meaningless, then your answer should be: It can't be *said*! (And if it can't be said, it can't be gainsaid either.) To support the argument that it can't be said, you need to call upon criteria of intelligibility. And, as one might expect, there is often much philosophical controversy over whether various assertions are merely false or nonsensical, for what is at stake are criteria of intelligibility —first-order philosophical theories.

No list of philosophical examples is respectable without one drawn from chess. One of the criteria that must be fulfilled for the intelligible application of the concept of a position in chess is that in no position can two pieces occupy the same square. If one picks up an account of a chess game, the tenth move of which reads "pawn and knight to king's bishop 3," one must reject the alleged tenth move as unintelligible and presume that the description contains a misprint. Again, an unintelligible or meaningless report should be distinguished from a false one. A record of a game in which Capablanca beat Keres in four moves is probably false, but not unintelligible. Imagine that before me is a board with large squares on which stand some small chess pieces. I notice that both the white king and white queen happen to occupy the same square. I may describe what I see without conceptual difficulty, as long as I do not speak of it as a *chess position*.

Since a chess game consists of a sequence of chess positions, there are thus no chess games in which, after *n* moves, a position is reached such that two pieces share the same square. An enormous number of games are possible, however, so it is likely that there are chess positions that have never been realized in the course of any game actually played. Let us assume that no game has ever occurred in which both sides lost all major pieces (except kings) before any pawn was moved. Such a game is possible, though to present a proof one would have to delve into the tiresome details of unfolding a sequence of legitimate moves that would terminate in the described position, which I shall call "position H." It is extremely probable, however, that position H has never been encountered in any game; to arrive at such a position would require stupid play amounting to a collusion in imbecility on the parts of the players. Now consider the following two propositions:

P1 No chess game has ever been played that contained a position in which two pieces occupied the same square.
P2 No chess game has ever been played that contained position H.

The grounds for asserting P1 appear to be quite different from those for asserting P2. To show that P1 is true, one needs to appeal to what I have termed "criteria of intelligibility," though there exists a plethora of standard philosophical jargon that could be used for making the point. One could say that, "by definition," there is no chess position wherein two pieces occupy the same square. Or one could maintain that P1 is true by virtue of "the logic" of the game. Or again, in more old-fashioned terminology, though admittedly stretching it a bit, one could call P1 an "analytic judgment" that is known "*a priori*" and P2 a "synthetic judgment" known "*a posteriori.*" As I am not concerned at the moment about making fine distinctions between technical philosophical terms, it doesn't matter to me what one says about P1 and P2, provided that one recognizes the difference in the grounds for asserting them. Unlike the reasons for maintaining P1, the grounds for asserting P2 are based, in part, on certain assumptions about the level of intelligence required if one is to play chess at all. To assert P2 with total confidence, one would need to know the details of every chess game ever played. Since most chess games go unrecorded, any assertion of P2 must contain a certain amount of conjecture. Yet it is always possible that there does exist somewhere a historical record of a game that included position H. Should such a document turn up, one would have a piece of evidence against P2. Not conclusive evidence, to be sure, for one might decide, on balance, that the document was spurious. Still, it makes sense, in this case, to talk about weighing the evidence presented against what one feels one knows about the level of human intelligence. To use another item of standard jargon, the grounds for asserting P2 are *empirical*. Not so with P1, apparently.

THE THREE EXAMPLES just discussed should convey a rough idea of what I mean by a criterion for the intelligible application of a concept. The phrase is so unwieldy, however, that some dissection of it seems worth undertaking. First, "criterion." A criterion is a test, rule, or standard by means of which things are judged, decided upon, or evaluated. A criterion is also that trait or characteristic which, singled out by some criteriological test, indicates whether or not an object possessing it has "passed" the test. (Entry in Johnson's *Dictionary*: "Criterion—a mark by which anything is judged of, with respect to its goodness or badness: 'By what criterion do you eat, d'ye think/ If this is priz'd for sweetness, that for stink.' Pope's Horace.")

One might, for example, ask the school psychologist what

criterion he employs in deciding how intelligent a child is. He would probably answer by citing some standard intelligence test—the Stanford-Binet, let us say. His reply would show that the term "criterion" refers to the testing procedure itself. One might object to the psychologist's use of standard intelligence measures by claiming that the ability to do well on an intelligence test is no criterion of intelligence. In this case, the term "criterion" refers to the trait singled out by the test rather than to the test itself. The two senses are of course related.

Although it is perfectly good English to use the term "criterion" to denote both test and trait, I intend henceforth to apply it in the latter sense alone. I shall employ the expression "decision procedure" to refer to criteriological tests. Instead of saying that an intelligence test is not a criterion of intelligence, I shall prefer to say that an intelligence test is not an adequate *decision procedure* for determining intelligence. When the word "criterion" is to be used, I should rather say that doing well on an intelligence test is no criterion of intelligence. It will become clear later why I prefer the expression "decision procedure" and what, philosophically speaking, hangs on the relationship between criteria and decision procedures. I shall argue that important problems of criteria arise when one is concerned with testing those general decision procedures that we employ, often only in a rough and ready way, in lieu of actually going through a process of evaluating, judging, or deciding upon something. And there are good reasons for preferring the expression "decision procedure" as the generic term for all such procedures, one of them being that the word "criterion" itself comes from the Greek *krino* meaning "to decide."

There is yet a third sense of the term "criterion." We sometimes speak of *formulating* criteria, and it is fairly clear that the term "criterion" is being used, in this instance, to refer to a *rule*. Thus the expression "Galois' criterion" in mathematics designates the rule that the solvents of irreducible equations must all be primes. If we ask someone to formulate the criteria for determining intelligence, the question can be interpreted as a request for the rules to guide one in deciding, let us say, which of two persons is the more intelligent. The following rule might then be proposed: if A can score higher than B on some standard intelligence test, then A is more intelligent than B.

Decision procedures, as well as criteria, can be classified as *positive* or *negative*. Roughly speaking, intelligence tests function as negative decision procedures when poor scores are considered to indicate low intelligence but high scores are not taken to signify high intelligence. Intelligence tests function as positive decision procedures when high scores are regarded as a token of high intelligence but poor scores are not necessarily thought to mean low intelligence. It too often happens, unfortunately, that intelligence testing in schools proceeds on the assumption that a particular test is both a positive and negative decision procedure.

So much for my use of the term "criterion." I must still cut through the formidable semantics of the whole phrase "criteria for the intelligible application of a concept." What is meant, for instance, by application of a *concept*? This mode of speech is admittedly vague—and deliberately so. It might have seemed preferable to talk about the application of *terms* or *expressions* and to define philosophy as the attempt to formulate criteria for the intelligible application of expressions. To apply words to things somehow sounds more manageable, rather like sticking labels on bottles. The sole criterion for pasting a "poison" label on a bottle, it would seem, is that the bottle contain or be used to contain poison. And if one creates some new stuff for the bottle, then all one has to do is to conjure up a new word to match. Here there are no criteria that must be fulfilled in order to apply a new word to a new thing. And when there are no criteria, to paraphrase Dostoievsky, then everything is permitted.

Two views of the nature of language correspond to the two modes of labeling bottles. The first takes language to be, at bottom, the product of a series of acts of will, in which names are assigned, at will, to things. Many logical positivists seemed to favor some variant of this position. The other view is that language is essentially the product of a series of acts of cognition. The criteria for the application of words are regarded, in some sense, as preexistent, to be unearthed by engaging in a bit of conceptual discovery. Plato held a position similar to this, and it was also, basically, the view of language taken by many ordinary language philosophers, who assumed that the criteria for the application of words were, in one way or another, built into the rules for the ordinary use of terms in a preexisting language. If philosophy is defined as the attempt to formulate the criteria for the intelligible application of words to things—if, that is, a philosophical problem is the kind which provokes one to worry about the criteria that govern the use of words—then, on either theory of language, philosophical problems are either solvable or soluble. With one theory, all philosophical problems can be solved by an arbitrary decision to use words in a certain way. With the other theory, all philosophical problems can be dissolved by making a minute inspection of preexisting rules for the ordinary use of the language one speaks.

If there were no disposition on anyone's part to adopt either of the two language theories just described, I should have no objection to defining philosophy as the attempt to formulate the criteria of intelligibility that govern the application of *words* to *things*. One could talk of the task of formulating criteria for the application of the *word* "intelligent," rather than of the *concept* of being intelligent, if it were understood that this manner of speaking did not commit one to either of the following two positions with regard to intelligence tests and testing: (1) Words can be used in any way one likes; we can arbitrarily define an intelligent person as one who does well on intelligence tests. (2) Words already embedded in a language can never be used as one likes. One must abide by the rules that govern the uses of terms in ordinary speech. The word "intelligent" does not ordinarily mean the ability to do well on an intelligence test; hence, scoring high on a test can never function as a criterion of intelligence.

It is easy to be seduced by either theory of language; in fact, some philosophers have bedded down with both, though not simultaneously. To help secure oneself from temptation, I think it preferable to speak of the intelligible application of concepts rather than of words. Being vague on the right occasions is one way of preserving virtue. And though I referred to (1) and (2) above as "theories of language," I could just as well have called them theories of philosophy, for philosophers have used one or the other to support certain views about the nature of philosophy and the validity of philosophical problems.

CHAPTER IV

Philosophy of History as the Search for Criteria of Historical Intelligibility

I HAVE FURNISHED the beginnings of an explication of what I mean by a criterion for the intelligible application of a concept, but I have as yet said nothing about why I use the word "intelligible" in the way I do or what its role is in the phrase "criterion for the intelligible application of a concept." It would be pointless, however, to continue by direct assault on the expression without further justifying its use as a characterization of philosophy and philosophizing. Accordingly, I shall attempt to anticipate and to answer certain objections to the fashion in which I have characterized philosophy.

For some people, doing philosophy is linked almost exclusively with the construction of philosophical systems in the style of Hobbes, Kant, or Hegel. Philosophical systems, however, must be based upon networks of criteria for the intelligible application of concepts. The system builders did not work in solitary confinement; they were of necessity influenced by the way the world was made intelligible at the times in which they lived. Systematic philosophy, in the grand manner, differs from the more modest undertakings of contemporary philosophers in scope. In the good old days, philosophy was nourished by the belief that everything intelligible hangs together coherently. Without such a belief, there would naturally have been no point in trying to construct philosophical systems. Philosophers now are much less sanguine and much more cautious. Yet contemporary philosophical practice closely resembles the venerable model in one absolutely crucial respect: philosophy has been, is now, and will always be associated with the posing of philosophical questions. Even when philosophy was in its most suicidal phase, when many philosophers really began to convince themselves that all philosophical questions are nonsensical, it seems to have been understood that, on the day people actually ceased from asking philosophical questions, philosophy would be finished. One way of mitigating the harshness of attempting to prove that philosophical questions are nothing but nonsense is to provide a role for philosophical questioning. Many of those philosophers who considered philosophical questions meaningless thought there was nonetheless some benefit to be derived from posing them. Philosophers differed, though, on whether the therapy offered by philosophical questioning was purely psychological or had a conceptual point as well.

Since the posing of philosophical questions is so distinctive and universal a practice of philosophers, it is necessary to square my view of philosophy with that practice. And certain objections come to mind at once when one seeks to accommodate my definition of philosophy to the philosopher's traditional habit of raising sticky questions. These objections can be summarized, perhaps, by means of two general questions: (1) Are *any* philosophical questions of the form "What are the criteria for the intelligible application of the concept of X?" (2) Are *all* questions of the form "What are the criteria for the intelligible application of the concept of X?" philosophical questions?

With regard to (1), the possibility that no philosopher has ever asked, in just so many words, "What are the criteria for the intelligible application of the concept of history?" should not count against using the formula as a way of characterizing certain kinds of philosophical questions about history that have in fact been raised. The objection that there have actually been no philosophical questions couched in these exact terms is unfair, for my intention is not to provide a handy recipe for generating all philosophical questions. Yet such an objection is not without point, because it inspires some interesting considerations. What is a philosophical question, after all? Is there a method of discerning whether a particular question is philosophical? How convenient it would be to have a machine that could sort out philosophical and nonphilosophical questions. In one slot the machine would deposit such queries as "Can the transcendental unity of apperception be directly experienced?" In another would go "Who was the first president of the United States?" Later I shall argue that the difference between philosophical and nonphilosophical questions is not one of form—that the same interrogative can often be used to pose either a philosophical or a nonphilosophical question. ("What are you?" One answer: "I am a philosopher." Another answer: "I am what I am not.")

With regard to (2)—whether *all* questions of the given form are philosophical questions—one might readily agree that a question such as "Can the number *pi* have a history?" seems philosophical (it can produce twinges of nausea, for one thing) but aver that not all questions about criteria are equally upsetting. And if a distinction must be made between kinds of concepts, then something further must be said about which concepts are fit to be objects of philosophical attention.

Nothing I have said so far gives any hint of what the difference between philosophical concepts and other kinds is supposed to be. Yet if there is such difference, it is pointless to characterize philosophy as the search for criteria for the intelligible application of concepts *simpliciter*; one must also know, to begin with, which concepts are philosophical. Various suggestions have been offered, but none are any good. Some have thought that philosophical concepts are more general than others, or more fuzzy, or more basic, to mention three possibilities. Such characterizations are not very helpful, particularly when one realizes that nonphilosophers, too, deal with basic or fuzzy or general concepts.

Surely, there must be a way of distinguishing a philosophical from a nonphilosophical concept, someone will say. Otherwise, how could one know where philosophy begins and ends? There must be a difference between history and the philosophy of history. Isn't it true that certain kinds of concepts interest the historian and other kinds the philosopher? Quite a number of historians, for example, have tried to provide an adequate characterization of the concept of the Renaissance; few, if any, philosophers have done so. On the other hand, philosophers *have* been concerned with the concept of history, the concept of cause in history, the concept of the great man in history. Doesn't this divergence in interests illustrate the distinction between philosophical and historical concepts?

It is very easy to slide from a consideration of history and philosophy to a consideration of professional historians and philosophers. Such transitions are usually innocuous. As an aid in surveying the relationship between philosophy and history, what better way than to commence with the activities of contemporary philosophers and historians? Note, though, that this approach presupposes that one begins with some notion of what history and philosophy are. Were all professional philosophers suddenly to cease whatever it is they do and start writing history instead, citing this switch would not constitute a proof that history and philosophy had become identical pursuits. If one is seriously concerned to discover what history is and what philosophy is and what the relationship between them might be, definitions in terms of what the professionals do cannot be adequate as answers without additional amplification. Can one remain satisfied long with the definition that philosophy is what philosophers do, or history is what historians do? (What is it that historians do when they are not doing history?) In fact, such definitions are usually advanced for the purpose of tabling a consideration of the initial questions. Even if it were true that no professional philosopher had ever tried to formulate the criteria of intelligibility that govern the application of the concept of the Renaissance (it is not true, by the way), it would not show that interests of this kind were nonphilosophical. Similarly, professional historians are not guilty of malpractice when they inquire about the criteria of intelligibility of the concept of cause, though normally it is the professional philosopher who is exercised about this matter.

If I am correct in asserting that a concern for the criteria of intelligibility of *any* concept is a philosophical one—that historians, as well as philosophers, have sometimes been interested in the criteria of intelligibility of historical concepts—then it appears that not all philosophy is carried on by professional philosophers. But this is hardly a radical thesis, after all. Why shouldn't historians have a stake in the philosophy of history? True, not all the concepts employed by historians have received attention from professional philosophers, but this circumstance is not important. There is more to philosophy of history than many professional philosophers have dreamt of.

Yet there are concepts and concepts, and in any particular inquiry some will be more crucial than others. It may even be that an entire discipline pivots around a certain concept, so that any change of concept would amount to a fundamental alteration in the nature of the discipline. It may also be that some concepts (such as space and time) are pivotal for many different disciplines. Couldn't philosophy be defined, then, as the attempt to provide criteria of intelligibility for pivotal concepts? One might not be able to say what makes a pivotal concept pivotal, but this inability neither disproves the existence of pivotal concepts nor provides an argument against defining philosophy in terms of them. Certainly, one can legitimately question whether philosophers should be interested in the criteria of intelligibility of *all* concepts (even those of mud and hair). That so many more philosophers have devoted attention to the concepts of space and time than to the concept of the Renaissance is a point one might use to support a pivotal concept contention. Need all philosophy be the philosophy *of* something? Even if it is granted that the philosophy of history deals with the criteria of intelligibility of historical concepts and the philosophy of mathematics with the criteria of intelligibility of mathematical concepts, why can't plain old philosophy be defined as a concern with the criteria of intelligibility of pivotal concepts? That philosophers teach courses called "Philosophy of Science" and not "Philosophy of Cytogenetics" suggests that some concepts are more deserving of philosophical attention than others.

It is certainly true that certain concepts, in certain important senses, are more important in certain ways than others. It is also true that there is a genuine need for sorting and comparison, for attempting to see how the various concepts exhibited by diverse disciplines hang together. Professional philosophers are not obsolescent. But the impulse to find a role for professional philosophers should not prevent one from seeing that there is more to philosophy than what interests professional philosophers at any given time. If one defines philosophy in terms of what professional philosophers are up to, then it might indeed seem more apt to designate philosophy a "second-order" concern—a concern for the intelligibility of criteria, perhaps, rather than for the criteria of intelligibility. Yet professional philosophy does become sterile when contact is lost with those first-order concerns about intelligibility that are the most essential ingredients of the philosophy *of* something. Even if one were to associate philosophy completely with the interests of professional philosophers, and even if it were true that philosophical aptitude shows itself best in a curious fascination with intelligibility per se, one would still have to admit that philosophers must pay attention to how mathematicians or historians make their respective domains intelligible. It is better to identify the philosophy of history with an interest in the criteria of intelligibility of *all* historical concepts than to restrict it from the outset to those concepts held to be pivotal in some sense or other. Not all philosophy is the philosophy *of* something, yet what I have termed "second-order" philosophy must feed on first-order philosophical concerns, on the attempts to formulate criteria of intelligibility in the philosophy of history, of mathematics, and so on. There does exist a philosophy of cytogenetics, though no course by that name is listed in any university catalog. The philosophy of cytogenetics is largely the affair of cytogeneticists, just as the philosophy of history is largely the affair of historians. Historians and cytogeneticists *are* sometimes vitally involved in the task of formulating the criteria of intelligibility of some of the concepts that make up their respective fields. And when they are, they are doing philosophy in a primary sense, though none of them would be tempted to exclaim "Now I am a philosopher!"

When professional philosophers turn their attention to the philosophy of something, their choice of topics and general orientation are bound to reflect second-order philosophical interests. Further, such philosophers have a tendency to justify their absorption in the philosophy of something by the claim that second-order "perennial" concerns must be sensitized to fit the particular first-order philosophy of interest. Philosophers of history, no less than philosophers of science, indeed have sometimes tried to identify *all* of philosophy with their particular first-order concerns. One must guard against such enthusiasms; still, one should also expect second-order philosophy to be affected in some way by first-order philosophy.

What should one expect, in particular, from the philosophy of history? The possibilities are enormous. R. G. Collingwood, who in various works explored many of them, bore down heavily on epistemological topics in *The Idea of History*. "Historical thought," he wrote there, "has an object with peculiarities of its own. The past, consisting of particular events in space and time which are no longer happening, cannot be apprehended by mathematical thinking, because mathematical thinking apprehends objects that have no special location in space and time, and it is just that lack of peculiar spatio-temporal location that makes them knowable. . . . Nor [can the past be apprehended] by scientific thinking, because the truths which science discovers are known to be true by being found through observation and experiment exemplified in what we actually perceive, whereas the past has vanished and our ideas about it can never be verified as we verify our scientific hypotheses."[1] By characterizing scientific and mathematical thinking in this hasty way, Collingwood supposed he had completely set them apart from "historical thinking," which, according to him, had something quite different to contribute to philosophy. Traditional philosophy, he thought, had been too closely affiliated with science, mathematics, or theology: "Theories of knowledge designed to account for mathematical and theological and scientific knowledge thus do not touch on the special problems of historical knowledge; and if they offer themselves as complete accounts of knowledge they actually imply that historical knowledge is impossible."[2] (Note that history cannot be distinguished from science in the way Collingwood suggests. Scientists—astronomers, geologists, etc.—as well as historians attempt to study "particular events in space and time which are no longer happening.")

While endeavoring to demonstrate, in *The Idea of History,* the epistemological autonomy of the study of history, Collingwood engaged in some special philosophical pleading: all history, he averred, is nothing but the history of ideas. One need not hold, however, that historical thought is *sui generis* in order to maintain that certain topics in the philosophy of history have a profound relevance to second-order philosoph-

---

[1] *The Idea of History* (Oxford: Clarendon Press, 1946), p. 5.
[2] *Ibid.*

ical concerns. Collingwood didn't quite succeed in showing the relevancies in *The Idea of History*, despite the obvious merits of that work. He was more on target in *An Essay on Metaphysics*, where he had the temerity to suggest that "Metaphysics is the attempt to find out what absolute presuppositions have been made by this or that person or group of persons, on this or that occasion or group of occasions, in the course of this or that piece of thinking."[3] "Absolute presupposition" was Collingwood's term for "first principle." According to him, the task of the philosopher or metaphysician is to try to discover the absolute presuppositions of an age. But he was ambivalent about whether the metaphysician's task is to excavate the absolute presuppositions of a bygone age (which would require him to be a kind of historian) or to unearth those of his own age (which would demand of him no more aptitude for history than the rest of us have). The first thesis is more radical than the second.

Collingwood's "absolute presuppositions" resemble in certain respects—though certainly not in all—what I have been terming "criteria for the intelligible application of concepts." At least, there are enough parallels between them to suggest that philosophy, on my conception of it as well as on his, is wide open to the waxing and waning of historical fashions. That Collingwood shifted between a radical and a less radical thesis indicates that he was having trouble grappling with the notion that absolute presuppositions, as he viewed them, change from one age to the next. For it is one thing to say that philosophical "first principles" undergo historical change; it is something else again to make sense of the saying of it. Nonsensical or not, these are fighting words among most Anglo-American philosophers, and one must smile when one utters them. Accordingly, I shall smilingly resort to parable in order to toy with some of the possibilities.

[3] *An Essay On Metaphysics* (Oxford: Clarendon Press, 1940), p. 47.

ONCE UPON A TIME there lived a famous historian whose works were admired as much for their volume and length as for their narrowness of compass. This historian suffered privately from bouts of philosophic melancholia, and only by secretly keeping a Rigid Philosopher in his employ could he continue to maintain that positive tone for which his historical studies were renowned. It came to pass that the historian was offered a huge sum of money by an addled but wealthy chess addict who desired to read a complete history of the game, from the beginning to the present and perhaps one step beyond. The historian, not having better prospects at the time, took on the assignment with his customary energy and zeal. Now the historian had to begin at the very beginning of the beginning, for he couldn't play chess at all. Common sense dictated that he should make his acquaintance with the game before proceeding to embark upon writing its history. The Rigid Philosopher, an avid player, thoroughly approved. In fact, he undertook himself to teach the historian the game, for he saw an opportunity to reinforce those proper philosophical habits which, weak as they often were, had nonetheless cost the philosopher much effort to implant in the historian.

Thus no sooner had the historian been presented with the absolute minimum number of rules necessary for a complete characterization of the set of permissible chess moves than there followed, hard upon, a lesson in the distinction between analytic and synthetic sentences. The Rigid Philosopher believed, of course, that a rigid distinction could be drawn between analytic and synthetic sentences. The Rigid Philosopher knew that he could not tell for *every* sentence whether it was indeed analytic or synthetic, but this limit to his powers did not prevent him from upholding the sanctity of the distinction. All the more reason for relishing the opportunity of showing what the distinction amounted to where sentences about chess were concerned, for in that domain the Rigid

Philosopher felt he knew not only what it meant to say that a sentence was analytic but also when it could be said truly.

He commenced by holding aloft a card on which was written: "No chess game ever contained a position in which more than one piece occupied the same square." After twirling it around twice, the philosopher proceeded to show that to suppose otherwise would lead to a contradiction in the application of those very rules of chess the historian had just so carefully memorized. Next the Rigid Philosopher flashed a card on which was neatly typed: "No chess game ever contained a position in which all major pieces (excluding kings) have been lost before a pawn is moved." By going through a strange sequence of moves, all of them nonetheless permissible, the Rigid Philosopher managed to arrive at the very ludicrous position described on the card. The moral, he explained in his didactic manner, was that an unbridgeable gulf loomed between sentences like the one on the first card and sentences like the one on the second: the truth of the latter, though probable, could not be confirmed without historical investigation, whereas the truth of the former could be established without any painful historical inquest at all. The historian, who thought privately that establishing the truth of the first sentence might be painful enough in its own way, had to admit that the Rigid Philosopher was right again. And just as soon as the philosopher believed the historian had learned to play chess with the minimum requisite ability, he turned him loose in the library. Said the philosopher epigrammatically: "One needs to know how to play chess in order to write chess history; one need not know how to play *good* chess in order to write *good* chess history."

The historian cast his nets wide and deep, and his luck ran as it usually did. In not too many days he began to find many curious chess facts flopping about in the daily catch. There were the Japanese Zen weightlifters who had played chess with pieces weighing two hundred pounds in order to combine spiritual with corporeal exercise. Hottentot kings had played on fields eighty yards square, with live warriors who would disembowel each other when captured. The Rigid Philosopher wore an indulgent smile when the historian reported on his progress; nonetheless, he remained interested.

One day the historian arrived at the philosopher's den quite out of breath. With loving care he took from his briefcase a fine old parchment. "One of the earliest records," he explained, "and quite remarkable in every way. Back in the fifth century, apparently, there were chess games in which more than one piece had occupied the same square at the same time." "And on what do you base this brilliant conclusion?" inquired the philosopher, a noticeable chill coming into the air. The historian pointed to the dated historical record, as solid a piece of parchment evidence as he had ever seen. There it was, black on yellow, the statement that after the 1,003rd move two pawns of the Satrap of Bandar Abbās had occupied the same square. "I suppose," sighed the historian, "that you don't approve of generalizing from only one piece of evidence; but documents like this do not grow on trees, you know." "Slip of the stylus," replied the philosopher curtly, for he had already proved that in no chess game could such a position possibly be reached. "Or a forgery," the philosopher added. "Just a bare-faced lie," he concluded.

Much as he was at sea in philosophy, the historian was very much on dry land when it came to documents. And since for him, as for all historians, the age of a document is directly proportional to a disposition to believe in its veracity, the historian continued his researches.

Before long he found reports of other games played during the fifth century in which it came about that more than one piece had simultaneously occupied the same square. But his elation vanished completely when he remembered his patron's injunction: to write a history of chess from the very beginning to the present and perhaps one step beyond. Where should he begin? Did people play chess before the fifth century? Could the very same game be played with different rules? The historian felt a migraine coming on, a symptom that presaged a bout of philosophic melancholia, and he hurried to see his philosophical alienist.

"Not a moment too soon," said the Rigid Philosopher after the historian had explained his problem. "Step one is to recognize that our little problem is philosophical and thus can be avoided. Step two is to adopt a linguistic point of view," the philosopher continued while forming a church steeple with his hands. "And so we must stop thinking about chess and think instead about what the word 'chess' means. Now what was the name of the game reported in those old documents?" "Apparently and improbably they called it 'chess,'" replied the historian. "They called it 'chess,'" repeated the philosopher thoughtfully as he thumbed his way through the pile of manuscripts the historian had laid before him. The Rigid Philosopher made some quick calculations on a piece of paper. "The problem is easily solved," he exclaimed; "it arose because you didn't realize that the same word is being used to refer to two different games. If the other game, the one reported in these documents, had been called 'pussycat,' you would not now be downing aspirin. To prevent confusion, we shall arbitrarily designate the game I taught you 'chess$_2$' and the game mentioned in those documents 'chess$_1$.' And to help keep the games apart, I have already devised a proof that chess$_1$ was played with at least three kings and at most seven." His voice trailed off as he began to examine the documents to see what else he could infer about chess$_1$. He quite forgot about the historian's philosophical problem, for he had found a better way to occupy his time.

"But I still don't know at which point to begin my history of chess," the historian timidly objected. "Why the answer is obvious," replied the Rigid Philosopher, without looking up.

"Are you writing a history of chess$_1$ or a history of chess$_2$? Make up your mind!"

"Perhaps the concept of chess itself changed," ventured the historian, "so that they are both different phases of the same game. Then the history of chess$_1$ would be part of the history of chess$_2$."

"*Um Gottes Willen*, what are you saying now? Haven't I already demonstrated that no game of chess could possibly contain such positions as the ones described in those damned parchments? What is to become of the distinction between analytic and synthetic sentences if we do not sharply distinguish between chess$_1$ and chess$_2$? Chess$_1$ and chess$_2$ cannot be phases of the same game because some of the rules of chess$_1$ contradict some of the rules of chess$_2$. There cannot exist a game with contradictory rules, can there?" cried the philosopher, afire with indignation.

The historian had never seen the Rigid Philosopher so upset. As he left the philosopher's den, he realized that the time had come to look for another philosophical alienist. The headache throbbed badly; if anything, it was a little worse.

Soon afterward the historian came across a Relaxed Philosopher among some lily pads. "It didn't do any good, did it?" said the Relaxed Philosopher sympathetically, for he had seen the direction from which the historian had come. "I was that way myself once, and such things have a way of recurring if not treated properly," the Relaxed Philosopher added, betraying only the faintest trace of a tic of the left eyelid.

"Can you help me?" asked the historian after presenting the philosopher with his particular perplex.

"Interesting case, that," the Relaxed Philosopher announced cheerfully. "You came to the right person. Your problem is philosophical, no doubt about that, but one can certainly cope." And thereupon the Relaxed Philosopher began to massage the historian's perplex.

He talked and talked and talked to the historian about the

various uses of the word "chess" and about how one should not expect chess to be played the same way all over the globe for all time, how silly. "Your philosophical problem arose because that other chap tried to get you to divide the various games of chess into watertight compartments," explained the Relaxed Philosopher. "It just can't be done. There are similarities and differences between each of the various kinds of chess games, just as there are similarities and differences between each of the various uses of the word 'game' itself."

The historian very much liked what he heard. "Do you mean that I can begin my history of chess with an account of chess$_1$?" he asked excitedly. He already had a pile of notes on the subject. "One would have thought that," said the Relaxed Philosopher nonchalantly, though he winced when he heard the expression "chess$_1$."

"But I also have discovered that before chess$_1$ there was a game played like chess$_1$, in a way, but with only five pieces on a board which contained four squares having three different colors—red, yellow, and purple. Should that be part of my history of chess, too?"

"If you like," murmured the Relaxed Philosopher as he stroked a lily pad.

Somehow the headache was coming back. The historian began to resort to the desperate expedient of inventing history when he no longer could discover it. "And before that a game was played with one board and one stone piece. And before that a game with one stone. Are all of these games part of the history of chess? Where *shall* I begin?"

The Relaxed Philosopher languidly drew out a well-worn copy of his favorite book and started to read aloud: "The White Rabbit put on his spectacles. 'Where shall I begin, please your Majesty?' 'Begin at the beginning,' the King said gravely, 'and go on till you come to the end: then stop.'"

CHAPTER V

Divergent Opinions of Philosophy and History

SOME PHILOSOPHERS and historians of science have recently become very much interested in the problems of characterizing conceptual change. We may speak blithely of "conceptual revolutions," but what constitutes one? Can concepts change? Do they have histories? Or is it the criteria of intelligibility of concepts that are subject to historical erosion? These are only two of the possibilities. In the last chapter I hinted at certain crucial difficulties that arise at this important point of intersection between philosophy and history, the fulcrum of a topic that might well be called "the impact of history on philosophy." Perhaps priority should be given, however, to a topic that was left hanging in the air—one that could be called "the impact of philosophy on history."

I have suggested that first-order philosophy of history concerns itself with criteria of intelligibility of the concepts that historians use in their attempts to make sense of history. I have also suggested that a fence should not be erected between lands traditionally belonging to professional philosophers and those belonging to professional historians—that, although at a given time some concepts may attract the attention of professional philosophers more than others, those concepts should not be treated as permanent boundary markers. Further, I have characterized a philosophical interest in history as a kind of concern about the intelligibility of history. Yet the historian, too, is concerned about the intelligibility of history. What is the difference between a *philosophical* interest in the past and a *historical* interest? How is the historian's task to be distinguished from the philosopher's? Does history ultimately collapse into the philosophy of history?

It is worth noting that those philosophers who were most involved with history—I am thinking of Hegel, Croce, and Collingwood—evidently found it extraordinarily difficult to draw a line between history and philosophy. Hegel began his lectures on the philosophy of history by categorizing various kinds of histories. He cited Herodotus and Thucydides as authors of "original history" (*die ursprüngliche Geschichte*), the kind which the historian produces by writing about events he himself has witnessed or events seen by people he can directly cross-examine. The aim of such history, according to Hegel, "is nothing more than the presentation to posterity of an image of events as clear as that . . . possessed in virtue of personal observation, or life-like descriptions."[1] Although Hegel professed admiration for great history of this kind, he seemed to value "original history" chiefly for providing source materials to the historian who "approaches his task with *his own* spirit; a spirit distinct from that of the element he is to manipulate."[2]

Hegel called this second kind of history "reflective history" (*die reflektierende Geschichte*) and distinguished various species of it, such as Universal History, Pragmatical History, and the various special histories, like the History of Art, of Law, and of Religion. That he lumped all these histories together in the class of "reflective history" (to which most histories belong) indicates that Hegel wished to emphasize the conceptual elements that were at work in their composition. When he came to Philosophical History—the philosophy of history proper—he defined it as "the conceptual consideration of history" (*die denkende Betrachtung der Geschichte*). One can see at once that, for Hegel, there could be no precise distinction between "reflective history" and "the conceptual

---

[1] *Lectures on the Philosophy of History*, p. 2 (Hoffmeister, p. 6).
[2] *Ibid.*, p. 4 (Hoffmeister, pp. 10-11).

consideration of history." The terms Hegel used reveal as much. Indeed, he said himself that the concept of special history "forms a transition to the Philosophical History of the World."[3]

Strictly speaking, then, Hegel did halfheartedly attempt to differentiate ordinary history from the philosophy of history, though the real basis of the distinction is far from clear. We might say the same about Hegel's contrast between original history and other kinds, a partitioning which evokes the distinction between perceiving something and reflecting about it. The chronicler of original history, unlike the historian who works from documents, writes in the "spirit of a recording witness." He is like a journalist. I cannot help thinking, however, that Hegel used his classification of kinds of histories merely as a rhetorical device, as a way of establishing an initial rapport with a nonphilosophical audience, for he did not suppose there were any important differences between perception and reflection, the former being considered more or less a species of the latter.

This point was picked up by F. H. Bradley, who attacked the notion that the historian's function is either to witness the past or to record that past witnessed by others. Not the latter because there are no records of "unadulterated facts," but only "divergent accounts of a host of jarring witnesses."[4] The historian cannot simply "correct the refraction of one medium by that of another, and in this manner . . . arrive at the bare and uncoloured reality."[5] And not the former because even the journalist cannot truly say: I am nothing but a camera. "We can not recall accurately what we have not rightly observed," wrote Bradley, "and rightly to observe is not to receive a series of chaotic impressions, but to grasp the course of events as a

[3] *Ibid.*, p. 8 (Hoffmeister, p. 22).
[4] *The Presuppositions of Critical History* (Oxford: James Parker & Co., 1874), p. 5.
[5] *Ibid.*, p. 5.

connected whole."[6] In short, even simple perception was for the idealist a conceptual affair and thus amenable to considerations of a philosophical nature. Even the simplest questions about plain matters of fact seemed to pose philosophical problems of fantastic difficulty, problems which evidently had to be resolved by a revolutionary metaphysical critique before one could be said to understand anything whatsoever.

The way was open for proclaiming a complete identification of philosophy with history, and Benedetto Croce took advantage of the opportunity. "Philosophy and History are distinguished," he argued, only "for didactic purposes, philosophy being that form of exposition in which special emphasis is accorded to the concept or system, and history as that form in which the individual judgment or narrative is specially prominent. But from the very fact that the narrative includes the concept, every narrative clarifies and solves philosophic problems. On the other hand, every system of concepts throws light upon the facts which are before the spirit."[7]

Yet Croce's attempt to marry philosophy and history in a shotgun wedding did not come off, though he sang many paeans to "History–Philosophy, of which the principle is the identity of the universal and the individual, of the intellect and intuition, and which regards as arbitrary and illegitimate any separation of those two elements, they being in reality a single element."[8] A hymen is not achieved by a hyphen. One must not be misled by the passionate claims of philosophical Irredentism into ignoring the obvious differences between history and philosophy. Nonetheless, it is prudent not to reject the proposed match out of hand and to continue the flirtation as long as possible.

[6] *Ibid.*, p. 12.

[7] *Logic as the Science of the Pure Concept*, tr. Douglas Ainslie (London: Macmillan & Co., 1917), p. 325.

[8] *History as the Story of Liberty*, tr. Sylvia Sprigge (New York: W. W. Norton & Co., 1941), p. 35.

A common route from history to philosophy, one traversed by many philosophers *and* historians, has its *terminus a quo* in the circumstance that the historian rarely has observed the events of which he writes; he works from other histories, documents, and artifacts. He must infer, it is said, from the documents before him what took place. Inference is a conceptual affair, allegedly requiring judgment on the part of the historian. And so, the argument runs, it is the historian who in the last analysis must decide *what* took place, to say nothing of *why* it took place. Of course, mistakes are always possible, especially when there is no way of checking up on the historian. The "perished past," as Bradley termed it, cannot be rerun like a film. Philosophical skepticism rears its head at this point; to submerge it necessitates, it seems, a radical shift in one's conception of what the historian really does. The historian, it now turns out, must be able to rethink the thoughts of historical personages (Collingwood); where he cannot manage this feat, the past becomes a blank screen. Or he must look upon himself as a man of action (Croce), whose view of the past is of necessity shaped by the practical requirements of his own day. At any rate, the *terminus ad quem* of the *via historia* often lies somewhere in the pastures of idealism, though not every historian is aware that he is grazing there. Yet some historians, such as E. H. Carr, have not shrunk from affirming that establishment of the basic facts of history requires "an *a priori* decision of the historian."[9]

This is, as I have said, a common route from history to philosophy, and one which I shall retrace more carefully, for it contains many pitfalls and traps for the unwary. Consider just one. That Adolf Hitler existed is, unfortunately, one of the basic facts of history. Does it really require a decision, *a priori* or otherwise, by a historian or group of historians, to establish that Hitler existed? That E. H. Carr uses the expression "*a priori* decision" indicates the presence for him

[9] *What Is History?* (New York: Alfred A. Knopf, 1962), p. 9.

of a philosophical problem. If this is a philosophical problem, however, what makes it so?

One difficulty with the common route is that it is a shortcut. We are faced with philosophical problems from the very beginning. If even the simple query "Did Hitler exist?" sets up a philosophical roadblock in the historian's path, then what interrogative does not? According to the idealist, this is precisely the point—every genuine question presents a philosophical puzzle. If one accepts this claim, then the identification of history with philosophy becomes breathtakingly simple; all that remains is to work out the particular variations. Another difficulty with the common route is that too much philosophical attention is focused on the historian's reliance on documents and artifacts. The study of history raises many genuine and interesting philosophical problems which are either overlooked or approached in oblique fashion if too much stress is laid on the document-artifacts theme. Not all philosophical issues would be resolved even if the historian had a time machine for witnessing the past. Most would, in fact, remain.

I have intimated that not all questions are philosophical— hardly a surprising thesis. What creates confusion, however, is that one and the same interrogative can be used to pose either a philosophical or a nonphilosophical question. The idealists blurred the distinction deliberately; they could make the most innocent queries occasions upon which to launch metaphysical rockets to alarming heights. Their strategy was, essentially, to argue that no question is really intelligible unless one can formulate the criteria of intelligibility of the concepts expressed by the interrogative. Naturally, every interrogative suggested philosophical questions at once, and the idealists treated even the simplest of requests for information as springboards for commencing the hunt for criteria of intelligibility. Now it frequently happens, as will be seen, that the quest for criteria of intelligibility leads into conceptual quicksand. Since it is often difficult to produce criteria, and since the results of such philosophical investigations often conflict, the idealists quite convinced themselves that a fundamental overhaul of our entire conceptual apparatus was necessary. They then proceeded to advance views radically different from those of common sense.

The analytic movement also made philosophic capital of the circumstance that one and the same interrogative can be used to pose a philosophical or nonphilosophical question. They erased the distinction from the opposite direction. Whereas the idealists believed every intelligible question to be philosophical, a main effort of the analytic movement was to spread the news that no intelligible question is philosophical. A favored gambit was to interpret philosophical questions in a nonphilosophical or "matter-of-fact" way. G. E. Moore, as we shall see, was a master of this technique, which he used to devastate his idealist opponents.

COMPARE the following two interrogatives: (1) Is the United States the same country that it was fifty years ago? (2) Are you driving the same car that you drove two years ago?

Sentence (2) certainly appears to be "matter-of-fact," admitting of a "yes" or "no" answer. Sentence (1), on the other hand, has a different ring. One is immediately wary, for a great deal of preliminary conceptual clarification is necessary before one can set about answering the question. Questions like (1) elicit responses of the "it all depends on what you mean by . . ." variety, whereas an official of the motor vehicle department would become suspicious of you at once if you began to answer question (2) in the same way. In such circumstances, philosophical circumspection has all the earmarks of criminal evasion. (Think of the impression Socrates must have made on his judges.) Sentence (2), then, is initially intelligible in a way that (1) is not; the need for criteria of intelligibility seems quite apparent for (1) but not so with (2).

Nonetheless, it is as difficult to formulate the criteria of intelligibility of the concept of sameness expressed by the second interrogative as it is for the first—despite the matter-of-fact and straightforward appearance of (2) and the mind-bending quality of (1). What is more, during the search for a philosophical theory of identity presupposed by "Are you driving the same car that you drove two years ago?" the question itself will begin to develop strange resonances. One can become genuinely puzzled over whether one is "really" driving the *very* same car, so that to say "yes" or "no" without further reflection will seem as simple-minded as responding in similar fashion to "Is the United States the same country that it was fifty years ago?" If one then concludes that no one properly understands the question "Are you driving the same car that you drove two years ago?" unless one can formulate the criteria of its intelligibility, it is only a short step to the proclamation that only philosophical questions are intelligible.

Let us take a rapid stroll through the philosophical quicksands surrounding the concept of identity, a terrain very well known to the ancients. There sits the family car in the driveway, looking somewhat the same as it did two years ago, when it was first purchased and registered with the motor vehicle department. There are, however, a few dents and scrapes, and it is no longer possible to peel rubber at 110. The old Ferrari will never be the same, we say. What do we mean? Are we really suggesting that the car in the driveway is not identical with the car purchased two years ago? Does it all depend on what you mean by . . . ? Some change, of course, is always taking place. How much makes a difference?

The most radical position, not surprisingly, is the Humean view of identity. According to it, the car, like any object, is "really" a different car from moment to moment. This position has the advantage of obviating the need to answer questions about how much change makes a difference. However, the Humean theory also has obvious disadvantages. Many conceptual dislocations are required to accommodate it. Consider, for example, the difficulties in even trying to *state* the view in an intelligible fashion. I said above that *the* car is a different car from moment to moment, to which the proper response, on the Humean view, is "Which car?" The use of the definite article here seems to commit us to a notion of identity quite different from the one we are trying to proclaim. A sentence like "The same car has been parked in my driveway for two days," in order to be intelligible on the theory being considered, has to be interpreted, roughly, as: "For any two point-instants in time, i_1 and i_2, where i_1 is not identical with i_2, and i_1 and i_2 both lie within the two-day interval, the car parked in the driveway at i_1 is identical with the car parked in the driveway at i_2." For the effort expended in reformulating the original statement, however, there is a reward. One no longer has to bother to look out the window in order to see whether someone has stolen or switched cars. The theory conceptually guarantees that no two objects at different instants of time can be identical with each other.

Something is wrong with the theory, one may say. The statement that objects at different temporal locations are not the same cannot function as a criterion for the intelligible application of the concept of sameness. How ridiculous if a negative reply is in order every time the motor vehicle department man asks whether one is driving the same car! How does the motor vehicle department decide such questions? To begin with, there is a certificate of title, on which is registered the motor and chassis numbers plus certain general characteristics of the car—the model, color, etc. When one first registers the car, an official notes these identifying characteristics on a form to be kept on file. So long as the defining characteristics are not changed, one can always prove to the satisfaction of the motor vehicle department officials that one is driving the same car. Well, then, why not elevate the identifying characteristics used by the motor vehicle department into a set of criteria of identity? The parts of the car can be conceptually divided, in the manner of Aristotle, into "essential" and "accidental." Changing the hubcaps is an "accidental" change; changing the piece on which the motor registration number is engraved is an "essential" change. In the latter case there is a change of identity, but not in the former. Looked at in this way, the identifying characteristics used by the motor vehicle department become part of the set of criteria of identity of the car; to challenge the criteria raises a philosophical problem because it threatens the intelligibility of sameness for those who accept the criteria.

This Aristotelian view of things is plausible to the extent that we are satisfied we have a reasonable way of demarking the essential from the accidental. If one asks for further criteria for defining the difference between the two, however, one is again faced with a philosophical problem. Any particular conceptual division of a car into essential and accidental components can be made to seem quite arbitrary. Suppose we replace the parts of the family Ferrari, one by one, until all are changed. If the first item replaced is the manifold head on which the motor registration number is engraved, then there has been a change of identity according to the motor vehicle department criteria; the new car may look very much like the old car, but it is a different one. The motor registration number, however, might have been located on the crankshaft—difficult to read, no doubt, but harder to change. Why should one's criteria of identity be dependent on the decisions automobile manufacturers make about where to put the registration number?

Would it be possible to convince the motor vehicle department men that one was driving the same automobile originally registered if one replaced all parts, including those parts used for identification purposes? Unless bureaucratic routines had hardened into a philosophy (as, in fact, often happens), they might be willing to register *the same car* under a different set of numbers. And this brings us to still another view of identity, one more interesting, perhaps, for historians.

Why can't we claim that the car really did remain the same, though all its parts were replaced *seriatim*? According to this conception, there can be no division of parts into accidental and essential, and in this respect the view resembles the Humean position on identity. Yet one is not required, as with the Humean view, to hold that a series of distinct cars present themselves from moment to moment. The identity of the car, let us argue, is a function of the temporal overlap of its parts. In tracing the history of the car, we are at the same time identifying it. Some such notion of identity would be called upon, I think, if one wished to persuade a government official that, though all the parts, including those containing the registration number, had been replaced at least once, the identity of the car had not changed. Let us call this view "the historical continuity theory" of identity. Note that it has certain peculiar features. Ordinarily, we would not distinguish between the following two procedures: (a) replacing the car parts gradually so that, after two years had elapsed, the car had a full set of new parts; (b) disassembling the car completely at some time during the two-year period, disposing of the old parts, and assembling on the spot a car composed of new parts. With (a) there is a temporal overlap of new parts with old, whereas with (b) there exists a temporal gap—a time during which any structural relationship between parts which identifies the car at any given moment is destroyed. With either procedure we apparently arrive, at the end of a two-year period, at the same point: the same structural relationship exists between new parts. If one accepts what I have called "the historical continuity theory" of identity, however, we should describe someone who follows procedure (a) as rebuilding his old car and someone who follows procedure (b) as building a new and different car. But what is to prevent us from describing (a) as *gradually* building a new and different car and (b) as *abruptly* building a new and different car? Nothing, at this stage, except a philosophical theory of identity.

To amplify the point, I shall choose a slightly different example. Consider now a child who is building a model windmill with the parts of a toy erector set. After the windmill is completed, the child decides to construct a model robot. As before, one could conceivably follow either of two procedures: (a) gradually transform the windmill into a robot so that there is a temporal overlap of the parts of the windmill-robot; (b) disassemble the windmill completely, put the pieces in a box, and start from scratch. Here, in contrast to the car example, the structural organization of parts undergoes radical transformation. Nonetheless, it makes sense, if one accepts the historical continuity theory of identity, to say that we are confronted in (a) by one object which undergoes radical change and in (b) by two objects, at different times, one of which is a windmill and the other a robot.

Is the difference between (a) and (b) trivial? With either procedure, one might argue, a robot has been built, and this is the important thing because our understanding of what the final object is rests solely upon our understanding of the structure and function of the parts of robots. This, of course, is the philosophical nucleus of the so-called functionalist position. Opposed to it are the historical evolutionists, who argue that our understanding of many things must be based on a historical knowledge of how they have evolved. The historical continuity theory of identity can serve as a criterion of intelligibility of identity to which the historical evolutionist can appeal.

Admittedly, in the examples presented so far, I have weighted the scales in favor of the functionalist, because it *is* difficult to see how the manner in which a particular toy robot is assembled can be necessary for understanding the nature of that robot. Examples more congenial to the historical evolutionist can be found, naturally, in the casebooks of biological evolution. And yet, even with the examples given, once one gets involved with such questions as whether the toy robot before us is the same object as, or a different object from, the toy windmill we saw yesterday, it may become conceptually enlightening to think about the manner in which the robot evolved, about the history of the robot. And when, in the future, perfect humanoid types are assembled in laboratories, our descendants will be able to differentiate themselves from the upstarts only be pointing to a difference in evolutionary history, a history of which we shall be a part.

THIS VERY BRIEF excursion into some of the problems of formulating criteria for the intelligible application of the concept of identity is sufficient, I hope, to lend a faint plausibility to the philosophical totalitarianism represented by idealism. The idealists capitalized on the circumstance that it is, apparently, always possible to dislocate matter-of-fact questions so as to give them philosophical overtones; for the idealists, it was always open season for hunting criteria of intelligibility. Thus F. H. Bradley, in his classic *Appearance and Reality* (1893), began by pointing to "the familiar instance of a lump of sugar. This is a thing, and it has properties, adjectives which qualify it. It is, for example, white, and hard, and sweet. The sugar, we say, *is* all that; but what the *is* can really mean seems doubtful."[10] Bradley then went on to ask whether we mean by sugar something existing apart from the properties of being hard, white, sweet, and so on, or just those properties "bound together" in a special relationship. He thought there were fearful obstacles to taking either view and concluded that, although "the arrangement of given facts into relations and qualities may be necessary in practice, . . . it is theoretically *unintelligible*. The reality, so characterized, is not true reality, but is appearance."[11]

[10] *Appearance and Reality* (Oxford: Clarendon Press, 1897), p. 16.
[11] *Ibid.*, p. 21 (my italics).

Neither the particular arguments Bradley used in support of his contention nor the details of the characterization of reality he proposed need detain us. The upshot was that, for Bradley, any attempt to describe the universe by simple statements expressing qualities and relations—such as "Sugar is sweet," "Fire-engines are red," "John is taller than Mary"—is unintelligible. "Our intellect, then, has been condemned to confusion and bankruptcy, and the reality has been left outside uncomprehended."[12] The kinds of characterizations of reality Bradley deemed intelligible involved the consideration of particular things as parts of absolute totalities, nonmaterial spiritual wholes. Bradley's technique is what concerns us. He began by questioning the criteria of intelligibility of the relationship of predicability expressed by such simple statements of fact as "Sugar is sweet." Because he found various criteria proposed by other philosophers or presupposed by common sense to be unacceptable, he denied that such statements are intelligible in the first place. In Bradley's language, what they describe is mere "appearance." He then went on to suggest criteria of intelligibility which he thought justified the position that things really are radically different from what they appear to be.

Among English-speaking philosophers, the reaction to idealism traversed two phases. In the first, led in England by Bertrand Russell and G. E. Moore, the conclusions about the nature of reality came under attack. The object of the attack was quite simple, and Russell has described it succinctly: "Bradley argued that everything common sense believes in is mere appearance; we reverted to the opposite extreme, and thought that *everything* is real that common sense, uninfluenced by philosophy or theology, supposes real. With a sense of escaping from prison, we allowed ourselves to think that grass is green, that the sun and stars would exist if no one was aware of them. . . . The world, which had been thin and log-

[12] *Ibid.*, p. 29.

81

ical, suddenly became rich and varied and solid."[13] The title of a famous article by G. E. Moore provides a handy summation of his and Russell's position at the time: "A Defense of Common Sense."

The second phase of the attack, as represented by logical positivism and the ordinary language philosophical styles, was an attempt to undertake a radical revision of philosophy itself. It is best understood, however, as an outgrowth of the initial reaction to idealism. An examination of Moore's philosophical tactics, accordingly, is particularly instructive as a way of putting recent Anglo-American developments into proper perspective.

I HAVE PRESENTED an account of the idealists' thesis that without philosophy our intellect is "condemned to confusion and bankruptcy," that without philosophy knowledge is impossible and "reality has been left outside uncomprehended." Croce developed one variation of this theme with his bold contention that history and philosophy are identical pursuits. Rather than enter into the technicalities of the arguments used by Croce or Bradley, I have tried to sketch a general picture of the kinds of considerations which led the idealists to thumb their noses at common sense and, I should add, science. It certainly seems in accord with common sense to say that anyone who claims he has been driving the same automobile for two years is asserting something perfectly intelligible. It also seems part of common sense to believe that we can often *know* we have been driving the same car for a certain period—that any question put to us about it would be a straightforward one, not involving any philosophical considerations. If, however, the question is interpreted as a philosophical one, as a signal to begin a quest for the criteria of the question's intelligi-

[13] "My Mental Development," *The Philosophy of Bertrand Russell,* ed. Paul A. Schilpp (Evanston, Ill. Open Court Publishing Co., 1946), p. 12.

bility—for some definition of identity presupposed in the question, for example—then it may no longer seem reasonable to say that the question was initially intelligible, at least until after a satisfactory definition of identity is produced. The question is only apparently but not really intelligible—or so an idealist would say. Nevertheless, we find that, as soon as we sally forth on the quest for criteria, we begin to founder. So many possibilities suggest themselves, none of them quite satisfactory and each raising further questions, that the way seems wide open for a radical revision of our concepts. We usually associate the term "idealism" with the results of such revision—with the denial of the existence of material objects or any object "external to the mind," with the view that reality must be comprehended as a spiritual whole, with the claim that by a philosophical contemplation of history one can prove that Reason is the Sovereign of the World and that the history of the world presents us with a rational process.

Moore and Russell attacked idealism by arguing that the conclusions drawn by the idealist were preposterous because so obviously false. The logical positivists and ordinary language philosophers argued that such conclusions were preposterous because so obviously meaningless. Although there is quite a difference between calling an utterance false and calling it meaningless, the work of Moore and Russell set the stage for the drastic overhaul of philosophy attempted by the logical positivists and ordinary language philosophers.[14]

[14] Consider, for example, the following, extracted from a logical positivist manifesto written by Rudolf Carnap, one of the leading figures of the movement: "In the first place I want to emphasize that *we are not a philosophical school and that we put forward no philosophical theses whatsoever.* . . . Any new philosophical school, though it reject all previous opinions, is bound to answer the old (if perhaps better formulated) questions. But we give no answer to philosophical questions, and instead *reject all philosophical questions,* whether of Metaphysics, Ethics, or Epistemology. For our concern is with *Logical Analysis.* . . . In traditional Philosophy, the various views which are

Consider again the kinds of problems encountered in pinning down a set of criteria for the intelligibility of identity statements. Take, for example, the statement "I have been driving the same car for two days." During the search the statement does appear to lose its straightforward, matter-of-fact appearance. Moreover, because its initial intelligibility depends in large measure upon its matter-of-factness, it may in turn appear to lose even this intelligibility. (Recall St. Augustine who, in a well-known passage from Book 11, Chapter 14 of the *Confessions*, wrote: "What, then, is time? If no one ask of

---

put forward are often mixtures of metaphysical and logical components. Hence the findings of the Logical Analysis of Science in our circle often exhibit some similarity to definite philosophic positions, especially when these are negative. Thus, e.g., our position is related to that of *Positivism* which, like ourselves, rejects Metaphysics and requires that every scientific statement should be based on and reducible to statements of empirical observations. On this account many (and we ourselves at times) have given our position the name of Positivism (or New Positivism or Logical Positivism). The term may be employed, provided it is understood that we agree with Positivism only in its logical components, but make no assertions as to whether the Given is real and the Physical World appearance, or *vice versa*; for Logical Analysis shows that such assertions belong to the class of unverifiable pseudo-statements. . . . The following article is an example of the application of Logical Analysis to investigating the logical relations between the statements of Physics and those of Science in general. If its arguments are correct, all statements in Science can be translated into physical language. This thesis (termed 'Physicalism' by Neurath) is allied to that of *Materialism*, which respectable philosophers (at least in Germany, whether in other countries also I do not know) usually regard with abhorrence. Here again it is necessary to understand that the agreement extends only as far as the logical components of Materialism; the metaphysical components, concerned with the question of whether the essence of the world is material or spiritual, are completely excluded from our consideration." Rudolf Carnap, *The Unity of Science*, tr. Max Black (London: Kegan Paul, 1934), pp. 21-29.

me, I know; if I wish to explain to him who asks, I know not.")[15]

Harried by possibilities, none of them very satisfactory, one may in desperation choose what is in many respects the purest theory of identity, namely, the Humean theory, according to which no objects at different temporal locations can be identical. Actually, the word "choose" does not bring out the captivating features of a philosophical theory, the way such a theory achieves its grip by functioning as an *idée fixe*. But whatever conceptual advantages the Humean theory may have, anyone who comes under its spell will have a hard time justifying its adoption on a practical basis. In particular, it runs counter to common sense; this, for G. E. Moore, was a sufficient reason to reject it out of hand.

Moore's technique consisted essentially in a brilliant use of the riposte. If it were true that no object at any moment is identical with any object at some other moment, he would say, then it would be false that the car I drove on Monday was the same car I drove on Tuesday. But I know it was the same car because it was my car to begin with, and I certainly did not sell it before Tuesday. So it must be false that no objects at different temporal locations can be identical. In similar ways, Moore defended common sense against any philosophical theory which had paradoxical consequences from the standpoint of common sense, paradoxical in that (1) it denied that something is the case which, according to common sense, we can say we know to be the case, or (2) it denied that something is intelligible which, according to common sense, is perfectly intelligible. Against the idealists' denial that material objects exist, Moore argued that he certainly knew that tables and chairs exist, and as these are surely material objects, that material objects exist. More important, against the idealists' claim that such statements as "Sugar is sweet" are unin-

---

[15] *The Confessions of St. Augustine*, tr. J. G. Pilkington (New York: Horace Liveright, 1927), p. 285.

telligible unless one can give a satisfactory account of their intelligibility, Moore held that such statements are *perfectly intelligible without such an account.* He would have admitted cheerfully that it is very difficult to analyze the concept of sameness in such sentences as "I have been driving the same car for two years," but he thought this no reason to suppose that the sentence is not perfectly intelligible.

The following passage, which is vintage Moore, brings out the latter point:

> In what I have just said, I have assumed that there is some meaning which is *the* ordinary or popular meaning of such expressions as "The earth has existed for many years past." And this, I am afraid, is an assumption which some philosophers are capable of disputing. They seem to think that the question "Do you believe that the earth has existed for many years past?" is not a plain question, such as should be met either by a plain "Yes" or "No," or by a plain "I can't make up my mind," but is the sort of question which can be properly met by: "It all depends on what you mean by 'the earth' and 'exists' and 'years': if you mean so and so, and so and so, and so and so, then I do; but if you mean so and so, and so and so, and so and so, or so and so, and so and so, . . . , then I don't, or at least I think it is extremely doubtful." It seems to me that such a view is as profoundly mistaken as any view can be. Such an expression as "The earth has existed for many years past" is the very type of an unambiguous expression, the meaning of which we all understand. Anyone who takes a contrary view must, I suppose, be confusing the question whether we understand its meaning (which we all certainly do) with the entirely different question whether we *know what it means,* in the sense that we are able to *give a correct analysis* of its meaning. The question what is the correct analysis of *the* proposition meant [. . .] by "The earth has existed for many years past"

is, it seems to me, a profoundly difficult question, and one to which, as I shall presently urge, no one knows the answer. But to hold that we do not know what, in certain respects, is the analysis of what we understand by such an expression, is an entirely different thing from holding that we do not understand the expression. It is obvious that we cannot even raise the question how what we do understand by it is to be analysed, unless we do understand it. So soon, therefore, as we know that a person who uses such an expression, is using it in its ordinary sense, we understand his meaning.[16]

Moore, as we shall see, had a great deal of trouble in trying to explain what it means to give an analysis of a concept. The term "analysis" suggests, among other things, the breaking down of a compound into simple parts, and Moore's use of the term in connection with philosophical enterprises carries with it the implication that concepts, like chemical compounds, are composed of simple elements. But whereas chemical theories make fairly clear what is meant by saying that chemical compounds are composed of chemically simple elements, one is in the dark about what could be meant by saying that complex concepts are composed of conceptually simple elements. Moore never saw his way out of this particular difficulty, and one must be allowed some leeway in interpreting his account of what philosophical analysis is supposed to be. However, there is enough of an analogy between what Moore called "giving an analysis of a concept" and what I call "formulating the criteria of intelligibility of a concept" to justify a partial rendering of one by the other.

It was characteristic of Moore's technique to treat a great many philosophical questions as if they pertained to matters of fact. Yet Moore did not have a satisfactory theory to account for the differences between a philosophical and a nonphilosophical question. Roughly speaking, he considered philo-

---

[16] "A Defense of Common Sense," in *Philosophy in the 20th Century*, II, 565-566.

sophical questions to be of two kinds: (1) substantive questions and (2) questions concerning the correct analysis of concepts or propositions. "Are there material objects?" is an example of the first kind. "What is the correct analysis of the concept of material object?" is an example of the second kind. Moore responded to the question "Are there material objects?" in the same way one usually responds to the question "Are there lions?" Of course there are lions, one says, I've seen them at the zoo. Of course there are material objects, Moore would have said, I've seen them at the zoo. For what is a lion if not a material object? Suppose one protests that one cannot really *know* that material objects exist unless one can state what it means to be a material object—that is, give a correct analysis of the concept—and that, in fact, it was the difficulty in the analysis of the concept that, in part, led the idealists to deny the existence of material objects. Moore would reply that, although someone might have a great deal of difficulty with the analysis of the concept of being a lion, this ought not dispose him to deny that lions exist.

I have said that Moore divided philosophical questions into (1) substantive questions and (2) questions about the correct analysis of concepts or propositions expressed in our language; but it is obvious that he did not believe that all substantive questions are philosophical. "Are there lions?" he did not think is a philosophical question, but he held that "Are there material objects?" is. How did he account for the difference? Putting this problem aside for a moment, one is assailed by another crucial uncertainty: did Moore believe *any* question about the analysis of *any* concept or proposition to be a philosophical question? To ask about the correct analysis of the concept of being a material object, or about the correct analysis of the proposition that there are material objects, one might say, is to ask a philosophical question. And Moore would have surely agreed. But what about asking for the correct analysis of the concept of being a lion or of the proposition that there are lions? Are these also philosophical questions for Moore? As far as I can tell, he never took up this problem directly, but my guess is that he considered all questions about the correct analysis of something to be philosophical questions. Thus he contended, in the long passage I quoted, that the statement "The earth has existed for many years past" is the "very type of an unambiguous expression, the meaning of which we all understand." Correspondingly, "Has the earth existed for many years past?" would have been considered by Moore an unambiguous question, the meaning of which we all understand. In contrast, "What is the correct analysis of the proposition that the earth has existed for many years past?" Moore held to be "a profoundly difficult question, and one to which . . . no one knows the answer" —in short, a philosophical question. But exactly what this latter question amounts to, and how it is supposed to be related to the former question, are puzzles Moore admitted he never satisfactorily explained or understood.

It seems as if all the philosophical perplexities exhibited at one level by philosophers before Moore emerged in him at another level. He claimed that he not only knew the meaning of the expression "Material objects exist" but also knew it to be true that they do exist. Nonetheless, he had grave doubts about what the expression means, about the correct analysis of the expression. The essential point for Moore was to take care that doubts about analyzing a concept or proposition not give rise to doubts about the intelligibility of statements expressing the concept or proposition. The business of analysis, according to Moore, is a totally different one from the business of understanding the world, or of understanding the language in which information about the world is communicated. In some notes taken of a lecture Moore gave in the early thirties, he is recorded as having said that "Our ordinary use of words is never affected by our philosophic analysis of their meaning"; hence, philosophical analysis does not lead to a clarification of the uses of language. It will lead to greater clarity, Moore contended, only when we are doing philosophy, which is worth doing for its own sake.[17]

Part of Moore's conception of analysis can be presented most clearly by means of one of his examples. "Suppose I say," he wrote, "the concept of 'being a brother' is identical with the concept 'being a male sibling.' I should say that, in making this assertion, I am 'giving an analysis' of the concept of 'being a brother'; and, if my assertion is true, then I am giving a *correct* analysis of this concept."[18] There are two things to note about this example. First, neither the analysandum nor the analysans is a linguistic expression; Moore argued that, in giving a correct analysis, one is stating an identity relationship between the concepts and propositions expressed by terms and sentences. But, second, the phrase that expresses the analysandum must, according to Moore, be synonymous with the phrase that expresses the analysans. Moore explicitly mentioned synonymity to be a necessary condition for giving an analysis. Hence, if one could show that the expression "brother" is not synonymous with the expression "male sibling," then one would also show that the concept of being a brother is not identical with the concept of being a male sibling; that is, one would show the analysis proposed above to be incorrect. Synonymity, of course, is a relationship that holds between linguistic expressions, but not between the concepts or propositions presumed to be conveyed by such expressions. Nonetheless, according to Moore, establishing that two expressions A and B are not synonymous is conclusive reason for rejecting any attempt to analyze the concept or proposition expressed by A by means of the concept or propo-

[17] "The Justification of Analysis" (notes of a lecture given by G. E. Moore, taken by Margaret Masterman and corrected by Professor Moore), *Analysis*, 1, no. 1 (Nov. 1933), 28-29.
[18] "A Reply to My Critics," *The Philosophy of G. E. Moore*, ed. Paul A. Schilpp, 2nd edn. (New York: Tudor Publishing Co., 1952), p. 664.

sition expressed by B, or vice versa. Thus, in the above quotation, Moore did not himself assert that the concept of being a brother can be correctly analyzed by means of the concept of being a male sibling. He put the matter conditionally, apparently because he thought there are grounds for holding that the expression "brother" is not synonymous with "male sibling." "It is obvious, for instance, that, in a sense, the expression 'x is a brother' is *not* synonymous with, has *not* the same meaning as, 'x is a male sibling,' since if you were to translate the French word *frère* by the expression 'male sibling,' your translation would be *incorrect,* whereas if you were to translate it by 'brother,' it would not."[19] If an expression A is synonymous with some other expression B and there is another expression C, in a different language, which expresses the same concept as that expressed by A, is it possible that C does not also express the same concept as that expressed by B? Moore evidently thought that, in such a case, either C was not a correct translation of A after all, or A and B were not synonymous in the first place. Moreover, if two different expressions, such as "brother" and "male sibling," are synonymous because they express the same concept, then it should be a matter of indifference which expression one uses when one asserts something. The only possible reason for choosing to say "My brother is married" instead of "My male sibling is married" would be a concern for style. The information communicated is the same whichever form is preferred.

Consider, in particular, the rather odd sentence: "The concept of being a brother is identical with the concept of being a brother." It is difficult to see how anyone using the sentence to make an assertion would be communicating anything at all; the informative content is null. But if "brother" and "male sibling" are a synonym pair, then replacing the second occurrence of the word "brother" by its synonym "male sibling" results in a sentence in which the informative content is also

[19] *Ibid.*, p. 667.

null—namely, the concept of being a brother is identical with the concept of being a male sibling. Moore held that, if he were to assert the latter sentence, he would be giving an analysis of the concept of being a brother, but now it looks as if giving an analysis amounts to saying nothing at all. What is the point of philosophical analysis as Moore conceived of it? One is faced with the following dilemma: all attempts to analyze a concept or proposition conveyed by some expression A by reference to a concept or proposition conveyed by some expression B will result in an incorrect analysis (if A and B are not synonymous) or in an utterly trivial statement (if A and B are synonymous). This dilemma is known in the literature as "the paradox of analysis," and Moore admitted that he didn't know how to get around it.

There was something wrong with identifying philosophy with "doing analysis," in Moore's sense of the term.[20] It is

[20] Wouldn't the paradox be neatly sidestepped if the synonymity requirement were dropped? Should a proposed analysis be rejected out of hand if it can be shown that the phrase expressing the analysans is not synonymous with the phrase expressing the analysandum? There is a simple answer to these questions—an answer which presupposes, however, that nonsynonymous expressions cannot express the same concept or proposition. Suppose one attempts to analyze the concept expressed by phrase A by means of phrase B, where A is not synonymous with B. Then if nonsynonymous expressions represent different concepts, the proposed analysis must be incorrect: the concept expressed by A is not identical with the concept expressed by B. But why insist that nonsynonymous expressions always represent different concepts? I do not think it necessary to so insist, but it would require too much of a detour to argue the point. One advantage of the synonymity requirement is that it functions as a negative decision procedure, an objective method for rejecting philosophical proposals. For whether or not an expression A is synonymous with an expression B in a given language is, presumably, a factual matter. Accordingly, the question "Can a correct analysis of the concept expressed by A be given by means of phrase B?" is matter-of-fact to the extent that correctness of analysis is a function of synonymy of expression. Given Moore's penchant for turning philosophical questions into questions pertaining to

true that Moore claimed he himself never "said or thought or implied that analysis is the only proper business of philosophy." "And, in fact," he added, "analysis is by no means the only thing I have tried to do."[21] Moore was right. His effort to defend common sense against the idealists did not consist in trying to analyze concepts or propositions. Far from it. Against them he played a waiting game. When *their* attempts at clarification led to conclusions at variance with common sense, Moore pounced. John Maynard Keynes has described the sheer physical impact of Moore's technique.

> In practice, victory was with those who could speak with the greatest appearance of clear, undoubting conviction and could best use the accents of infallibility. Moore at this time was a master of this method—greeting one's remarks with a gasp of incredulity—*Do* you *really* think *that*, an expression of face as if to hear such a thing said reduced him to a state of wonder verging on imbecility, with his mouth wide open and wagging his head in the negative so violently that his hair shook. *Oh!* he would say, goggling at you as if either you or he must be mad; and no reply was possible.[22]

Moore's philosophical position produced an entirely unsatisfactory state of affairs, and for a number of reasons. Moore had to assume that certain substantive philosophical questions differ from substantive nonphilosophical questions only by way of generality. In a set of lectures delivered in 1910-11, Moore stated that the first and most important aim of philosophy is to give a general description of the whole universe. Thus, for him, statements like "There are material objects in the universe" and "There are minds in the universe" differ from "There are lions in the universe" and "There are feelings

---

matters of fact, it is not surprising that he tried to impose synonymy as a checkrein upon philosophical analysis.

[21] "A Reply to My Critics," pp. 675-676.

[22] *Two Memoirs* (New York: Augustus M. Kelley, 1949), p. 85.

of pain in the universe" in that the former two are more general descriptions than the latter two. On this view, philosophy is a kind of science, related to such empirical sciences as biology and psychology but in some sense more general. It is quite obvious, however, that philosophy is not a science in its own right and that the question "Are there material objects as well as minds in the universe?" is not an empirical one to be answered by empirical observation. If Moore were correct, then to deny the existence of material objects (as the idealists did) would be as fatuous as denying the existence of mammals; the existence of lions proves them both. The difference between a substantive philosophical question and a substantive nonphilosophical question is not a matter of generality. Moore's approach is reminiscent of the story in which someone is asked whether he believes in baptism. The person replies that of course he believes in baptism, because *he has seen it done!* Moore's defense of common sense, like the reply about baptism, avoids the issue.

Then what is the point of a philosophical question? The logical positivists after Moore argued that no intelligible question can be both substantive and philosophical. All substantive questions are either scientific questions or else pseudoquestions having no point at all. Philosophical questions purporting to be substantive fall into the second class. Even if the positivists were correct about substantive questions, there would remain on Moore's view questions about the correct analysis of a given concept or proposition. But we have seen how, with Moore's conception of analysis, responses to questions of this kind are reduced to trivialities. In order to preserve the initial intelligibility of such questions as "Has Jones been driving the same car for two days?" and still provide a place and function for philosophical questions, Moore would have contended that the question "What is the correct analysis of the concept of sameness expressed in the first question?" is philosophical and that there is a point in the philosopher asking it, but that neither the latter question nor its answer *has any bearing on the intelligibility of the former question.* The philosopher *is* engaged in the work of conceptual clarification, according to Moore, but it is of a curious kind and at one remove. Again, in the long passage quoted earlier, Moore wrote: "It is obvious that we cannot even raise the question how what we do understand . . . is to be analyzed, unless we do understand. . . ." So unless we understand completely what it means to say that Jones has been driving the same car, we apparently cannot raise the question of what is meant by it. Yet if we understand completely what it means to say it, and also the conditions under which we can say it truly, then it is difficult to see what further understanding can be gained about the matter. Moore insisted, however, that our "ordinary use of words is never affected by our philosophic analysis of their meaning."[23]

It was just here that the ordinary language school found its fulcrum. In essence, the message was that, if we really do understand the ordinary uses of language, the philosopher cannot furnish further conceptual clarification of a different kind. Moore was hunting animals which didn't exist: there are no such things as concepts or propositions, and it is fruitless to ask whether this concept is identical with that concept, this proposition identical with that proposition. The meanings of expressions are their uses in a language; therefore, Moore was mistaken in supposing a distinction could be drawn between asking what is the meaning of the expression "The earth has existed for many years past" and asking *what is meant by it* (that is, what is the correct analysis of the proposition expressed by it). As a consequence, a large class of what, for Moore, constituted genuine and important philosophical questions—questions about the analysis of concepts and propositions—was jettisoned as pointless by most members of the ordinary language school.

[23] "The Justification of Analysis," p. 28.

I began by considering the idealists' thesis that every intelligible question is philosophical and concluded with a sketch of some of the strains of recent philosophy, the *leitmotiv* of which is that no intelligible question is philosophical. If philosophy is the attempt to formulate criteria of intelligibility and if philosophical questions create the need as well as the occasion for such attempts, then showing the pointlessness of philosophical questions is tantamount to destroying philosophy itself. Moore's effort to distinguish between asking for the analysis of a concept and asking a question that involves its application in a particular use of language was, on my interpretation, an attempt to distinguish straightforward, matter-of-fact questions from philosophical ones which would, at the same time, justify the asking of philosophical questions, *at least by professional philosophers*. Moore's habit, however, of treating philosophical questions as if they pertained to matters of fact—curious matters of fact, to be sure—as well as his insistence that the intelligibility of matter-of-fact questions is not affected in any way by the attempt to answer philosophical questions growing out of them, led to the collapse of the very distinction between philosophical and nonphilosophical questions that Moore had so desperately tried to maintain. Moore was right in supposing that there must be a distinction between the two. But we need a different kind of retaining wall to separate philosophical from nonphilosophical questions in order to prevent the study of history from sliding into the philosophy of history.

CHAPTER VI

Philosophical and Historical Questions About the Past

THE PRECEDING CHAPTER opened with a brief examination of some of Hegel's views on the nature of history and closed with a lengthy discussion of Moore's views on the nature of philosophy. The coupling may strike one as odd, particularly since Moore had little or nothing to say about history. Yet the history of the philosophy of history—at least that part controlled by professional philosophers—is of necessity controlled by the history of philosophy. What a philosopher says about the philosophy of history is shaped, however subtly, by what he believes to be the nature of philosophy and philosophizing, and Moore has had an enormous influence on Anglo-American philosophers. Philosophical styles in England and America are so radically different from those on the Continent that historians who wish to converse with Anglo-American philosophers on topics of common interest in the philosophy of history will usually do better to read Moore than to read Croce or Hegel. Choose at random a historian and an Anglo-American philosopher—it will be far more likely that it is the historian who has read Croce or Hegel. Philosophy, which traditionally had transcendent and transcendental expectations, is at present more regional than history. There is little disposition to peruse the works of philosophical foreigners. The popular conception of the historian as one peculiarly vulnerable to cultural pressures, certainly more than the philosopher, is sadly wide of the mark.

Throughout his career Moore was a philosopher's philosopher. Moore's philosophical parochialism, a total involvement with professional philosophy, quite clearly influenced his own conception of the nature of philosophy. He was not interested in the philosophy of mathematics or the philosophy of science, and certainly not the philosophy of history. Moore was concerned only with what I have termed "second-order" philosophy. As he once wrote, "I do not think that the world or the sciences would ever have suggested to me any philosophical problems. What has suggested philosophical problems to me is things which other philosophers have said about the world or the sciences."[1] Moore's preoccupation with second-order philosophy and professional philosophers drove him to characterize philosophy solely in terms of second-order considerations. Yet if one is to find a more intimate relationship between philosophy and history than that suggested by Moore's delineation, one must look beyond the recent history of second-order philosophy to first-order philosophy of history. Is it possible to steer a course between, on the one hand, the states' rights view of recent Anglo-American philosophy and, on the other, the federalism of idealism? Let us begin by scrutinizing the differences between philosophical and non-philosophical questions. The kinds of philosophical questions I shall examine for this purpose pertain to the general problem of attaining knowledge about the "perished" past. Historians as well as philosophers have had a keen interest in such questions. The consideration of these questions makes up an important part of the philosophy of history; for some writers, in fact, philosophical problems centering on our knowledge of the past make up *the whole* of the philosophy of history.

What, then, are the differences between a historical problem about the past and a philosophical problem about the past, between a matter-of-fact question and a philosophical question?

Let us take, to begin with, a historical and matter-of-fact question about the past: did Martin Bormann survive those

---

[1] "An Autobiography," in *The Philosophy of G. E. Moore*, p. 14.

last days in the Zoo Bunker beneath the *Reichskanzlei*? This is of some concern to historians and nonhistorians alike. Furthermore, it is a real question, an open one. The evidence given by those on the scene is conflicting. Some witnesses claimed Bormann was killed in a tank explosion on the Weidendammer Bridge on the night of May 1 or the early morning of May 2, 1945. One witness said he had seen Bormann's body. Another maintained that Bormann was never in the tank at all. Still another witness testified that he saw Bormann alive after the explosion, that Bormann changed into civilian clothes at the Hotel Atlas and then vanished. Trevor-Roper, who had the opportunity to interrogate many of the witnesses, was inclined to think when he wrote *The Last Days of Hitler* that the evidence, on balance, suggested that Bormann survived. Other historians may think otherwise. A few years ago a reporter wrote in *Der Spiegel* that Bormann was living in Paraguay. Rumors continue to flourish in the Sunday supplements. The question will remain open, perhaps, until that standard denouement, when Bormann is cornered as a waiter in Buenos Aires.

Why is Bormann's death a historical and open question? Is it because no one at present knows whether Bormann survived the night of May 1-2? This is certainly not a necessary condition. Suppose that Bormann did in fact escape, is now alive and of sound memory. Then at least one person knows whether Bormann escaped—Bormann himself. Nonetheless, the historical question of his death remains. Is it because no *historian* knows now, or ever knew, the answer? Again, this is not a necessary condition. Suppose Trevor-Roper, through some great British intelligence coup, had himself been secreted in the Zoo Bunker and had seen Bormann escape by another route entirely. Surely, the fate of Bormann in 1945 would under these circumstances no longer be a historical mystery, because at least one historian, Trevor-Roper, would know the truth.

Admittedly, Trevor-Roper's testimony would be given far more weight by his colleagues than the testimony of other "witnesses." I call attention to the word "witness" because, if Trevor-Roper had seen Bormann slip through the Russian lines, let us say, then no one *witnessed* his death in a tank explosion on the Weidendammer Bridge or saw him change into civilian clothes at the Hotel Atlas. But perhaps Trevor-Roper was mistaken. The man he saw was not Bormann. He was not a witness to Bormann's escape.

There seems to be a conflict in conjectures here. We hypothetically introduced a historian to the scene as the one true witness, only to whisk him immediately offstage by suggesting that he might have been mistaken in what he saw and not a witness after all. The point is that the problem of whether Trevor-Roper was mistaken and, in turn, the historicity of Bormann's escape would be a different one for Trevor-Roper than for other historians. Of course, either he was mistaken or he was not; there is no middle course. If he was not mistaken, then Bormann did escape, and this is what we first supposed. But we have no right to suppose anything of the kind—to take a point of view that goes beyond any to which every historian, not just Trevor-Roper, has access—if we are really concerned about the *historical* question of whether Bormann escaped. Trevor-Roper, had he been on the scene and were he later to have any misgivings about what he had seen, would be primarily doubting the reliability of his own memory or his own powers of perception, and only incidentally worrying about Bormann's escape. If other historians, though, continue in the face of Trevor-Roper's testimony to puzzle over the fate of Bormann, they will be predominantly concerned, not about the dependability of memory or perception (which must be assumed reliable under normal conditions), but about whether Bormann escaped.[2] Other testimony besides Trevor-Roper's will have to be considered; other evidence will have

[2] For further discussion of this point, see Chap. X.

to be weighed. To put it another way, even admitting that Trevor-Roper once *knew* that Bormann escaped would not require us to grant that either he or we now know it. In history there can be no such thing as a privileged position, even when some historian is alleged to occupy it.

The reason Bormann's survival is a historical question is not simply that no one knows the answer or, obviously, that no historian knows the answer. It would remain a historical question even if there were at present a privileged few (Bormann himself, perhaps, and his family) who really do know the answer. *Bormann's fate is a historical question because the usual procedures and methods used by the historian do not at the moment enable him to decide the matter.* There is not enough evidence, the existing evidence is conflicting; the reliability of the witnesses is dubious, their motives impugnable.

Contrast the very real question of what happened to Martin Bormann with another: namely, did Martin Bormann exist? Unlike his survival, Bormann's existence is not in question so far as historians are concerned. Bormann's existence is a historical fact. It is quite difficult even to imagine a conversation in which Bormann's existence would come into question and be debated seriously. It may happen that, when Bormann's name is mentioned, someone declares that he has never heard of him; but this is, of course, not the same as denying his existence. Anyone who required convincing could be shown evidence of such magnitude, such great variety, from so many different and independent sources, that only a crank, it would seem, could hold out in the face of it. Public newspapers and private memoirs refer to Bormann; official decrees and inter-office memos bear his signature. It would take more than a lifetime to inspect personally all the evidence which supports, directly or indirectly, the conclusion that Bormann existed. Consider just one piece of evidence: Hitler's proclamation, reported in the German newspapers, naming Bormann successor to Hess as head of the party chancery. Could these reports have been false? Then why didn't Hitler correct them? Perhaps Hitler didn't read the papers and so didn't know. . . ? One question so quickly leads to another that one is soon overwhelmed by the effort involved in merely trying to conjecture what possible evidence could be discovered that would prove superior to the evidence already in the possession of historians. Any evidence supporting the conclusion that Bormann succeeded Hess would also, it might seem, support the conclusion that Bormann existed. And Bormann's appointment was just one episode in his career. Think of all the other major episodes there are to be cited, each supported by evidence which in turn apparently supports the conclusion that Bormann existed. Unlike his survival, Bormann's existence is not doubted by historians. It is simply not an open question.

Both the interrogatives "Did Bormann survive?" and "Did Bormann exist?" express, in their ordinary employment, matter-of-fact questions. The question expressed by the former is not at present decidable; the latter is decidable. Both could be called "questions about the past," but only one is really a historical question. Some people have thought that it is the "undecidability" of a question that makes it philosophical. Yet as we have just seen, though philosophical questions may be undecidable, not every undecidable question is philosophical.

I suggested earlier that the form, the shape, or the size of an interrogative does not always signal when a philosophical question is being raised, that one and the same interrogative can be used to express either a philosophical or a matter-of-fact question.

Consider again the interrogative "Did Bormann exist?" In ordinary usage this would be construed as a question that is not only matter-of-fact but decidedly decidable. What makes the question of Bormann's existence decidable? It is the availability of a decision procedure which, for the issue at hand, yields unequivocal results: no examination of the historical record, in the ordinary way, has yet turned up any discrepancies in the record, any grounds for doubting Bormann's existence. Accordingly, one can use the interrogative "Did Bormann exist?" to pose a philosophical question only if one can twist it in such a way as to bring into question the validity of the decision procedure which would normally be taken to decide the matter. (Of course, one can often introduce a little skepticism just by adopting a suitable tone of voice. Inserting the word "really" with the proper inflection—"Did Bormann *really* exist?"—works wonders. Simple repetition of the question each time one is shown a piece of evidence will indicate that one is either a lunatic or a philosopher.)

One can be skeptical in many ways, some of them philosophically significant and some not. One is playing neither the philosopher nor the crank in suspending judgment about Bormann's escape. On the other hand, one *would* be dismissed as a crank if, having remained skeptical about Bormann's existence while being shown evidence that would convince any historian, one suddenly capitulated when presented with Bormann's birth certificate—for it surely is an eccentric idea that only birth certificates validly establish the existence of people.

In more cynical moments, when one is tired or contemptuous of philosophy, it is easy to dismiss the philosophical skeptic as a crank. And there are ways of playing the skeptic that make it appear as if the skeptic were nothing but a crank. Philosophers have philosophized not only with hammers but sometimes, unfortunately, with meat cleavers. There is no point in being a skeptic, however, just for skepticism's sake; one might as well be a crank. Even philosophical skepticism must lead somewhere, must have a point and direction.

Consider an example of meat-cleaver skepticism. One merely points out that it is *logically* possible that any document is a forgery. Therefore, it is logically possible that all the documents pertaining to Bormann's life have been forged. *Logically* possible, yes, but what about the usual procedures employed to distinguish a forgery from the genuine article? These procedures as well can be questioned, and so on.

One trouble with this mode of playing the skeptic is that we are allowed no time to catch our breath. We are bounced from a consideration of one kind of decision procedure to a consideration of another and are given no explanation why we should become concerned with such matters in the first place. Is the general point supposed to be that no one ever really knows anything about empirical matters of fact? Then why pretend that one is focusing on a particular decision procedure used by historians or is involved with skepticism about the past. If no one knows anything at all, then no one knows anything about the past. Q.E.D.

Philosophers often engage in a kind of game that has held some fascination for themselves but is of little interest to anyone else. It is played by attempting to formulate so-called incorrigible statements, statements which would be immune from any skeptical attack whatsoever. Descartes, one of the masters of the game, came up with "I exist" as an example of a sentence that can be used to make statements which can be known to be true by those who make them. How can one be skeptical of one's own existence, Descartes thought, if on each particular occasion when one is skeptical of one's own existence one cannot help but be aware that one exists, if only for the perverse purpose of being skeptical of one's own existence on that particular occasion? Although this sort of talk is all very entertaining, the fact of the matter is that no philosopher has ever proposed an incorrigible statement—a statement impregnable to attack from *any* skeptical quarter— that was of the slightest interest either to scientists or to historians. Scientists do not worry about whether a sentence like "It seems to me as if I am seeing a reddish tomato right now" can be used to make an incorrigible statement. Historians are not exercised about their own existences, though they could conceivably become concerned about Bormann's. Descartes, of course, had a reason for hunting incorrigible statements; he believed that only incorrigible statements could serve as the proper deductive basis to which all other truths could be safely moored. Yet if there is no connection, deductive or otherwise, between incorrigible truths and other kinds, then the search for incorrigibility is of second-order philosophical interest only. Moreover, only philosophical skepticism of the kind that bears directly on the particular decision procedures used by the historian is really relevant for the philosophy of history.

It is most unsubtle, then, and fatuous as well, to base one's skeptical leap into the philosophy of history on the bare logical possibility that all the documents supporting the conclusion that Bormann existed are forgeries. Before examining this matter further, I should like to show that there are more subtle routes for a skeptic to take when confronted by the overwhelming mass of evidence which points to the conclusion that Bormann existed. When the skeptic inquires "Did Bormann *really* exist?", let us suppose that the historian attempts to deal with the skeptic as he would with another historian—an aborigine historian, say, from the Australian outback who has not yet heard the news. The historian may exhibit a German newspaper in which is reported Bormann's succession to Hess. He may display a letter written by Goering, in which Goering comments on the way young Bormann is directing construction at Hitler's chalet, the Berghof. And so on. The aborigine sitting across the table, however, is not a historian but a skeptic. And perhaps he complains that he did not ask "*Who* was Bormann?" but whether Bormann existed. All the historian has done, he charges, is to provide answers to the question "*Who* was Bormann?": Bormann was the man who succeeded Hess, the man who directed the construction of the Berghof, and so on. In similar fashion, every school boy knows *who* Robin Hood was, but no historian knows whether Robin Hood ever existed.

One can see that no evidence of the kind usually provided

by historians will do the trick. And as the attestations and depositions continue to mount, the skeptic's question—"Did Bormann exist?"—begins to acquire a different ring. The question will have become "detached," as it were, from the ordinary decision procedures that historians follow in answering such questions. The question will not only have become undecidable but will no longer be matter-of-fact. The interrogative "Did Bormann exist?" will have been employed to pose a philosophical question, though we have yet to learn what such a question is or what the purpose of posing it might be.

What aim could be served by playing the skeptic? What is the point of turning a simple matter-of-fact question into a philosophical one? What is at stake, conceptually speaking, when one deliberately uses the interrogative "Did Bormann exist?" as an excuse to begin some philosophical exercise?

A number of things come to mind. Once one has succeeded in detaching a question from the ordinary decision procedures that would normally be used in answering it, the meaning of the question shifts, and one can exploit it for a number of philosophical purposes. But no matter what particular philosophical aim a philosopher or historian may have in mind, any transformation of a matter-of-fact question into its philosophical counterpart challenges the decision procedure to which the question is normally attached, for it is the decision procedure that gives the matter-of-fact question its original point and direction. Thus if we treat "Did Bormann exist?" as a straightforward, matter-of-fact question about the past, we are bound to abide by the methods historians use to decide it. And the verdict is unanimous: Bormann did indeed exist. Any refusal to accept the outcome, therefore, must bring into question the methods employed to arrive at that verdict, that is, the proffering of evidence by historians in the usual way. One general purpose, then, of posing what can be called "grassroots" philosophical questions is to challenge, in some way, the decision procedures normally used to decide the matter-of-fact counterpart to a philosophical question. The kind of skeptical challenge and the specific purpose of issuing it vary from one occasion to another, of course. Someone who contends that the evidence historians use to establish Bormann's existence succeeds only in establishing *who* he was, not *that* he was, could be suggesting that the historical past is as unreal (or real) as the fictional past—that Gladstone is "at present" as real as Pickwick. Or the point could be that only those who have seen Bormann with their own eyes can know *that* he existed; all others, including soon all living historians, can know of Bormann only by virtue of a set of descriptions which, strictly speaking, establish *who* Bormann was, but no more. These examples scarcely begin to exhaust the possibilities, but what is important is that each possibility raises a question which "transcends" the normal evidence in such a way that it is undecidable by means of that evidence. There are at least two senses, then, in which a question is unanswerable or undecidable: (1) the decision procedure (or procedures) ordinarily used to resolve similar questions fails to resolve it in the *particular* case; (2) the decision procedure ordinarily used to resolve such questions is itself put into question for *all* cases to which it is normally applicable.

Both the interrogatives "Did Bormann survive?" and "Did Bormann exist?" are customarily used to pose matter-of-fact questions. Both, in common usage, are intimately attached to the decision procedures that historians employ to decide such questions. The existence of such procedures gives the interrogatives their normal direction and point, their "matter-of-factness." The questions raised by both differ, however, in one important respect. The matter-of-fact question "Did Bormann survive?" is open; the matter-of-fact question "Did Bormann exist?" is not. Although the former is undecidable at present and may indeed always remain so, its matter-of-fact status is not affected. Its undecidability does not controvert the validity of the decision procedures with which it is connected. The historian knows what kind of evidence *would* be conclusive; the difficulty is that he does not have it and may never get it. Bormann's survival may always be in doubt.

Grass-roots philosophical questions arise in the normal course of any positive inquiry. In fact, they are often expressed by interrogatives that usually would be interpreted as posing matter-of-fact or decidable questions. It is this feature of many grass-roots philosophical questions that creates confusion; sometimes it is not easy to tell whether someone is posing a matter-of-fact or a philosophical question. Although it is extremely important that historians become aware of the philosophical penumbra surrounding the study of history, they must not mistake philosophical shadows for the substance of positive inquiry as it exists at the time at which they engage in it. To guard against this error does not mean, of course, that historians ought never to traffic in shadows; philosophical shadows, after all, sometimes prefigure the shape of the future path of positive inquiry.

Consider again the distinction between an open question such as "Is Bormann still alive?" and one that is not open— "Did Bormann exist?" Now a skeptic who does not accept the historical verdict as an answer to the latter question may, by his deliberate refusal to consider the evidence in the same way historians do, be suggesting that both questions are "really" open, that both are historical questions, and that to neither of them do historians really *know* the answer. There are always degrees of evidence, the skeptic may argue, and corresponding to degrees of evidence there are only probabilities, not certainties. Hence, one ought to speak of Bormann's existence as being only "probable"—highly probable, to be sure, and of course more probable than Bormann's survival, but still not certain. The skeptic may be hinting, then, that all questions about the past are really open but that some are more open than others.

The skeptic's recommendation—that we ought to think of all questions about the past as really being open—may appear innocent, but it is not. The skeptic is proposing a philosophical theory—moreover, one that is in many respects very attractive, for it can be couched in such terms that few historians will be aware of its skeptical intent. The word "certain" is often associated with attitudes of bigotry and intolerance. The word "probable," on the other hand, carries with it a suggestion of moderation and proper caution. Thus there is something initially palatable about any view which recommends that we ought never (or hardly ever) say we are certain about things. Then, too, the skeptic's argument may stimulate gloomy thoughts about the frailty of reason, and the introduction of probabilities rather than certainties may appear more seemly in light of that frailty.

Despite its innocent appearance, however, the skeptic's point —that the difference between a question about the past that is open and one that is not is only a matter of degree—is philosophically upsetting. It corrodes the distinction between what is "decided" and what is "undecided" about the past, between "historical fact" and "historical hypothesis," between "proof" and "conjecture," between the "certain" and the "probable," between historical "knowledge" and historical "belief," between historical "truth" and historical "fiction" (for there is surely *some* probability, however minuscule, that even Mr. Pickwick existed).

I have called attention by the use of quotes to a number of pairs of expressions, for it is the concepts represented by these expressions that come in for reexamination when a decision procedure, in which they are embedded in a certain way, is shaken. These pairs of expressions figure prominently in the lexicon of epistemology, and the criteria for the intelligible application of the concepts expressed by these pairs are what are being challenged by the skeptic. That is why the skeptic's theory is a philosophical one in the first place. His suggestion that all questions about the past are really open comes down to a proposal to formulate new criteria for the intelligible application of the concepts of historical fact, historical fiction, historical knowledge, and so on.

Of course, the skeptic's proposal may not appear to be philosophical, and appearances here may be deceiving. For if the skeptic had alleged instead that there is *no* evidence for the occurrence of *any* event in the past, everyone would have been able to recognize a philosophical thesis, if only because of its outlandishness and radical rejection of the usual decision procedures employed by historians. Still, it is important to realize that a theory which urges the treatment of the occurrence of *any* past event as more or less probable is philosophical also and is, as well, a departure from the application of concepts as they are normally embedded in the historian's decision procedures.

Now it is true that there are degrees of "openness," that there are many questions about the past where the evidence points more or less strongly in one direction or another, but not conclusively in any single direction; and with regard to such questions, the historian does use the language of probability. "Did Lee Harvey Oswald fire a rifle at President Kennedy?" "Yes, probably." "Was Jack Ruby a conspirator in a plot to assassinate President Kennedy?" "Probably not." Because so many questions about the past do require answers of this kind, it may seem reasonable to suppose that all do. Yet it would be a radical departure from the ordinary application of concepts in the standard decision procedures used by historians if it were held that the evidence sanctioned the historian to answer only "Yes, probably" when asked whether President Kennedy existed. One can attempt to make the claim more plausible by recommending that the historian say "very, very, very, . . . *very* probably President Kennedy existed." It is apparent, however, that no control can be exercised over the number of "verys" to be considered appropriate for this particular question about the past. The evidence certainly does not warrant any distinction between, say, the probability that JFK existed and the probability that FDR did. One might wish to maintain that they are equally probable; but then one might as well say that they are equally certain, that is, certain *simpliciter*.

The skeptic's thesis—that the distinction between open and nonopen questions about the past is a matter of degree—is a philosophical one: it amounts to a proposal that the present criteria for the intelligible application of such pairs of concepts as historical fact–historical hypothesis, historical truth–historical fiction, and so on, should be revised. And what are the present criteria for the intelligible application of these concepts? They are embedded in the ordinary employment of the standard decision procedures used by historians to decide questions about the past. The evidence at the historian's disposal does not conclusively establish that Martin Bormann survived the night of May 1-2, 1945; it does conclusively establish that Bormann existed. That Bormann survived is a hypothesis; that Bormann existed is not a hypothesis, but a historical fact. If we adopt the skeptic's point of view, then we are bound to say that the difference between fact and hypothesis is only a matter of degree, that the difference between historical truth and historical fiction is only a matter of degree. We can in theory assign degrees of probability to the occurrence of any event whatever, both events described in so-called fictional narratives and those recounted in so-called historical narratives, so that the difference between what is history and what is fiction would, on the skeptic's proposal, become a matter of degree.

The skeptic's position presents a perspective that, in its center of curvature, seems natural enough—probably Oswald fired a rifle at Kennedy, probably Ruby was not involved in any assassination plot—but that, as one moves along the axis of curvature, causes things to appear more and more distorted. If there is a very high probability that Kennedy existed, then there is a very low probability that he did not exist, but a finite probability nonetheless. And there is also a probability (higher or lower?) that all the events I believe happened last week—or yesterday, or five seconds ago—did not really happen.

If one is totally in the grip of this theory, it does not seem strange to say that there exists a probability that all the events which one thinks happened did not actually happen. For it is a characteristic of philosophical theories that they impose views of reality which make all other views seem warped and unintelligible to a certain extent. Once one takes on the probability style of discourse, one wonders how one could have been so blind as to suppose that even Kennedy's existence could be certain.

Which is the correct view then? Is Kennedy's existence certain or merely probable? One is faced here with competing criteria of intelligibility, and that is why such questions are baffling. No decision procedures exist that can be called on to decide issues like this one.

The philosophical conservative will prefer to stick to the criteria of intelligibility embedded in existing decision procedures. He will remind us (conservatives are forever *reminding* people about things) that the evidence the historian has at his disposal *entitles* him to say that he *knows* Bormann and Kennedy existed. The conservative will point out that the skeptic's proposal contains no guidelines for distinguishing degrees of probability. And if we are not equipped to answer such questions as whether or not Kennedy's existence is more probable than Adolf Hitler's, Moby Dick's more probable than Mr. Pickwick's, then any talk about probability and probabilities is without substance. Does it make any difference if we say it is *certain* that Kennedy and Hitler existed, instead of saying it is equally certain that both did?

The philosophical conservative, by defending existing criteria and procedures, can often make it look as if only his opponent, the skeptic, is playing the philosopher. He can make it appear that philosophical skepticism—and, by implication, philosophy itself—is a wrongheaded or foolish thing. F. H. Bradley's jibe, however, is still deadly accurate: an antimeta-physician is a metaphysician with a rival theory of his own. The conservative's philosophical wares are prepackaged by existing criteria and procedures. He sells only name brands. His philosophical position is entrenched quite firmly in the way we ordinarily think about things. The conservative phi-losopher offers us only the stock or common garden varieties of intelligibility—in short, common sense.

CHAPTER VII

Skepticism: Benign and Malignant

IN THE PRECEDING CHAPTER some of the disconsolations of philosophy were presented in the form of a morality play, with "skeptic" and "historian" as the principals. These epithets should not mislead one into thinking that the skeptic is necessarily played by a professional philosopher and the historian by a professional historian. Historians, as we shall see, are perfectly capable of taking on for themselves the role of philosophical skeptic. Professional philosophers (and particularly those who speak philosophy in the accents of the vernacular), for their part, can derive great satisfaction from playing historian, at least to the extent of defending what they consider to be the historian's proper intellectual *Lebensraum* from attacks by philosophical aborigines. In clever hands ordinary history, like ordinary language, really does seem all right. Being a historian, however, involves more than a defense of methods. Both the decision procedures and the concepts employed by the historian represent the positive study of history only as it exists at a given time. Professional philosophers may be able to afford the luxury of indulging themselves in various clarifications; professional historians, however, are responsible for the *future* of their own discipline. They must get on with it. For them, ordinary history can never really be all right.

Philosophical skepticism, provided it is of the right sort and is administered on the right occasions, has always been an important prelude to fundamental conceptual reappraisal. But what is the right sort, and when are the right occasions? A skepticism that is too broad, too pervasive, will not allow one to get a proper grip on the concepts embedded in the decision procedures of the particular positive inquiry in which one is interested. How do we know, wondered Bertrand Russell in his *An Outline of Philosophy*, that the whole world did not come into existence five minutes ago complete with memories, records, and fossils.[1] He answered the question himself, asserting that we have no valid reason for believing that the world is more than five minutes old.

> I might have come into existence a few moments ago, complete with just those recollections which I then had. If the whole world came into existence then, just as it then was, there will never be anything to prove that it did not exist earlier; in fact, all the evidence that we now have in favor of its having existed earlier we should then have.[2]

Skepticism of the Russellian kind leaves the study of history quite intact, even though most of the beliefs held by historians about the past would, on that hypothesis, turn out to be false. Yet historians need pay no attention to possibilities of this sort. Neither the methods nor the concepts they employ in making sense of the past need come up for reevaluation. Contrast this general skepticism with the more "temperate" kind contained in the suggestion, discussed in the last chapter, that the difference between historical fact and historical fiction is only a matter of degree. On the Russellian skeptical hypothesis, the sentences "Mr. Pickwick once skated on thin ice" and "Mr. Gladstone once skated on thin ice" would both be false; nonetheless, the distinction between historical fact and historical fiction remains, to all intents and purposes, what it always was. It is true that one way of describing the difference

---

[1] *An Outline of Philosophy* (London: George Allen & Unwin, 1927), p. 7.

[2] *Human Knowledge: Its Scope and Limits* (New York: Simon and Schuster, 1948), p. 212.

between fact and fiction would no longer be available—we could not characterize it in terms of truth and falsehood. There should in any case be little disposition to portray the difference between fiction and fact in such straitlaced terms. Is it really enlightening to be told that all sentences in *Pickwick Papers* are false? What is wrong with reserving a right to use both the concepts of falsehood *and* truth even in such "fictional" contexts. (The sentence "Mr. Pickwick was over seven feet tall" is false; the sentence "Mr. Pickwick was *not* over seven feet tall" is true.) Were the more general skeptical thesis accepted, the historian would still be forced to go after the facts about Mr. Gladstone in the same old ways. And there would still be conclusive evidence that Mr. Gladstone existed but no evidence that Mr. Pickwick did. Neither the historian's decision procedures nor his use of concepts connected with them would be affected. In contrast, the more modest proposal—that the difference between fact and fiction is only a matter of degree—does bear in a direct and crucial manner upon the study of history and is, therefore, relevant to the philosophy of history in a way that Russell's proposal is not.

One might attempt to dispute this contention by arguing that the suggestion that all statements about the past are only more or less probable also leaves intact the historian's usual employment of concepts. Presumably, the probability that Gladstone existed would be extremely high and the probability that Pickwick existed extremely low; one could accordingly say that sentences in novels have low probability values attached to them, whereas assertions in history books have (let us hope) high probabilities. A distinction between fact and fiction could be discerned; one could still draw a line somewhere. One could, of course, arbitrarily draw a line between what is to be termed "fact" and what "fiction," even with the modest proposal. Justifications would have to be found for making the distinction, however, and the new concepts of fact and fiction would perforce be different from the old. Russell's conjecture, on the other hand, is of no consequence for the study of history precisely because the criteria for the intelligible application of the *historian's* concepts are not affected by it. To make this claim is not to assert, of course, that a skeptical thesis of this kind has no bearing on any concept whatever. It could serve, for example, as a spur to examine the concept of time—of what it might mean to say that the universe began at some point in time (never mind if it was only five minutes ago). In the study of history, however, time is not of the essence.

Is the discipline of history peculiarly vulnerable to skeptical attack? Many writers have thought so. The historian is confronted with stacks of dusty documents, heaps of corroded coins, locks of hair, shards—dead traces of things once active and vital. An impenetrable wall, it seems, frustrates the historian from ever achieving an epistemological consummation with the object of his intentions. Sometimes, if lucky, the historian manages to hear snatches of conversations from the other side of the wall. Sometimes bits of trash and garbage are thrown over the wall. From these scraps he must reconstruct what has taken place in those delightful walled gardens to which he is forever denied access. It is not surprising, given the potency and currency of the image, that some have succumbed to a foolish theory, a theory that proposes to substitute the traces of past events for the events themselves as the only fitting objects worthy of historical attention. The historian's task, it has been suggested, consists solely in the attempt to predict, from the documents and artifacts in his possession, what documents and artifacts he is likely to find if he looks in the right direction. On this view, the historian is made out to be rather like a sulking boy who, having been denied admission to the walled garden, avers that he had no desire to enter in the first place, being content to play with the leavings of the past.

True, the historian does not always find enough scraps of

the right sort; he must continually be on the lookout for more. Then, too, he often gets too many scraps of the wrong sort. Nonetheless, it is a mistake to suppose that he can never know what has been happening on the other side of the temporal barrier—that he can never come upon enough scraps of the right sort. Would a person who sees bits of orange peel sailing over the wall be wrong to conclude that someone is peeling an orange on the other side? Well, of course, it is possible that some crazy inventor has devised an orange-peel-throwing machine, which has just been installed. But would it not be better to climb over the wall and see with one's own eyes whether someone actually is peeling an orange, or whether it is only an orange-peel-throwing machine, before hastily concluding from the flimsy evidence of flying orange peels that *someone* is peeling an orange? On the other hand, one might be confronted with someone peeling a wooden orange and mistakenly suppose that he is peeling a real orange. One far-fetched possibility deserves another. Perhaps the prevalence of the view that the historian's knowledge about the past is inferior to other kinds of knowledge is rooted in the belief that perceiving something to be the case is always more certain than remembering that something was the case, and that remembering that something was the case is always more certain than being told that something was the case. This belief, in turn, nourishes those philosophical theories that attempt to draw a line between "direct" and "indirect" knowledge, the former kind presumed to be more "valid" than the latter. One may disagree about the point at which to separate the two kinds of knowledge—about whether remembering that something was the case should be considered an example of direct knowledge or relegated to the status of indirect knowledge. Philosophers have also questioned whether so-called indirect knowledge is, properly speaking, knowledge at all. No matter what the variant, the historian is invariably shortchanged, since he is presented as a person who gets his information from someone else; historical knowledge, accordingly, is classified as being of the most indirect sort—if, indeed, it can be dignified by the term "knowledge" at all.

Despite its charming simplicity (which perhaps accounts for its plausibility), the theory just sketched is fundamentally mistaken. According to it, the historian's knowledge (if we can call it "knowledge") of the battle of Trafalgar, say, is necessarily inferior to the knowledge possessed by those who wrote firsthand accounts upon which the historian ultimately must base his narrative. Again, according to the same theory, the knowledge possessed by those who wrote the accounts was necessarily inferior, at the time they wrote, to the knowledge they possessed at the time of the actual battle (for surely, by the time they sat down to write the accounts, they had already forgotten part of what they had observed). Something is amiss. We have not given sufficient weight to the consideration that a knowledge of what it was that happened at the battle of Trafalgar presupposes conceptual integrations of various kinds. This is why it is so obviously false that those who drew up firsthand accounts of the battle necessarily knew less when they wrote than when the battle was proceeding. Suppose that all they perceived during the battle was powder and smoke, alarums and excursions—the view of history that can be called "Tolstoyan," the chaos of individual happenings. Still, even the writing of a simple report requires one to sort things out. Should we say therefore that the battle did not take place the way it was reported because any report, to be intelligible at all, must introduce some kind of unification? For all that was "directly" observed, after all, was chaos.

Consider an analogy. Suppose it were true that every green surface is composed of minute yellow and blue specks that can be seen only with the aid of a microscope. Some would be disposed, no doubt, to take the "close-up" view of reality and claim that green surfaces are not *really* green. Those who favored this position would still have to find a way of specifying the difference between green apples, say, and those which are spattered with globs of blue and yellow paint. "In the end," they might assert, "a difference in quantity amounts to a difference in quality." Others would be inclined to let common sense be their guide: green apples are green and "that's an end on't." No amount of philosophical talk about quantity and quality, they would say, can eliminate the greenness of things.

Yet one is not really required to adopt one orientation to the exclusion of the other. Both have their uses and abuses. Similarly, the "up-front" or Tolstoyan picture of history—history unadorned by conceptual embellishments—if it can be grasped at all, does not have priority over other kinds. There may even be conceptual advantages, for some purposes, in taking a view of history precisely the opposite of Tolstoy's—namely, the Hegelian historical perspective, history as seen from the standpoint of some overriding master plot. Could you write a coherent history of mankind without having one?

A delightful cartoon depicts a tourist with a bewildered expression surveying the ruins of ancient Rome. "What *happened?*" he exclaims. His question strikes us as comical because it seems that he has no conceptual grasp of what he is observing. He is not looking at the aftermath of some explosion that happened just that morning. Describing what transpired at the battle of Trafalgar depends upon the historian's getting a correct conceptual hold on the events whose concatenation makes up the battle of Trafalgar. Eyewitnesses are not necessarily in a better position to describe what is taking place at the time they are eyewitnesses. Nor is the historian necessarily in a worse position one hundred and fifty years later. The conclusions one reaches while actually observing something are not necessarily more authoritative than conclusions based on recollection or reflection. Historical knowledge is not more vulnerable to skepticism than, and hence epistemologically inferior to, other kinds.

Yet if I am right that historical knowledge is not peculiarly

open to skeptical attack, why have so many thought otherwise? One reason, already mentioned, is that insufficient
weight has been given to the role of concepts. One's knowledge
that something took place often presupposes a knowledge of
what it was that took place. The point can be overemphasized;
nevertheless, the greater error is to underemphasize it or to
forget it altogether. Knowing what it was that happened in
history requires conceptual organization; part of the historian's
task is to provide it. Cannot the historian have a better *knowledge* of what occurred than those who witnessed the events
of which he writes? Do we not often expect this of the historian? Is it not true that we often wonder what future historians will say about the present, particularly when we lack
an adequate perspective on the events we are living through?
Is there, then, any basis for the common prejudice about the
peculiar epistemological vulnerability that historical knowledge is supposed to have?

Imagine a man stealthily removing a sheet of blue paper
from his desk drawer, carefully placing it in an envelope, ty-
ing the envelope to a stick of dynamite, and burying the pack-
age thirty feet underground. He and only he knows the
color of the paper buried in his garden. When we attempt to
become privy to his knowledge, he triumphantly pushes the
plunger of the magneto that explodes the dynamite. Now he
has us at his mercy. Who could know better than he the color
of the paper which has presumably been blown to smith-
ereens? Who but he could possibly know, in the first place, the
color of the paper? Our historical "knowledge" of the color of
the paper is entirely "secondhand." We must rely on an informant. Do we really want to say that we, too, *know* that
the paper is colored blue, if our informant says it is blue? Why
speak about historical knowledge at all when, as this example
shows, any opinion on the matter, even to qualify as informed
opinion, depends upon there being an informant?

The charge that historical "knowledge" is an inferior brand

will stick if one can use the above example as a skeptical die. Yet one can use it thus only to the extent that one can generalize from certain features of the example. Consider a variation. The informant tells us that the paper is colored blue. He presses the plunger. Nothing happens. The dynamite fails to explode. We race him to the garden and dig it up before he can destroy it. But the paper we dig up is red! Did the informant lie? He seems to be quite astonished and dismayed and gives every impression of being a man upon whom a trick has been played. Have his powers of recollection failed him? Did he mistake the color in the first place? None of these conjectures need be true. The paper is blue litmus paper, its color changed by the acids in the soil. Thus even where only the "simplest" kind of perception—"direct" color perception without any apparent conceptual overlay—is involved, knowing *that* an object is a certain color can turn out to be a function of knowing *what it is* that is so colored.

The past becomes a blank screen when no traces of past events are available. If the dynamite had gone off, then of course we would have had to rely upon the informant. But it is a mistake to suppose that what this consideration shows is that the *historian* is in a particularly bad situation, epistemologically speaking, vis-à-vis his colleagues in other disciplines. The picture of the historian as a man trying to live in the past and being forever denied his wish—unlike his scientific colleagues, who live entirely in the present and are interested only in events they can directly observe—is nothing but a caricature. Geologists and astronomers, just as historians, investigate the "perished" past, and their knowledge too is often limited by the lack of traces. Yet no one imagines that the geologist or astronomer is in an impossible epistemological situation.

Perhaps, it will be argued in reply, the central concern of the historian is with human transactions, with events that often leave no physical trace but must be witnessed by eyes and ears.

Yet any information which comes from using one's own eyes and ears is more certain than information which depends on another person's experience and interpretation, or so it might seem. And that is why, to return to the example considered before, one desires to see for oneself the color of the buried paper, rather than merely to take the word of the informant. This kind of argument, however, is plausible only to the extent that it can succeed in ignoring the conceptual overlay upon so-called raw experience. Does one check on the doctor who reports hearing a heart murmur by demanding the use of the stethoscope to hear for oneself? Certainly not. One goes to see another doctor!

The widespread belief that "historical" knowledge is inferior and is peculiarly vulnerable to skeptical attack achieves a good part of its hold, I think, because of an uncritical generalization upon one epistemological model. One elevates the kind of knowledge one has when experiencing pain, or when tasting something sour, and so on, into the very paradigm of all knowledge. Pain is direct and immediate. One cannot be mistaken when one is in pain (a psychosomatic pain is still pain). Naked pain needs no conceptual clothing to be recognized for what it is; knowing that one is suffering a pain in the throat requires no inferences, unlike the knowledge that one has a streptococcus infection of the throat. Knowing that one is presently in pain is surer than knowing that one was in pain three weeks ago. Knowing that one was in pain three weeks ago is surer than knowing that someone else is (or was) in pain.

A too eager acceptance of the model has led some philosophers to reconstruct every epistemological situation in its image. They have supposed that all knowledge is based upon inferences from naked smells, looks, sounds, and the like; that one really sees, not tomatoes, but bulging reddish patches; that one feels squishes and hears plops when one throws bulging reddish patches on hardish-looking white planes. And from all these sensations one must *infer* that a tomato was spattered, a knowledge less secure than the knowledge that one had been confronted by bulges, squishes, and plops. If a philosopher accepts this account, it is not surprising that he will pity the poor historian, who admittedly cannot experience the bulges, squishes, and plops of the past. Yet we might well wonder who is the more to be pitied.

I trust I have said enough to give one pause before granting that history is more vulnerable to skeptical attack than, say, astronomy—that the historian cannot claim to know, for example, that Napoleon was defeated at Waterloo because neither he nor anyone else alive today was present at that affair. (Nobody knows the trouble I have seen because nobody can know my sorrow. This is surely one of the most perennial of philosophical laments.)

To attempt to anticipate all possible rejoinders would, at this point, be otiose. I have, I think, dealt with the more likely ones. Assume for the moment, however, that I am wrong, that the historian does provide an easy mark for the skeptic. What difference does it really make? Skeptics are just as prone to attack knowledge claims based on so-called direct perceptual experience as they are to harp upon the documents and artifacts theme. We may think, for a time, that the physicist is better off than the historian because he can confirm with his own eyes Galileo's report of the rate of falling bodies. (He cannot confirm with his own eyes that *Galileo* saw what Galileo said he saw. Some recent *historical* analysis suggests that Galileo, like many a good physics student today, "dry labbed" some of his experiments.) Yet even the study of physics, as we saw in considering some of Hume's arguments, has its soft epistemological underbelly. Why worry about degrees of vulnerability?

Some philosophers, and some historians as well, convinced by skeptical arguments that it would take heroic labors to protect history's position on the tree of knowledge, turned around and attempted to locate history on a different tree of knowledge altogether. R. G. Collingwood's view of history, as we shall see, was premised on the assumption that historical remains must be authenticated "from within," that the historian has to be able to enter the minds of historical figures in order to know that actions imputed to them in documents really did take place. And this, in turn, led Collingwood to proclaim the methodological autonomy of historical study.

Collingwood's conclusion may be sound. The historian's major concepts, as presently employed, may turn out to be so radically different from those of the physicist that it would be incredible to suppose they could share any but the more superficial criteria of intelligibility. I shall suggest in Chapter XV that, if one contrasts history with geology rather than physics, there is less of a disposition to believe in the existence of a radical break in continuity between history and science. For some, however, this consideration will provide scant comfort. Are human actions the same as geological processes? What about free will? I said that Collingwood's general conclusion may be sound; many of the arguments used to arrive at that conclusion, however, are unsound. One should be very wary about deriving such important consequences from premises that seem of such slight moment. Are we really prepared to proclaim the methodological autonomy of history simply on the ground that the historian works from documents and artifacts? If the historian is not epistemologically vulnerable merely because he does not himself experience the events of which he writes, then every philosophical examination of the criteria of historical concepts need not begin from the same point of departure. The documents and artifacts theme has been highly overrated in the philosophy of history.

Skeptical challenges, like Russell's, can be so general that they leave the study of history quite intact. So far as a particular positive inquiry is concerned, skepticism plays a useful role only when it is in some way relevant to that inquiry. Skepticism can act as a catalyst for the philosophy of history to the extent that it succeeds in provoking reflection about the criteria of intelligibility of historical concepts. That the historian is rarely a direct witness of the historical events in which he is interested does not, I strongly submit, mean that he is in an epistemologically inferior position. Thinking otherwise encourages one to suppose that the primary purpose of skepticism in the philosophy of history is to show just that—to prove that no one can have knowledge about the past. Similarly, it is a mistake to think that, if a particular skeptical probe can be turned aside, it must have failed its purpose. There is, in fact, no single axis in the philosophy of history around which all debates between skeptic and antiskeptic turn. The philosophical issue is not simply "Can we have knowledge about such and such?" with the skeptic saying "no" and the antiskeptic answering "yes." Or, to put it another way, the question of whether we can have knowledge—about the past, say—is not a simple one.

CONSIDER the example of Charles Beard. Most people are under the impression that Beard's sole purpose, in his famous article "That Noble Dream," was to show the impossibility of ever attaining an "objective" knowledge about the past. This impression is strengthened by the very title of the article, for Beard used the expression "that noble dream" to refer to a belief in "the possibility of finding and stating the objective truth in history."[3] The most dramatic part of Beard's argument, to be sure, consists in bringing philosophical skepticism to bear in questioning that possibility. He points out that "the historian is not an observer of the past that lies beyond his own time"[4] and concludes from this circumstance that the historian "cannot see it [the past] *objectively* as the chemist sees his test tubes and compounds."[5] Furthermore, "multitudinous events and personalities escape the recording

---

[3] "That Noble Dream," in *The Varieties of History*, p. 323.
[4] *Ibid.*   [5] *Ibid.*

of documentation." Nor can the historian be "reasonably sure that he has assembled all the documents of a given period, region, or segment."[6] Moreover, "since the history of any period embraces all the actualities involved, and since both documentation and research are partial, it follows that the total actuality is not factually knowable to any historian. . . . History as it actually was, as distinguished of course from particular facts of history, is not known or knowable, no matter how zealously is pursued 'the ideal of the effort for objective truth.' "[7] Beard then goes on to remark that the "events and personalities of history in their very nature involve ethical and aesthetic considerations,"[8] leaving the reader to draw the conclusion (as most will from this observation) that objectivity in history is impossible. (Presumably, Hitler's mustache objectively belonged to him, though his wickedness did not, since wickedness, it seems, unlike a mustache, exists only in the eye of the beholder.) Then, too, the historian's mind is not a neutral medium through which stream his ideas about history, unaffected by his personality, his hopes, desires, fears, and aspirations. Even those "overarching" hypotheses and conceptions "employed to give coherence and structure to past events in written history" are "an interpretation of some kind, something transcendent."[9] Beard ends by contending that "the validity of the Ranke formula . . . is destroyed by internal contradictions. . . . The historian's powers are limited. He may search for, but he cannot find, the 'objective truth' of history, or write it, 'as it actually was.' "[10]

Given the variety of skeptical arguments that Beard exploits, as well as his eloquence in presenting them, it is no wonder that most readers recall only the most dramatic thesis of "That Noble Dream": that objective historical knowledge is impossible. Yet there is a more subtle thesis contained in Beard's article. It must be remembered that Beard's own economic

[6] *Ibid.*, p. 324.   [7] *Ibid.*   [8] *Ibid.*
[9] *Ibid.*   [10] *Ibid.*, p. 325.

interpretation of constitutional history was at that time under attack and that he wrote "That Noble Dream" partly by way of replying to his critics. He was accused of being "partial and doctrinaire" in his interpretation of constitutional history. Why? Apparently because he was taken to be merely interpreting historical events when he should have been trying to discover what had really happened. Constitutional history was presumed to be composed of certain political events, and any analysis in place of a political analysis was counted as a mere interpretation, unqualified to be the true statement of what had actually taken place.

Although Beard did assume a skeptical stance regarding the possibility of objective historical knowledge, he did not do so solely to indulge himself in certain philosophical thrills. He was a working historian, and he employed philosophical skepticism as a lever in the attempt to pry his fellow historians from the notion that history is in essence political history and that any other kind has to be regarded as mere interpretation. If philosophical skepticism could show that the past is unknowable as it actually was, then, Beard thought, the writing of *any* kind of history necessarily becomes an interpretive affair. Orthodox constitutional history, no less than economic "interpretive" history, imposes an interpretation upon historical events. "A book entitled *An Economic Interpretation of the Constitution*," Beard asserted, "like every book on history is a selection and an organization of facts; but it serves advance notice on the reader, telling him what to expect." "A book entitled *The Formation of the Constitution* or *The Making of the Constitution*," Beard went on, "is also a selection and organization of facts, hence an interpretation or conception of some kind, but it does not advise the reader at the outset concerning the upshot to be expected."[11]

To pick up the philosophical issue here, ask yourself why it does not seem quite right to describe someone who is writing

[11] *Ibid.*

a standard history of England as working on a *political* interpretation of the history of England, though there is nothing
odd about describing someone as writing an *economic* interpretation of the history of England. The expression "a political
interpretation of the history of England" suggests a history
written from the point of view of one political party—say, a
Whiggish history of England. The phrase "the history of
England" apparently refers to a certain set of political events,
so that in its ordinary employment explicit mention of the
political aspect of the history of England implies a certain political partisanship toward a certain set of political events.
Similarly, because the expression "the history of England"
antecedently refers to a certain set of political events, turning
out an economic interpretation of the history of England
means attempting to explain such political events as the decline in power of the monarchy in terms of particular economic
developments that took place at the time. Note, in addition,
that we still tend to contrast specialized histories, such as the
history of art, science, or music, with history *simpliciter*—the
history of political events.

The practical purpose of Beard's skeptical arguments was
to liberate the concept of history from "political" criteria of intelligibility. He was out to show that the concept of history is
not identical with the concept of political history, that economic interpretations have, philosophically speaking, just
as much right to be considered history, properly speaking, as
the more orthodox kinds of history.

Were all of Beard's skeptical arguments really needed to
make that point? The answer depends upon how deeply in-
grained are conceptual habits; sometimes only the most vio-
lent of skeptical assaults will provide the necessary shock
therapy. Yet after Beard had used them, the very same skeptical arguments were obviously a source of embarrassment
to him. Beard, as a historian, could not easily remain content
with the view that his own version of constitutional history

was just as good as, but no better than, any other version. He did firmly believe that the events described in his *An Economic Interpretation of the Constitution of the United States,* as well as in his *Economic Origins of Jeffersonian Democracy,* had taken place more or less as he had portrayed them. If he had thought otherwise when he wrote his histories, he would not have been a historian but a charlatan. And so, in the very same essay in which he argued that "the possibility of finding and stating the objective truth in history" is nothing but a "noble dream," he also claimed that economic interpretations of history do not necessarily violate "the ideal of the effort for objective truth." "The historian who searches out and orders economic aspects of life, events, and interests," Beard contended, "may possibly be as zealous in his search for truth as any other historian searching out and ordering facts in his way."[12]

Was Beard inconsistent? Note first that he was shrewd enough to leave himself an exit line or two to use when it came time to lay aside his skeptic's mantle. In a passage cited earlier, Beard stated, more or less parenthetically so as not to distract attention, that "history as it actually was, *as distinguished, of course from the particular facts of history,* is not known or knowable. . . ."[13] This hedging seems like philosophical pussyfooting to those who are more metaphysically inclined than Beard. Is it really possible to separate, conceptually, historical fact from historical interpretation so completely that a skeptical x-ray treatment will kill a theory deemed philosophically cancerous while leaving intact the "particular facts of history"? Yet Beard's instincts were sound. As a working historian, he knew that, although he might be able to give a good shake or two to existing decision procedures (the use of documents and artifacts in the ordinary way), he could not abandon them altogether. Every man can be his own his-

[12] *Ibid.*
[13] *Ibid.*, p. 324 (my italics). Cf. note 7.

torian only up to a point, for it is the existence of common decision procedures that creates the possibility of history by creating the possibility of attaining objectivity in history. And so objectivity in history on at least one level—the level of "particular facts"—was implicitly acknowledged by Beard to be something more than a dream. In addition, Beard could not allow his own narrative focus, his concentration on the details of economic life, to be dismissed as just one more way of doing history, no better if no worse than any other. Having fought hard to liberate the concept of history from political criteria of intelligibility, Beard sought to anchor it in economic criteria. He called for "exploring the assumptions upon which the selection and organization of historical facts proceed."[14] He maintained that "there is nothing in the nature of an economic interpretation of history that compels the interpreter to take any partisan or doctrinaire view of the struggle of interests."[15] And he concluded with a plea that historians examine the criteria by means of which they might hope to "bring the multitudinous and bewildering facts of history into [a] coherent and meaningful whole." "Through the discussion of such questions the noble dream of the search for truth may be brought nearer to realization, not extinguished."[16]

"That Noble Dream" actually contains two themes. One is that objectivity in history is only a noble dream, but the other is that the historian should not abandon that noble dream. Was Beard, then, an incurable romantic, urging the historian on to strive, strive, strive for the unattainable? I have suggested a more complicated resolution. As a historian, Beard's skeptical leap into the philosophy of history had to be qualified. He could not in the process kick away his springboard—the historian's decision methods—altogether.

He was committed, by the nature of his calling, to the possibility of attaining historical truth (the discovery of the "particular facts of history") as well as involved in the task

[14] *Ibid.*, p. 328.   [15] *Ibid.*, p. 326.   [16] *Ibid.*, p. 328.

of making history intelligible. History, as Beard saw it, was not intelligible in purely political terms. And so he plumped for a different narrative focus, one in which attention was centered on economic events.

Was Beard, then, really a skeptic? Well, perhaps on Saturday nights, when he was not working on some history or other. He could not in good conscience be both a historian and a skeptic simultaneously, even though his skepticism had a practical relevance to the study of history as a stimulus to the examination of the criteria of intelligibility of concepts. This tells us nothing about whether Beard's Saturday-night philosophical orientation toward life was one of Pyrrhonic skepticism, objectivism, Neoplatonic post-rational eclecticism, or whatever philosophical school you care to invent or name. I have been concerned only to investigate Beard's involvement with the philosophy of history, and I am suggesting that it is quite possible for a while, at any rate, to do philosophy of history—to examine and formulate criteria of intelligibility of historical concepts—without committing oneself to any particular second-order philosophical position. It is when one starts worrying about what is involved in a quest for criteria of intelligibility, or what is to be done when there are conflicting criteria for a given concept, that one begins to cast about for some general philosophical position.

CHAPTER VIII

Use and Abuse of Skepticism in Philosophy of History

ONE CAN NEVER really be certain that p; it is impossible to *know* that p—these are some of the more common skeptical schemata. Perhaps the very simplicity and regularity in form of such skeptical openers encourage the mistaken belief that the philosophical issues exposed by skepticism are equally simple and regular. Because a great deal of philosophical thinking takes place in an epistemological matrix, one can easily be fooled into imagining that the holy grail of skeptical yearning is a unitary concept called "*the* concept of knowledge," in quest of which a philosopher must always be prepared to take leave of his senses. The kinds of philosophical issues exposed by skepticism, however, are at least as numerous as the kinds of concepts expressed by the different sentences that might be represented by the letter p in the above schemata—if one knows how to look. Philosophical interrogations are successful when they manage to provoke reflection about conceptual frameworks, expressed as criteria of intelligibility, which are often so deeply embedded in habitual routines and procedures that one is not aware of their presence at all. Yet although a philosopher may succeed, by a clever use of the skeptic's scalpel, in calling attention to certain important and largely unnoticed features of a conceptual landscape, he is prone to cutting himself on his own instrument. Instead of being content with an examination of criteria of intelligibility of concepts, made possible by his exploratory incision, a philosopher will be sorely tempted to perform radical surgery in order to gain a quick access to knowledge and truth. René

Descartes and R. G. Collingwood, who differed vastly in temperament and philosophical orientation, are two philosophers who succumbed to the temptation.

Descartes's *Meditations* has been admired, from the time of its publication until today, by almost all philosophers as the embodiment of the very paradigm of philosophical reasoning. Yet, in fact, only the first two "Meditations" excite contemporary philosophical interest. By the end of "Meditation II," Descartes succeeded in attaining his main philosophical objective—namely, to provide certain suggestions or hints of suggestions about some of the criteria of intelligibility for the concepts of belief, knowledge, mind, body, sensory experience, dream, and a few more as well. Descartes's skeptical technique exposed these concepts by challenging, in the right way, some of the knowledge claims in which they find much of their ordinary expression. In "Meditation III," Descartes thought it philosophically necessary to overcome the skepticism introduced in the first two, and so he made the mistake of treating a question like "Can I really know that there doesn't exist a powerful evil genius who has employed his whole energies in deceiving me?" as a simple question, involving a single issue. Admittedly, given the criteria of intelligibility Descartes suggested, the question is crucial. It is not a simple question, however, to be resolved by proving the existence of *le bon Dieu*, who in His infinite benevolence could not permit so evil a genius to torment Descartes in such a delicious, if philosophically malicious, manner.

Descartes found it philosophically upsetting to make room for the possibility of a demon because one of his proposed criteria of knowledge amounts to the following: it is unintelligible for anyone to claim that he knows something while admitting at the same time that he could be mistaken. Therefore, if anyone asserts that he knows, say, that the addition of two and three makes five, he cannot allow that his addition could possibly have been at fault. Yet how can anyone really guarantee his computational decision procedures, even in the solution of simple problems, especially when there may be demons about to jiggle his pencil or gremlins to foul his computer? Descartes writes: "And, besides, as I sometimes imagine that others deceive themselves in the things which they think they know best, how do I know that I am not deceived every time that I add two and three, or count the sides of a square, or judge of things yet simpler, if anything simpler can be imagined?"[1]

It is a good question, but it cannot be answered in the way that Descartes goes about answering it. An argument for the existence of God does not settle a question of this sort, even if such an argument should turn out to be a genuine proof. Gods and devils are quite capable of existing side by side. Although Descartes held that without a knowledge that God exists and is no deceiver "I do not see that I can ever be certain of anything,"[2] he could not, even with such knowledge, conceptually eliminate the possibility of error altogether. Is it really unintelligible to admit that possibility when one claims to know something? *That* is the question which should be considered when one is faced with the skeptical imputation that gremlins may exist. Descartes's failure to reconsider it goes a long way toward explaining why the final three "Meditations" are, for the most part, historical curiosities only. No matter. Descartes's main philosophical objective—to provoke reflection about the criteria of intelligibility of certain concepts—had been reached.

Descartes went astray at precisely the point at which he began to treat skeptical questions in literal fashion. He was overcome by the temptation to take the question "Can one really know when one is not mistaken?" as one which required a direct answer. The function of this question, however, is to

[1] "Meditation I," in *The Philosophical Works of Descartes*, I, 147.
[2] "Meditation III," *ibid.*, p. 159.

stimulate interest in the criteria of intelligibility of certain concepts.

The letter *p* in a skeptical matrix like "Can one really ever know that *p*?" has to be replaced by a *sentence* (rather than by a noun phrase, say) in order to generate an interrogative that can, in turn, be used to pose a skeptical question. Now if the purpose of the philosophical question were solely to investigate a unitary concept called "*the* concept of knowledge," then it wouldn't much matter which sentence one substituted for *p*. The emphasis would be upon what it means to *know* something, never mind what. But it obviously does matter. Replacing the letter *p* by the sentence "This is a robin's egg" generates the interrogative "Can one really ever know that this is a robin's egg?" Replace the letter *p* by "All robins' eggs are blue," and you obtain a quite different interrogative: "Can one really ever know that all robins' eggs are blue?" These different interrogatives can be used, in turn, to provoke quite different kinds of philosophical issues. No one is surprised when a skeptical opener like "Can one really ever know that all robins' eggs are blue?" is advanced by way of introducing a philosophical problem about induction. A quite different response is elicited, however, and a quite different set of philosophical problems suggested, by the question "Can one really ever know that *this* is a robin's egg?"

Logicians call sentences like "This is a robin's egg" *singular* sentences and sentences like "All robins' eggs are blue" *general* sentences. Here again it would be a mistake to think that all singular sentences or all general sentences, when located within the skeptical matrix, are bound to pose the same kind of philosophical issue. Both "This document was written by Gustavus Vasa" and "This is a robin's egg" are singular in form; yet, within the skeptical matrix, each can raise different philosophical issues. Similarly, the interrogative "Can one ever really know that no robin's egg is nonblue?" suggests an entirely different philosophical problem from that inspired by "Can one ever really know that nothing attains a greater velocity than the speed of light?" Both of the *p*'s within the matrix, however, are general in syntactical form.

Other kinds of sentence classifications may lead to different philosophical partitionings. Sentences have tenses. Would it be judicious to adopt as one's guide a classification of sentences by tense and lump together all philosophical problems about the past simply because all the *p*'s within the skeptical schema are expressed by means of the past tense?

One hesitates when the matter is put so unguardedly. I am afraid, though, that inadvertent acceptance of sentential classificatory principles has legislated, by default, a great deal of philosophical thinking and that, in particular, even those philosophers who have been most sensitive to the philosophy of history have attempted at times to structure their philosophical investigations around what they call *the* problem about the past. There is no problem about the past in general, not even an epistemological one. To think otherwise impairs one's philosophical acumen in analyzing historical concepts; every issue is approached by one predetermined route. The interrogative "Can one ever really know that the discovery of the printing press was instrumental in the development of the Renaissance in Northern Europe?" suggests a different kind of philosophical problem than the interrogative "Can one ever really know that Bormann existed?" Yet recognizing the difference will not, I fear, check a disposition to try and arrange both problems along one epistemological continuum— to think that one could not, logically speaking, be skeptical about such "simple" facts as Bormann's existence without also being skeptical about such "complex" facts as the contribution of the printing press to the development of the Renaissance in Northern Europe.

There is, I contend, no one epistemological problem that can be labeled "*the* problem about knowledge of the past." Skeptical issues, moreover, are not simple, though sentential classificatory principles will give the false impression that they are easily classifiable. Skepticism about historical knowledge is useful when it manages to arouse an interest in criteria of intelligibility of historical concepts. He who is not aware of this utility will misunderstand one of the main functions of philosophical questions. In fact, it often happens that a philosopher will penetrate a particular decision procedure, uncover some of the concepts largely unnoticed in its ordinary employment, but then, after having attained the main objective, think that some wholesale vindication or replacement of the original decision procedure is absolutely necessary. It is at this point that one begins to hunt for shortcuts to knowledge and truth.

Now LET US turn to R. G. Collingwood. His book *The Idea of History* is pivoted around an attack on a historiographical style that he summarized with the label "scissors-and-paste history." Scissors-and-paste history, according to Collingwood, is "history constructed by excerpting and combining the testimonies of different authorities."[3] It was against this notion of "authority" that he rebelled—against the view that the historian stands in an essentially passive relationship to his authorities, that to all intents and purposes the historian can only maneuver by playing off one authority against another. One of Collingwood's objectives was to bring out the conceptual aspect that underlies both historical description and explanation. On the scissors-and-paste view of history, reading a document is analogous to making a simple observation, and constructing historical theories and making historical interpretations an affair of adding or subtracting documents. Collingwood's attack on scissors-and-paste historiography is reminiscent of Croce's criticism of Taine's maxim: *Après la collection des faits, la recherche des causes.* Both Collingwood and Croce maintained that the historian does not first collect

---

[3] *The Idea of History*, p. 257.

facts and then cast about for explanations. What is to be called "historical fact" is always subject to an "overarching" conceptual control. There is a great deal of truth in this way of looking at the matter, and I shall argue something in a similar vein later on.

If finding out what happened in history is not like experiencing a toothache, if a conceptual hegemony must be exercised over the way even "simple" historical events are portrayed, then it is obvious that one must meet a document more than halfway. Any interpretation of a document or artifact requires an implicit appraisal of its value as evidence in the first place. Philosophical skepticism can be a dramatic way of making that very point. Does the historian really know, one may ask, whether any event ever takes place as reported in a document? Is documentary evidence ever sufficient? These questions can provide the occasion for a reexamination of the concept of historical evidence, for a critical look at what is presupposed in the ordinary use of the historian's standard decision procedures. One point that can easily escape notice, for example, is that the "amount" of evidence provided by a set of documents and artifacts is not a function of some simple additive process.

How much evidence would be needed to convince historians that the Napoleonic wars occurred before the French Revolution? Can anyone even conceive of the kind or amount that would do the trick? Carbon dating perhaps? Suppose that a new refinement of carbon-dating techniques allows one to estimate the age of an object to within one year and that, when any document or artifact from the Napoleonic Wars is compared with any document or artifact from the French Revolution, the former is always found to be older than the latter—according to the new carbon-dating process, that is. Here, indeed, would be a real issue between science and history on which one could choose sides. If the Napoleonic Wars took place after the French Revolution, then certain very important laws of nature would have to be considered false; if, on the other hand, the laws of radioactive decay are true, then the Napoleonic Wars must have taken place before the French Revolution. Yet the significance of the French Revolution and its relationships to the rise of Napoleon, and the role given to both sets of events in the development of the course of modern European history, make it literally inconceivable, as far as historians would be concerned, that Napoleon could have flourished *before* the French Revolution. It would be for them much less shocking to suppose that the universe itself is no more than five minutes old.

If historians lost the fight, if history had to give way to physics, the only recourse left for historians would be to jettison the evidence. Locks of hair presumably plucked from Napoleon's head which show him, according to carbon dating, to have been two hundred years old in 1821 would have to be plucked from the body of evidence bearing on Napoleon's existence; and so on for each item. One can almost imagine each document and artifact now regarded by historians as primary source material on the French Revolution and the rise of Napoleon being rejected as spurious without casting serious doubt upon the general outline of history as commonly conceived, until the received view, like the grin of the cheshire cat, came to float without visible support in any particular set of documents and artifacts. Almost, but not quite. In the end, the historian would have to fall back upon the use of existing decision procedures until he was in a position to replace them by something better. A carbon-dating challenge of the kind imagined would not do the trick because a radical alteration of historical calendars would not of itself provide the means for a reconstruction of the historical past. The intelligibility of history would have been shattered almost beyond repair. Philosophical skepticism works, in a hypothetical sort of way, much as an actual carbon-dating challenge would in fact. Both can certainly bring to light the utilization of historical concepts and conceptualizations for performing even the most mundane of historical tasks. Yet both challenges would have to be, for much the same reason, conveniently forgotten afterwards if no better procedure were forthcoming for deciding questions about the past.

Philosophical skepticism, I am contending, can play a useful function in at least one of two ways: in helping to expose concepts or in preparing the ground for a replacement of existing decision procedures. Yet, without resorting to science fiction devices such as time machines, it is difficult to imagine what decision procedures could prove superior to those the historian already has in his possession. It is, then, reasonable to assume that, if skepticism is to contribute at all to the study of history, its main aim must be to bring to light historical concepts and conceptualizations. The common mistake of philosophers is to conflate two functions: to suppose that, because skepticism about decision procedures provides a handy route for commencing a fundamental examination of concepts, the decision procedures themselves need to be immediately replaced. Collingwood's *The Idea of History* provides a beautiful illustration of this common pitfall.

Scissors-and-paste history, according to Collingwood, presupposes that "historical truth, so far as it is at all accessible to the historian, is accessible to him only because it exists ready made in the ready-made statements of his authorities."[4] "The criterion of historical truth," Collingwood pointed out, cannot consist in a simple "agreement of the statements made by the historian with those which he finds in his authorities."[5] Accordingly, the historian is not acting improperly if he refuses to accept the testimony of *any* authority, no matter how authoritative an authority that authority may be. The historian must, of course, have his reasons. Part of Collingwood's point, however, was that the historian can legitimately question a particular authority without having to produce a counter-

[4] *Ibid.*, p. 235   [5] *Ibid.*, p. 238.

authority of equal stature. Weighing evidence is not a matter of balancing one document off against another. One does not construct history with scissors and paste.

Collingwood was surely right in contending that the criteria for the intelligible application of the concept of historical truth (or of historical fact) cannot consist in some simple correspondence between what the historian says and what his authorities say—even if authorities never disagree. But authorities do disagree, and so in the nature of the case the basis upon which the historian can justify his choice of the particular authorities that he decides to back must be a complicated affair. The relationships between historical evidence and the versions of history that can be legitimately constructed upon that evidence must, of necessity, be fantastically tangled—so tangled that some have despaired of ever finding any intelligible relationship between them at all and have espoused, accordingly, some variety of historical relativism. Collingwood was well aware of the complications. To expose some of them, he developed in *The Idea of History* an analogy between history and crime detection. A detective need not take any piece of evidence at face value—sometimes he is more interested in why *x* said *p* than he is in the truth value of *p* itself. The detective develops hypotheses, cross-examines witnesses, inquires into motives, and so on. And just as detectives do, in fact, often solve crimes correctly, so historians, Collingwood maintained, can by historical examinations force secrets from their authorities that the latter did not know they were revealing.

To be sure, the relationship between historical evidence and historical truth is complicated. If one did not suspect as much at the outset, a consideration of some skeptical arguments would soon alert one to that fact. Yet there are dangers here, for a misconstruing of the skeptic's questions about the use of historical evidence can actually disguise the complex nature of the relationship between evidence and truth. In granting that the historian need not accept *on someone else's authority* that the facts are as they have been reported by that authority, one should not be tempted to proceed to ask on whose authority the historian does accept or reject testimony. The question is misguided because it poses the issue in too simple a way. If the historian does not reject or accept a document on his authorities' authority, then, almost inevitably, it will seem as if the only alternative left is that the historian must do so solely on his own authority. But if the exercise of the historian's authority is not to be a matter of whim or caprice, it would seem that the historian must somehow be able to confront historical truth directly so that he can exercise his own authority to reject or accept historical evidence in an intelligent manner. A fantastic notion? Yet that is exactly what Collingwood suggests:

> I began by considering a theory according to which everything is given: according to which all truth, so far as any truth is accessible to the historian, is provided for him ready made in the ready-made statements of his authorities. I then saw that much of what he takes for true is not given in this way but constructed by his *a priori* imagination; but I still fancied that this imagination worked inferentially from fixed points given in the same sense. I am now driven to confess that there are for historical thought no fixed points thus given: in other words, that in history, just as there are properly speaking no authorities, so there are properly speaking no data.[6]

Such an impasse should provide strong inducement to retrace the steps that led up to it, particularly if one is not disposed to throw in the towel by coming down on the side of historical relativism, thus abandoning the concept of historical truth altogether. Collingwood, like almost all professional philosophers, was constitutionally unable to accept philosophical relativism as the last word. Yet, instead of ask-

[6] *Ibid.*, p. 243.

ing himself whether the impasse could be avoided, he took the heroic path of attempting to dismiss historical evidence altogether as awkward impedimenta in the search for historical truth. He proposed to bring about "a Copernican revolution in the theory of history" by means of the "discovery that, so far from relying on an authority other than himself, to whose statements his thought must conform, the historian is his own authority and his thought autonomous, self-authorizing, possessed of a criterion to which his so-called authorities must conform and by reference to which they are criticized."[7]

Yet if "the historian has no direct or empirical knowledge of his facts, and no transmitted or testimoniary knowledge of them,"[8] how, according to Collingwood, could the historian really know anything at all? "My historical review of the idea of history has resulted in the emergence of an answer to this question," wrote Collingwood in *The Idea of History*: "The historian must re-enact the past in his own mind."[9]

Now Collingwood used this cryptic formula for a number of conceptual purposes and for the resolution of a number of problems. Some of the Collingwoodean resolutions covered by the formula were brilliant. As a response to historical skepticism, however, the formula misses the mark completely. What, in fact, did Collingwood mean by "reenacting the past in one's own mind"? How, in particular, could such reenactment overcome the unbridgeable hiatus alleged to exist between historical evidence and historical truth?

AN ILLEGIBLE TABLET and a document written in an undecipherable language are pieces of historical evidence, the very physical existence of which can provide certain clues about the historical past. Yet everyone will admit that, were the tablet legible and the document decipherable, their utility as historical evidence would be increased immeasurably. Why? Collingwood's answer might run somewhat as follows: The

[7] *Ibid.*, p. 236.　　　[8] *Ibid.*, p. 282.　　　[9] *Ibid.*

physical existence of a tablet is by itself not important. An illegible tablet is of use to a historian when and only when he can determine something of its purpose, what the person who made it had in mind. Were the tablet legible, certainly something more of its purpose would be manifest; hence, other things being equal, a legible tablet is always a better piece of historical evidence than an illegible one. The final historical objective, Collingwood would tell us, must be to discover the thought that lay behind the construction of the tablet. All history, ultimately, is the history of thought.

The matter becomes more complicated, of course, when one considers not only the tablet maker and his thoughts but also the person or persons whose deeds are chiseled upon the tablet. The historian is almost invariably more interested in the activities described on tablets than in the activities of tablet makers. Yet even though the problem is more complex, Collingwood's thesis remains the same. The historian's objective is to see events from "the inside," to penetrate the thoughts that lie behind the deed, the thoughts of a hero as well as the thoughts of a scribe. And, according to Collingwood, there is only one way that the historian can achieve this perspective: "To discover what this thought was, the historian must think it again for himself."[10] When the historian cannot rethink the thoughts of historical personages, their actions become opaque, and the utility of the document describing such actions, as historical evidence, is impaired.

Consider, as an analogy, an archeologist confronted by a stone artifact whose use he does not fathom. Suppose the evidence that it is an artifact is based entirely on observation of its physical characteristics. Could nature have produced those scalloped edges? Compare this with a borderline case. A curious stone is found in an ancient barrow amidst a heap of oyster shells. Suppose that its physical characteristics do not establish whether it is natural or man-made. Will it open

[10] *Ibid.*, p. 283.

oysters? One discovers that it does, handily. Establishing that it was a tool means establishing that it had a use. To determine if it had a particular use in the past, one must "reenact" that use in the present. In the borderline case, then, one must wait to discover the purpose of an artifact before one can say that it is an artifact in the first place. What is more, one cannot consider it a piece of historical evidence until its function as an artifact has been established. To establish its status as evidence, one must see its purpose, reenact its use.

It is no accident, I suppose, that an archeological example provides an excellent illustration for Collingwood's thesis; Collingwood was himself an archeologist as well as a philosopher. But just how good is the example? Does Collingwood's thesis work so neatly for all domains of historical inquiry? Let us consider a nonarcheological example, yet one which is fair to Collingwood. Collingwood maintained that histories of warfare are possible because "the intentions of a military commander are easy to understand . . . and from the recorded account of his acts we can reconstruct in our own minds the plan of campaign which he tried to carry out."[11] Of course, we must presuppose, Collingwood warns us, that the commander's acts were done on purpose because, "if they were not, there can be no history of them; if they were done on a purpose that we cannot fathom, then we at least cannot reconstruct their history."[12]

The criterion of historical truth that Collingwood proposed would, if sound, restrict the historian's activity very severely. Much of what is commonly accepted as historical fact—in general, that which could not be construed as pertaining to purposive, rational actions—would have to be jettisoned, even though the historian's ordinary decision procedures might appear to establish such facts beyond reasonable doubt. These limitations would, no doubt, upset historians; still, they might be persuaded to take a philosophical gain at the

[11] *Ibid.*, p. 310.   [12] *Ibid.*

expense of a historical loss if historical truth were promised as compensation.

Let us confine ourselves, then, to the history of warfare. To simplify further, let us choose a military hero who was also a scribe, so that we do not have to worry about the possibility of mistaking the thoughts of historical authorities for those of historical personages. Consider, if you will, the task of writing a true account of the actions of Vice-Admiral Cuthbert Collingwood at the battle of Trafalgar, an account that would transcend historical evidence by overcoming historical skepticism and would get at historical truth directly. The evidence in question would include eyewitness reports by British, French, and Spanish observers, private journals, log books, battle plans, and the like. As recently as 1914 a British Admiralty committee was convened to examine the evidence relating to the tactics employed by Nelson at the battle of Trafalgar.[13] There were, it seems, serious discrepancies in the various records of that most important British naval victory, and the task of the committee was to sift the evidence and prepare a definitive account of the battle.

One of the problems was that of reconciling the plan of attack, as drawn up by Nelson in the so-called Nelson Memorandum, with eyewitness reports of observers aboard the combined fleet of French and Spanish naval units. According to the battle plan, Vice-Admiral Collingwood was to launch a perpendicular assault against the column formation of the combined fleet and to engage the last twelve ships of the line, while Nelson dealt with the forward part of the column. According to some eyewitnesses, however, Collingwood broke through astern of the Spanish flagship, the "Santa Ana," on Monday, October 21, 1805, and in fact cut off at least fifteen ships from the main body of the combined fleet. One question that the Admiralty committee wished to settle was how many

---

[13] "The Evidence Relating to the Tactics Employed by Nelson at the Battle of Trafalgar," *Parliamentary Papers*, vol. 54, cmd 7120 (1914).

ships were actually engaged by the British forces sailing under Collingwood's direct command.

Some of the discrepancies in the record were, in fact, resolved by fiat. The clocks aboard the various vessels were neither accurate nor synchronized; different logs on different vessels listed different times for the occurrence of the same event. The committee arbitrarily assumed that Collingwood's flagship, the "Royal Sovereign," opened fire at noon and accordingly fixed the position of the individual ships at the moment each log stated that the "Royal Sovereign" opened fire, regardless of the particular times recorded in the logs.

We shall never know the exact time at which the "Royal Sovereign" commenced action—not an important detail, to be sure, but worth noting if only as an example of a problem beyond the reach of evidence, and one resolved by fiat. Moreover, here is a beautiful illustration indeed of what it might mean to say that historical truth is a matter of convention. "It was exactly noon on October 21, 1805, and the battle of Trafalgar was on," states the author of a recent account of the battle written for children.[14] How convenient for the battle to have started precisely at noon! Suppose, though, that all historical truths are really, at bottom, conveniences of a similar nature. Generations of children will believe that the battle of Trafalgar started at 12:00 sharp, as they will believe that it occurred on October 21, 1805. We may smile at an account that presents as historical fact what has been decreed by an Admiralty committee. Yet couldn't the belief that the battle took place on October 21, 1805—or that it even took place at all—rest on similar foundations? Once more, it seems, we find ourselves stalked by a sphinx just as we thought ourselves safe on the sane path of positive historical inquiry.

Suppose, then, we should suddenly fall prey to a doubt about the efficacy of historical evidence, used in the familiar

[14] A.B.C. Whipple, *Hero of Trafalgar: The Story of Lord Nelson* (New York: Random House, 1963), p. 160.

way, as a means of attaining historical truth, yet, like Collingwood, refuse to countenance any position that would relativize historical truth to the point of making it a matter of convention only. Let us see now whether the criterion of historical truth that Collingwood proposed provides us with a way of escaping our difficulties. Could that criterion have been applied—was it in fact applied—by the Admiralty committee in its endeavors to produce a true account of the battle of Trafalgar?

A historian who wishes to *know* what Cuthbert Collingwood's actions were on October 21, 1805, must somehow manage, according to Robin Collingwood, to rethink the thoughts of the Vice-Admiral as he performed his duties as a proper Englishman on that day of days. Suppose we direct attention at one of the questions facing the committee: how many of the ships of the combined fleet did Collingwood's forces actually cut off from the main body? Was the total twelve, according to plan, or fifteen, as some eyewitnesses had it? How would rethinking the Vice-Admiral's thoughts provide the answer? Indeed, could Robin Collingwood ever rethink the very thoughts of Cuthbert Collingwood without Collingwood becoming identical with Collingwood?

Let us dispose of one objection right away. No one can know the thoughts of another, it may be said, because thoughts are private to the thinker. My thoughts are mine, yours are yours, and they can never be shared. I can have *similar* thoughts to yours, but not the *same* thoughts. Therefore, the objection runs, the one Collingwood could never rethink the very thoughts of the other Collingwood; the philosopher's criterion of historical truth has no possible application to the deeds of the Vice-Admiral.

The objection proves too much, however. Using the same logic, one might argue that Robin Collingwood could never rethink even his own earlier thoughts. But surely Collingwood, like anyone else, was often capable of picking up his train of thought when reading on Monday what he had written the Friday before. Now it doesn't much matter whether you depict Collingwood as rethinking on Monday the very same thoughts he had had on Friday or as having different but quite similar thoughts on Monday. These modes of description are, after all, only figures of speech and should not distract attention from the important fact that we often do know on Monday what we were thinking the Friday before, simply by reading on Monday what we had written on Friday. And if Robin Collingwood could become apprised of the earlier thoughts of Robin Collingwood, why couldn't Robin Collingwood rethink the earlier thoughts of Cuthbert Collingwood as well?

Following up this deceptively promising lead, we seem to strike pay dirt at once, for the Vice-Admiral did, in fact, keep a journal, the appropriate entry in which reads:

> First, and middle parts light Winds, inclineable to Calm, latter part Fresh breezes, and Squally, with a heavy Swell from the Westward, about noon the Royal Sovereign opened a fire on the 12th, 13th, 14th and 15th Ships from the Enemy's Rear, and stood on with all sail to break the Enemy's Line. 1/4 past 12, altered Course to port, and in passing close under the stern of the Santa Ana, a Spanish three deck Ship, with a Vice-Admiral's Flag, raked her, and sheering up on her Starboard Quarter, began a very close Action;—at this time the Mars, Tonnant, and Belleisle had just broke thro' the Enemy's line, and were beginning to engage warmly: the smoke soon became so thick, that more of the Management of other Ships could not be distinguished....[15]

The entry suggests that Collingwood was under the impression that he had proceeded according to a plan drawn up by Nelson on the ninth of October, twelve days before the battle began:

[15] *Parliamentary Papers*, Appendix I, p. 3.

The Divisions of the British fleet will be brought nearly within Gun Shot of the Enemys Centre. The Signal will most probably [then] be made for the Lee Line to bear up together to set all their sails even steering sails in order to get as quickly as possible to the Enemys Line and to Cut through beginning from the 12 Ship from the Enemies rear some ships may not get through their exact place, but they will always be at hand to assist their friends and if any are thrown round the Rear of the Enemy they will effectually compleat the business of Twelve Sail of the Enemy. Should the Enemy wear together or bear up and sail Large still the Twelve Ships composing in the first position the Enemys rear are to be [the] Object of attack of the Lee Line unless otherwise directed from the Commander In Chief which is scarcely to be expected as the entire management of the Lee Line after the intentions of the Commander In Chief *is* [are] signified is intended to be left to the Judgement of the Admiral Commanding that Line.[16]

Note that Nelson thought it very important that the lee line engage twelve and only twelve ships, that the lack of an effective communications system between the lee line and the main body made it imperative that Collingwood stick as closely as he could to the original intention once the battle was under way, hewing to the "plan of the campaign which he tried to carry out," the knowledge of which, moreover, is supposed to provide the historian with a criterion of historical truth— at least, according to R. G. Collingwood. Note also that Vice-Admiral Collingwood's very description of his own actions was prefigured by Nelson's plan; he related what happened using almost the same language that occurred in Nelson's Memorandum. Nonetheless, other eyewitnesses, stationed on vessels in the combined fleet, reported the "Santa Ana" to be located fifteen ships from the rear of the column. Hence, Col-

---

[16] *Ibid.*, Appendix II, p. 65.

lingwood (if his French and Spanish opponents are to be believed) actually engaged at least fifteen French and Spanish ships, instead of the twelve he had thought. What is more, the Admiralty committee came to the same conclusion.

Was the committee wrong *a priori* in preferring to believe the point-blank reports of enemy observers rather than heed Nelson's intention and Collingwood's own description concerning the working out, in action, of that intention? If not, then what becomes of R. G. Collingwood's claim that knowledge of an actor's intentions puts us in touch with a criterion of historical truth, a criterion to which historical evidence must conform or be judged wanting?

Do we have the right in this instance, however, to assume that we know the Vice-Admiral's true intentions? Why should we suppose that he really meant to cut off no more than twelve ships? Why should *his* testimony be our authority? In order to know what an actor intended to do, according to R. G. Collingwood, the historian must see that intention as representing a solution to a problem posed by the situation confronting the actor at the time. The historian must "see for himself, just as if the [actor's] situation were his own, how such a situation might be dealt with; he must see the possible alternatives, and the reasons for choosing one rather than another; and thus he must go through the process which the [actor] went through in deciding on this particular course. Thus he is re-enacting in his own mind the experience of the [actor]; and only in so far as he does this has he any historical knowledge. . . ."[17]

Did the Vice-Admiral really intend, then, to isolate for special engagement no more than twelve of the enemy fleet? A simple statement of his intentions will not provide us with a conclusive answer, according to Collingwood, unless we can show that that particular naval maneuver was the best possible

[17] *The Idea of History*, p. 283.

strategy under the circumstances, as these circumstances were appraised by Nelson and Collingwood at the time. If we cannot recapitulate the strategy, then we have no right to assume we *know* how Nelson and Collingwood intended to fight the battle. Thus it seems we are not yet in a fair position to judge Collingwood's criterion of historical truth. Let us suppose, in addition, that a careful study of all of the circumstances confronting the British fleet lying off Cape Trafalgar would convince anyone who knew anything about sailing ships of the time, methods of battle, and so on that the Nelson strategy was far and away the best possible plan of action; that, in particular, isolating twelve and only twelve ships for separate engagement gave Nelson the greatest likelihood of winning; and that, if more than twelve ships had been separated from the main body, the probability of a British victory would have decreased radically. Only under these special circumstances, according to R. G. Collingwood, can we justifiably claim to know that Vice-Admiral Collingwood really did intend to isolate twelve ships for separate engagement.

What we must bank on, of course, is that the person whose actions we are trying to understand made his decision to act in a rational manner. We can then, theoretically, retrace some of the steps that led up to the particular decision. When one is following the actions of a chess player who, move for move, does exactly the right thing, the feeling that one knows just what the player is thinking soon becomes irresistible. One might even, on the strength of that feeling, reject a player's own statement of what he was thinking when it conflicts with a continual and successful anticipation of the player's moves according to sound principles of play. When, on the other hand, one cannot see for oneself why a chess player made a particular move, one has only the player's own word for what he intended to do. Considerations such as these, I think, led Collingwood to declare that the historian possesses "a criterion to which his so-called authorities must conform and by reference to which they are criticized."[18]

Suppose we accept Collingwood's contention that to know a person intended to do something necessitates rethinking his thoughts. Let us not challenge the claim, either, that we are always justified in rejecting testimony on that kind of ground (he *said* he was trying to trap his opponent's queen, but his moves showed he had an entirely different purpose in mind). We are still not in possession of a criterion of historical truth, one that will withstand a really corrosive skepticism about the efficacy of historical evidence for its attainment. Consider the following two questions: (1) Did Collingwood engage more than twelve ships? (2) What was Collingwood thinking at the time? If we seriously question the use of historical decision procedures—the ordinary appraisal of evidence which includes, as a proper part, the Nelson Memorandum as well as Collingwood's own journal—we have no basis for saying that the battle of Trafalgar took place at all. If we set aside the evidence, then we have, with one stroke, prevented ourselves from answering either question (1) or question (2). We could not say that we knew what the Vice-Admiral was thinking when he did such-and-such because we could not even say that there was a Vice-Admiral to do or think such-and-such. If, on the other hand, we stay within the confines of existing decision procedures, then the answer to question (1) need not be a function of the answer to question (2). The Admiralty committee was not doing anything philosophically improper by giving more credence to the reports of enemy observers than to Collingwood's own descriptions of the engagement. Moreover, the committee would not necessarily have been wrong to do so even if it could be shown that the Nelson strategy was the best of all possible strategies.

The relationship between historical truth and historical evi-

18 *Ibid.*, p. 236.

dence is tangled, perhaps hopelessly so. One cannot cut the Gordian knot, however, by supposing that there is a simple method of dispensing with the evidence, a method that brings one to grips with historical truth directly. The use of philosophical skepticism as a preliminary to a fundamental overhaul of decision procedures is not its only use. Philosophical skepticism can also provide the occasion for examining criteria of intelligibility of the concepts that lie embedded in existing decision procedures. Collingwood made the common philosophical mistake of conflating the two functions, of thinking it incumbent upon him to replace the customary decision procedures of historians with something better. All his philosophical cunning, wasted in the desperate attempt to find a general criterion of historical truth, could have been more suitably employed in teasing concepts from decision procedures—the latter being something that Collingwood, a good philosopher, did superbly well.

CHAPTER IX

Decision Procedures and Concept Formation

DECISION PROCEDURES provide natural matrices for concepts; to pry away the concepts, it is often necessary to impugn the procedures. In this and the following two chapters, I shall examine more closely the relationship between concepts and decision procedures. Having hitherto relied quite heavily on the metaphor of embedment in referring to that relationship, I think it time to take a closer look at what underlies the metaphor.

Thus far my defense of philosophical skepticism has consisted in justifying its use as a propaedeutic to the search for criteria of intelligibility of historical concepts. I have as yet said little about the role of philosophical skepticism in bringing about fundamental changes in decision procedures. Unlike science, the study of history affords few, if any, examples of such changes. Change has occurred more or less by accretion, by the addition of certain procedures to those already in use; there has been little conflict between the new and the old. In this sense, the study of history is a much more conservative affair than science. One should not suppose, however, that the lack of radical alterations of decision methods has blocked revolutions in conceptual style. There is an enormous difference between pre-Marx and post-Marx historical thought, even though the differences between pre-Marxist and post-Marxist historiography are not nearly so extreme. True, there have been important innovations in historiography since Marx, but they are not of a revolutionary nature.

Jean Jaurès' *The Socialist History of the French Revolution,* one of the first serious histories thoroughly Marxist in approach, contains in its Introduction a program for reform in the historiography of the French Revolution. Hitherto, Jaurès complains, historians like Taine, when they concerned themselves with economic matters, did little more than search the archives "to count the number of windows broken during the Revolution by the rioting populace."[1] Jaurès called for the collection of statistics on prices, wages, sale of properties: "If one could ascertain accurately into what kinds of stores and shops many abbeys, refectories or chapels were transformed, one could discover the details of an extraordinary economic effervescence caused by the Revolution."[2] Jaurès was instrumental in persuading the French Government to establish a commission charged with the task of collecting economic and social source material that bore on the French Revolution, a commission to which Jaurès himself was appointed. Without Marx, of course, such shifts in historiographical attention might never have occurred; to grant this point, however, does not commit one to the view that those changes which did take place are as fundamental as the changes in modes of historical thought that brought them about initially. In commenting on pre-Marx historians of the French Revolution, Jaurès remarks that "what even the greatest among them have lacked is not the documents but rather a concern with and insight into economic evolution as well as into the depth and movement of social life."[3] That insight into economic evolution had to wait for Marx to be born. It is quite possible, I contend, for fundamental conceptual revolutions in historical thought to occur without being preceded or accompanied by fundamental changes in the modes of historiographical production.

Without resorting to fictive science or downright science fiction (time machines and the like), it is difficult to imagine

[1] "Critical Introduction to The Socialist History of the French Revolution," in *The Varieties of History*, p. 162.
[2] *Ibid.*, p. 161. [3] *Ibid.*, p. 163.

radical alterations taking place in the historian's basic decision procedures. Skeptical assaults against them seem to hold little promise of eventuating in revolutionary action at that level. Nevertheless, it should not be supposed that such limitations confine the philosophy of history to being nothing more than a series of passive exercises in conceptual appreciation. Significant conceptual revolutions in both history and science have taken place without correspondingly revolutionary changes in the use of decision procedures. Moreover, significant changes in the use of decision procedures are not always accompanied by equally fundamental changes in the concepts traditionally attached to them, nor are all important changes in the use of decision procedures of serious philosophical interest.

I have cited Marx's contributions to the study of history as a partial illustration of this general thesis. I am aware, though, that many will disagree with my assessment of Marx's contributions to historiography. To some, the use of social and economic statistical data in the study of history will seem so radical a departure from the more traditional historiography that it will be thought deserving of being denominated a fundamental change of decision method. To find less contentious illustrations, perhaps, one must turn to examples outside the normal purview of the philosophy of history.

In a previous chapter, I suggested that the concept of time is not pivotal for the study of history. The point has to be qualified if one regards geology as a form of history. To understand most geological processes, one must reorient one's thinking along a time scale whose smallest unit is one million years.[4] The study of human history does not make such

---

[4] "We would suggest that the reader never lose sight of the fact that all geological phenomena obey laws whose time-scale is very different from the one used for human history or even for geography. A geologist will feel quite justified in applying to slowly developing phenomena (whose duration must be measured in millions of years)

demands upon one's everyday temporal *Anschauungen*. A consideration of the concept of time and some of the methods of measuring time provides an excellent illustration of the double-barreled thesis that (1) decision procedures can change fundamentally without affecting the concepts embedded in them and (2) concepts can be altered without fundamental revision of the decision procedures to which they are attached. These points must be established decisively because it is necessary to demonstrate that defending the historian's decision procedures does not commit one to defending the status quo employment of the concepts attached to them. In Chapters VII and VIII, for example, I defended the philosophical legitimacy of the traditional use of historical evidence in attaining historical truth. It is something else again to defend the traditional use of historical concepts in attaining historical intelligibility. Ordinary history is never all right.

Was the duration between that flash of lightning you just saw and the thunder you heard afterwards longer or shorter than that which you heard between the first and fourth notes of the opening movement of the Klemperer recording of Beethoven's Fifth Symphony? This question, though complicated, is perfectly intelligible; it would have been intelligible even if clocks had never been invented. Men had the capacity to estimate and decide upon the passage of time long before they got around to manufacturing clocks. To consult a watch is to resort to the use of a decision procedure for determining duration. Exchanging an old watch for a new one is, strictly speaking, a substitution of one decision procedure for an-

---

dynamic terms which we are accustomed to use in describing what may be called almost instantaneous events. The man in the street sees a river sweep by, the geographer notes the flow of a glacier, the student of tectonics reconstitutes the movement of rock-sheets." H. and G. Termier, *The Geological Drama* (London: Hutchinson, 1958), p. 13.

other. Yet reflections upon the exchange of clocks and watches do little to stimulate an interest in the concept of time.

The example is not germane, it may be objected, because exchanging an old watch for a new one is not a *fundamental* alteration of decision method; that is why the transaction is not philosophically interesting. Let us see if this reply is adequate.

Before 1956 physicists used the rate of spin of the earth as the basic standard for determining the passage of time. In 1956 the standard was changed to the length of time it took the earth to circle the sun in the year 1900. In 1964, at the Twelfth International Conference of Weights and Measures, the standard was changed once more to the vibration rate of the cesium atom. No one will dispute that each of these changes in the measurement of time is fundamental: certain sentences that are true according to one basic system of measurement become false according to another. If, for example, the rate of spin of the earth serves as the primary criterion for deciding questions about duration, then the vibration rate of the cesium atom must be deemed to be accelerating. If the vibration rate of the cesium atom is taken as the standard, then the rate of spin of the earth is seen to be decelerating.

Have these incompatibilities provoked great philosophical *Angst* among scientists? Not at all. Fundamental changes in the decision methods for measuring time were accepted without serious controversy. This absence of philosophical acrimony cannot be dismissed by attributing it to a distaste, shared by many scientists, for philosophical wrangling. The explanation, rather, is that there existed a consensus among physicists on the criteria for evaluating the various decision procedures for measuring time. According to one well-established physical theory, there are forces at work that decelerate the rate of spin of the earth—for example, the counterforces exerted by the motion of the tides. According to another established theory, the vibration rate of the cesium atom is constant. These theories provide the criteria by which physicists judge the validity of decision procedures for measuring time; in so doing, they are setting forth some of *the criteria of intelligibility for the concept of time.* This is why transitions from the use of one standard "clock" to another took place so smoothly.

Fundamental changes in decision methods can occur without affecting the concepts attached to them as long as there is agreement about the criteria for evaluating those methods. Philosophical interest is aroused at that point at which the criteria of intelligibility themselves are brought into question. A striking illustration occurred in 1905 when Einstein published his Special Theory of Relativity. It is instructive to consider the issues provoked by Einstein's theory because here one finds the very obverse of the example just considered. In the previous example, the concept of time was preserved intact through a series of fundamental changes in the decision methods for applying that concept. The Special Theory of Relativity, on the other hand, suggested a radical alteration of the concept of time itself for the sake of preserving the decision procedures used to determine its passage. Consequently, Einstein's proposals were of much greater philosophical importance than those advanced by the Twelfth International Conference of Weights and Measures.

Let us imagine Harry driving his car along a straight road from a point A to a point B. His speedometer reads a steady twenty miles per hour for the entire journey. Being a rather compulsive type, Harry insists upon driving from B to A in the same amount of time that it took him to drive from A to B. His compulsion also extends to velocities: the return journey must be accomplished not just at an average velocity of twenty miles per hour but at a constant velocity throughout. His car is equipped with a governor to regulate the velocity precisely. His watch is a perfect timepiece. Not surprisingly, Harry discovers that the return journey takes the same amount of time as the original journey.

Now he decides to repeat the adventure. He begins at point A and sets his governor for twenty miles per hour. The trip from A to B, according to his watch, takes one hour. After reaching point B, he turns his car around for the trip back. The setting of the governor is left unchanged; his speedometer reads a constant twenty miles per hour. An hour passes, but point A is not yet in sight. Another hour, and still no point A. To his horror, Harry finds that the return journey takes three hours to complete. What is more, although the distance from A to B, according to his odometer, is twenty miles, the same instrument records the distance from B to A as being sixty miles. What happened?

Harry's first impulse is to blame the instruments for the discrepancy, yet he is loathe to give up his fine decision procedures and decides that the fault does not lie there. His second hypothesis is that points A and B have been moved during the journey; but since both points are marked by buildings sixty stories high, that is highly unlikely. His next thought (a rather desperate one) is that the road itself was some sort of moving platform, traveling at a constant velocity of ten miles per hour in a direction from A to B. Harry reasons that, if the platform were moving from A to B at the rate of ten miles per hour, then his total velocity, relative to stationary points A and B, would be thirty miles per hour on the journey out but only ten miles per hour, relative to A and B, on the return. If the distance between A and B were thirty miles, then it would take one hour to get from A to B at thirty miles per hour, and three hours to drive back at ten miles per hour. His odometer should read eighty miles, for his wheels rotated much more often while moving "against the current" on the way back. All the facts would be explained—why the speedometer recorded twenty miles per hour, why it took him an hour to get to B and three hours to return to A, why the odometer registered eighty miles—*if* the road from A to B were, in fact, a platform moving at ten miles per hour in the direction of B.

Harry alights from his car and examines the road very carefully, but the road turns out to be just an ordinary road, as mobile as the Pennsylvania Turnpike. Is such a state of affairs even conceivable? Not when using everyday concepts of space and time. The situation as outlined becomes intelligible only when one alters those concepts radically. If the concepts of time and space are relativized and considered to be functions of velocity and direction, then one may hypothesize that "a contraction" of space occurred on the journey from A to B, that "an expansion" of space occurred on the return trip, that time "sped up" on the trip out, and that time "slowed down" on the way home. One would be forced to make conceptual maneuvers of this kind if "the facts" were as literally described and one were concerned about fitting them all into one conceptual landscape.

The universe, or at least that portion of it with which we are familiar, is not quite so queer as it is made out to be in the example. But it is almost as queer, according to Einstein's Special Theory of Relativity.[5] Suppose, to return to our example, that there *is* a moving platform from A to B but that the time it takes a person to drive, at a constant velocity, between A and B is exactly the same from A to B as it is from B to A. Suppose that, no matter how fast the platform moves relative to stationary points A and B, one can cover the distance from A to B only in the same amount of time as from B to A, both jour-

---

[5] The main difference between the concepts of space and time presented in the Special Theory of Relativity and the concepts of space and time presented in the hypothetical example is that, on the Einsteinian view, space and time are not functions of the *direction* in which an inertial frame is moving but only of the rate of velocity with which it is displaced.

neys taking place at the same velocity. Impossible? According to the Special Theory of Relativity, the closer one can attain the velocity of light, the closer one can approximate this curious feat. A photon of light, in the limiting case, moves from B to A in the same amount of time that it takes to move from A to B, regardless of what the velocity of any moving platform or system through which it passes may be. The general phenomenon was first noted in 1881 by Michelson and Morley, in the famous experiment in which they attempted to measure the extent to which the motion of the earth affects the speed of light. What they discovered, in fact, was that the velocity of light is constant no matter what the velocity or direction is of any platform from which light is emanated or received. In the Michelson-Morley experiment, the earth played the part of the moving platform of our example.

A clock is, among other things, a physical process. To hold that the rate of spin of the earth or rate of vibration of the cesium atom or of any clock could be physically affected by the velocity at which the earth or the atom travels through space would be to presuppose some very serious qualifications of several fundamental laws of nature. If the motion of a clock could be physically affected by the velocity of a system which contained it, then someone who used a clock to time other physical processes while traveling in a rocket ship at high velocities would get experimental results different from those obtained on earth. The Special Theory of Relativity postulates that time itself is "retarded" by velocity, a retardation that, it is assumed, would go unnoticed by an experimenter in a rocket ship because all processes, including his own heart beat, would be retarded systematically. Rather than give up the ordinary use of clocks as decision procedures for marking time, Einstein proposed a radical alteration of the concept of time (as well as that of space) in order to fit all known facts into one conceptual picture. Time and space were relativized, and new criteria of intelligibility for those concepts were formulated. According to the relativity concept of time, for example, it is not intelligible to speak of the simultaneity of two events which occur in systems moving at different velocities. It is *conceptually* impossible, according to relativity theory, to synchronize clocks in different systems. Similar considerations apply to the relativity concept of space. Relativity theory alters the criteria of intelligibility of the concepts of time and space while leaving intact the decision procedures for measuring time and space.

REFLECTION on the concept of time and its measurement should establish that concepts and decision procedures, though intimately connected, are not logically dependent upon one another; it is quite possible for new concepts to be attached to old procedures and for new procedures to be attached to old concepts. Although the historian may perforce continue to decide in the same old manner—undaunted by the failures of philosophers like R. G. Collingwood to invent conceptual time machines—such issues as the number of ships engaged by Cuthbert Collingwood at Trafalgar, he is not condemned to think about history in the same old ways. And though it is difficult to imagine how fundamental changes in the historian's traditional decision procedures could come about, it is not impossible. I shall consider one such possibility now—one, moreover, that would be accompanied by a conceptual revolution in historical concepts. (Before the wrong expectations are aroused, let me state at once that I am not about to exhibit the preliminary sketches of a time machine. Some of my examples of decision procedures may have inadvertently produced the impression that all decision procedures are mechanical devices. My next example should correct that impression. Although it is true that decision procedures enable one to make decisions in a mechanical way, a decision procedure is not necessarily a machine.)

In Chapters VI and VII, I introduced a modest skeptical

proposal that would substitute "probabilistic" historical concepts for "polar opposite" concepts in such a way that the distinctions between fact and hypothesis, truth and fiction, and so on, would turn out to be matters of degree. Whatever its initial appeal, the main deficiency of the modest proposal, it will be remembered, was that, like spun cotton candy, it contained more promise than substance. It gave no hint of how to estimate the numerical probability values of historical hypotheses, nor did it even so much as suggest how historical hypotheses could be objectively ranked, relative to each other, as more or less likely. *What was missing in the proposal was a decision procedure for determining the likelihoods of historical hypotheses.*

I should like to reiterate that the decision procedures now used by historians do not allow one to arrive at such estimates of likelihood. Furthermore, although there is a natural disposition to attempt to arrange "uncertain" hypotheses along a probabilistic continuum, one must not confuse an estimation of the truth of various nonprobabilistic assertions with the assertion of probability hypotheses. Meteorologists used to make statements like "rain tomorrow" when predicting rain. Nowadays they present us with forecasts like "the precipitation probability tomorrow is .9." How they express themselves does make a difference. Formerly one could blame the meteorologist for the unnecessary cancellation of a picnic, but now he gets off scot free by phrasing his prognostications in terms of precipitation probabilities. A .9 or even .999 probability of rain is not the same thing as rain. It is quite compatible with the fairest of skies.

We are obliged to excuse the meteorologist for his prognosticatory cowardice only if he can produce a reasonable decision procedure for the calculation of precipitation probabilities. For the same reason, we shall not allow the historian to indulge in retrodictory pusillanimity unless he can display a decision procedure for estimating the likelihoods of historical hypotheses. The modest skeptical proposal must be backed by a method that can generate such assertions as: Robin Hood existed with probability .324; Moby Dick existed with probability .00000342; JFK existed with probability .999997; FDR existed with probability .999992. The decision procedures currently at the historian's disposal do not permit such sport with historical reality. The historian really has only three options: he can assert that Robin Hood did exist; he can assert that he did not exist; or he can assert nothing at all. There is no difference, conceptually speaking, between affirming the existence of Robin Hood in ringing tones and affirming it in a whisper. Without a decision procedure for arranging hypotheses along a probability continuum, the word "probably" in such sentences as "Probably Robin Hood did not exist" has to be taken as referring to the doubts of the speaker, as meaning something like "I do not think Robin Hood existed." As long as probabilistic decision procedures are lacking, a cavil cannot be incorporated as a part of the very structure of reality but only assimilated to the assertorial act of a particular speaker.

How would one go about constructing and institutionalizing a decision procedure that could serve as a proper matrix for probabilistic historical concepts? One way would be to find and enshrine a good judge of historical probabilities, a sort of oracle or hunch player of historical horse races. The decision procedure would consist, simply, in consulting the oracle to get the day's betting odds on the existence of Kennedy, the landing of the Vikings at Newfoundland, and so on. Historians might never know how the historical oracle estimated these likelihoods: as happened with the rocking horse winner in the D. H. Lawrence short story, the answers might just come to the oracle after he had worked himself up to a sufficiently feverish pitch. Even if the oracle calculated the odds in a highly idiosyncratic or subjective manner, however, it would not follow that consulting the oracle would necessarily be an idiosyncratic and subjective procedure. Whether that were so would depend upon the extent to which oracle-consulting was institutionalized. The main theoretical advantage of using a decision procedure is that it provides a way of securing objectivity of judgment. If historians could agree to consult the historical oracle, they then would have an objective method of determining historical probabilities. The only drawback to this proposal, really, is a practical one: good oracles are always in short supply.

Failing to find historical oracles, the only other way one could develop decision procedures for estimating historical probabilities would seem to be via the construction of a logic of historical evidence. Everyone has certain intuitions about how to rank the likelihoods of various historical hypotheses in light of various kinds of evidence. If such intuitions could be codified into a logic, the historian would have at his disposal a set of recipes to consult as an aid in determining historical probabilities.

An early attempt at codification can be found in John Craig's *Theologiae Christianae Principia Mathematica* (1699). Craig wished to develop a logic of historical evidence for evaluating in a rational and scientific manner the probability of certain events reported in the Bible. He reasoned that there are two kinds of probabilities: "Natural probability," which is "probability deduced from arguments conforming to our own observation or experience," and "historical probability," or "probability which is deduced from the testimonies of others who are affirming their own observation or experience."[6]

Craig endeavored to devise a logic of "historical" probability based on a set of principles that he set forth. One of these postulated that "historical probability increases in proportion to the number of primary witnesses who describe the event."[7]

[6] "Craig's Rules of Historical Evidence," *History and Theory*, IV (1964), 3.
[7] *Ibid.*, p. 5.

Another stated that historical probability is diminished in proportion to "the number of witnesses through whom the history is successively transmitted" and in proportion to "the space of time through which the history is transmitted."[8]

Principles like the above are acceptable, perhaps, in proportion to the quantity of *ceteribus paribus*'s with which they are sprinkled. Still, they are relatively harmless; some are still being reproduced in historiographical manuals. Craig went a bit further, however. He tried to introduce numerical parameters by means of such rules as the following: "Let s be the total suspicion which we have concerning the trustworthiness and other virtues of an ideal witness: then if one witness should give s, two witnesses will give $2s$, three witnesses will give $3s$; and universally a number of n witnesses will give ns suspicions."[9] Using this and several other principles of equal dubiousness, Craig computed the probability of the story of Christ to be "as great as that which a man (in the times of Christ himself) would have had who received the history by only word of mouth from 28 disciples of Christ."[10] This was the probability for the written history of Christ in 1699; Craig also calculated that "after 3150 years from the birth of Christ the probability of his written history will vanish."[11] According to Craig, this figure fixed the upper boundary of the time of the second coming, "for it is necessary that Christ come before the probability of the Gospel story vanishes."[12]

Craig's assessments of the probability of the story of Christ are amusing because his numerical principles are absurd. Is it absurd, however, to attempt to compute the historical probability of the story of Christ? Absurdity is often a relative matter. Is it absurd to inquire into the probability that a man who survives his one millionth birthday will go on to live to be a billion years old? If there is zero probability that anyone will ever have to face up to a million birthday candles, then it

8 *Ibid.*   9 *Ibid.*, p. 7.   10 *Ibid.*, p. 27.
11 *Ibid.*   12 *Ibid.*

would be absurd to ask for the probability of living to be a billion years old, conditional upon living to be a million years old. The particular conditional probability can be expressed as the probability of living to be a million years old and then going on to live to be a billion years old divided by the probability of living to be a million years old. If the latter probability is zero, however, the fraction representing the conditional probability would be "0/0," which is a meaningless expression.[13] Thus if the probability of living to be a million years old is zero, the concept of living to be a billion conditional upon living to be a million has no intelligible application. If, on the other hand, the probability of living to be a million years old is not zero, but a fraction above, then it is intelligible to inquire into conditional probabilities—as intelligible as asking after the probability that a thirty-year-old will survive his fortieth birthday. The conceptual sleight-of-hand can be brought off by an introduction of sampling considerations. Why not suppose that the class of human beings who have lived (and died) hitherto is only a relatively small sample drawn from a population containing not only a Methuselah but also a few chiliagenerians, one or two retired million-year-old pensioners, the odd billion-year-old senior citizen, and so on. It is extremely unlikely, of course, that anyone will collect a million years' worth of social security benefits; nonetheless, there is no contradiction in supposing that there exists a small probability that someone one day will do so. In fact, the mortality rate tables used by insurance companies are based upon the presupposition that, for any n, there exists a finite probability that you will live to be n years old. One could theoretically purchase a million-year-term life insurance policy —at a price, of course. One should be cautious in making final judgments about what must be absurd and what isn't. Sometimes a simple conceptual trick will make all the difference.

Craig's desire to compute the historical probability of the

[13] See above, Chap. III, pp. 44-45.

story of Christ is not as bizarre as it may at first appear. If one really is bent on replacing "deterministic" two-valued historical concepts with "probabilistic" multi-valued concepts, one must take seriously the problem of providing an objective procedure of application for them. I have argued that the decision procedures historians now use cannot accommodate probabilistic concepts. Without historical oracles, it would appear that the only way to anchor probabilistic concepts in a decision procedure is by constructing a logic of historical probability. The principles of the logic would then function as the main ingredient of the method. I should like to emphasize again that the conceptual change brought about in the study of history would be revolutionary. I mentioned before that under the new conceptual system the difference between historical truth and historical fiction becomes a matter of degree. Yet that is not the only novel feature. One is accustomed to thinking of the past as fixed and the future as fluid— that Jack Kennedy was President of the United States is determined, one feels, and that Ted Kennedy will be President is only probable. If one of the principles of a logic of historical probability, however, is that historical probability tends to decrease with the passage of time, then one must view both past and future as fluid: that Jack Kennedy was President of the United States is very probable, no doubt, but it is getting less probable every day.

CHAPTER X

Evidence, Knowledge, and Belief

Philosophy has its playful side. There can be great exhilaration in seeing through a decision procedure, in spiking the engines of practical deliberation and positive inquiry. Plato, who in one way or another seems to have anticipated the entire history of Western philosophy, noted that "youngsters, when they get their first taste of it [philosophical discussion], treat argument as a form of sport solely for purposes of contradiction . . . delighting like puppies in tugging and tearing at anyone who comes near them."[1] One risk that philosophers run, according to Plato, is that, "after . . . proving others wrong and being proved wrong themselves, they rush to the conclusion that all they once believed is false; and the result is that in the eyes of the world they discredit, not themselves only, but the whole business of philosophy."[2] Philosophical discussion is not to be entrusted to anyone under thirty, Plato advised. Plato did not himself follow this severe stricture. He had a better suggestion. A philosopher should always "take for his model the conversation of one who is bent on seeking truth. . . ."[3] In these days of specialization, there are many different models from which to choose: physicists, historians, psychologists, mathematicians are all bent on seeking truth. The philosopher of history must choose for his model the conversation of the historian, whose primary business it is to seek out historical truth.

There is no shortcut to historical truth. The historian ap-

[1] *The Republic of Plato*, tr. F. M. Cornford (New York: Oxford University Press, 1945), p. 261.
[2] *Ibid.*   [3] *Ibid.*

proaches it by means of the decision procedures at his disposal. Probing into the details of what actually happened, conducting minute examinations of historical evidence, is often a rather tedious affair. Not surprisingly, many historians see themselves as sober, practical men with little use for high-flown theories. Intellectual history, where the employment of concepts is more visible than in other branches of the field, is regarded by many historians as history *manqué*—"ineffectual history" was one historian's term for it. Usually, though, the historian's conceptual apparatus is so deeply entrenched in his decision procedures that it passes unnoticed.

In any positive inquiry, truth takes precedence over intelligibility. And that priority, perhaps, provides the ultimate basis for distinguishing between historians and historical novelists. The novelist, unlike the historian, must declare for intelligibility over truth. It is quite possible for a historian to confess that he cannot make sense out of some data, cannot fit the data into a more general framework. This failure of itself does not disqualify the data. The novelist's art, on the other hand, requires that episodes coalesce into meaningful stories. Were a historical novelist to pretend that he did not understand the meaning of the incidents about which he was writing, he would be considered merely artful and his confession an unnecessary intrusion into the story.

All the same, even though historical truth takes precedence over historical intelligibility, one must not go overboard in proclaiming its primacy, simply because one really cannot in the end distill off all historical theory from some hard-core residue of historical fact. Yet it is just because historical theories and conceptualizations are so deeply embedded in the historian's decision procedures that it is easy to declare them not present at all; it is this feature which provides much of the ammunition for historical positivism of the kind expressed in Taine's maxim.

Imagine a situation in which two historians, equally skilled in the uses of historical evidence, are set the task of examining all the evidence that bears on some more or less well-defined historical event—the proceedings of the First Continental Congress, let us say. Imagine further that one of the historians is non-Western and is not at all acquainted with the history of Western Europe and America, with anything that came before or after the First Continental Congress. Accordingly, his knowledge of what happened at the Congress would have to be based entirely on what historians would regard as primary source materials, which we may suppose to have been placed before him. The second historian, we shall suppose, is fully versed in the history of the United States and of Europe, is in fact a specialist on Colonial history, but has not yet had the occasion to examine the primary historical documents relating to the First Continental Congress. The example need not be elaborated; everyone will agree on which historian has the edge. Why?

The answer seems to be that a specialist in Colonial history already knows a great deal about the First Continental Congress before being assigned the task of sifting any primary evidence. His broad familiarity with what the First Continental Congress was about gives him a plan of attack, a *modus operandi* in examining the evidence. He has a long head start because his view of history guides his use of decision procedures right from the beginning and, in fact, is so much a part of them that that very point can be overlooked. Once recognized, however, his advantage is so easily explained that the unequal contest hardly seems worth considering further. The Colonial specialist knows in general what happened before he examines the data; his knowledge of the event, when compared with the point from which his poor colleague begins, can be called *a priori*. The non-Western historian has no more chance against the Colonial specialist than did the tortoise against Achilles.

A race between Achilles and a tortoise becomes interesting

only when one can handicap Achilles. Can one do for the non-Western historian what Zeno did for the tortoise? There is nothing easier, one might think. Why not even up the unequal contest by conjuring up a Colonial specialist whose knowledge of Colonial history has but one curious lacuna: he knows nothing about the First Continental Congress. Let us now match him against our non-Western historian who, though knowing nothing at all about the *Abendland*, knows a thing or two about working with primary sources of all kinds. Has the tortoise been allowed a sufficient advantage?

A moment's reflection will show that Achilles has just been eliminated from the race altogether. The situation outlined above is inconceivable. How could a Colonial specialist know about the Second Continental Congress, say, without knowing that there was a First Continental Congress? Could he know that Benjamin Franklin was a new delegate to the Second Congress and Washington not, without knowing that Franklin was not present at the First Congress and Washington was? There is no point in arguing the case, which is obvious. The question is what to make of it.

A great deal, philosophically speaking, can be hung on this particular peg. It can be used to support a "seamless web" view about the nature of knowledge or a "coherence theory" about the nature of truth. But, whatever else might be made of the example, I think it shows at the very least that the historian's conceptualizations of history are so deeply entrenched in his decision procedures that they effectively define the procedures themselves. To all intents and purposes, the Colonial specialist and his hapless colleague are working with different procedures, though they were both presumed to make use of the same set of documents and artifacts.

This point is reinforced when one realizes that the race could not be held even if neurosurgery could do what logic cannot —namely, sever from Achilles' brain just the information he has of the First Continental Congress while leaving intact all else. In any case, I have perpetrated a conceptual illusion: can one really suppose that the two historians would have set before them *all* the evidence that bears on the First Continental Congress and then compete to see who would produce the most credible history? The total body of evidence bearing on the First Continental Congress is not a well-defined set. With a second glance at the phrase "the total body of evidence," one sees that the words have no clear reference. Of course, one feels instinctively that evidence pertaining to the affairs of Hideyoshi Toyotomi, let us say, cannot be part of the total evidence bearing on the First Continental Congress. Yet although the total body of evidence that bears on the First Continental Congress does not include every item of historical evidence, the concept is still open-ended enough to defy any attempt to provide clear-cut rules of reference. The reason is that what one considers to be a part of the total body of evidence bearing on a certain event is, in fact, a function of how one conceptualizes the event, of how one interprets its significance and relationships to other events making up the history of the *Abendland*. (One need not settle for the *Abendland* perspective, of course. A general history of mankind might place the First Continental Congress in quite a different landscape.)

We may approach the same resolution along a slightly different route. Which of the two historians is in a better position to pass judgment on what is or is not to be included in the total body of evidence pertaining to the proceedings of the First Continental Congress? Again the answer is obvious. Knowing that a document or artifact is a piece of evidence bearing on the proceedings of the First Continental Congress is often a function (though not always an obvious one) of knowing what it was that happened at the First Continental Congress. Furthermore, the inverse function holds as well. A historian's conceptualizations are in fact so finely meshed with the use he makes of his decision procedures that, to all intents and purposes, they can be considered to be part of those procedures themselves.

This view of the nature of historical evidence is not unlike that proclaimed by R. G. Collingwood and by F. H. Bradley before him. The historian's use of evidence, Bradley wrote, "implies a preconception, and denotes in a sense a foregone conclusion."[4] "The more historical knowledge we have," Collingwood observed, "the more we can learn from any given piece of evidence; if we had none, we could learn nothing. Evidence is evidence only when someone contemplates it historically. Otherwise it is merely perceived fact, historically dumb."[5] Inasmuch as I have been somewhat critical of Collingwood's attempt to secure for the historian an absolute conceptual hegemony over his use of evidence, it might be helpful to outline the main differences, as I see them, between Collingwood's position and the one I have sketched above. Like Collingwood, I am impressed by the extent to which historical conceptualizations shape the raw data with which the historian deals. Yet, unlike Collingwood, I do not think it possible to conjure away decision procedures altogether. True, the Colonial specialist of our example had great freedom of action because of his prior and general knowledge of Colonial history, a freedom of action denied his plodding colleague. Still, the picture of the proceedings of the First Continental Congress possessed by the Colonial historian, no less than the one conceived by his colleague, must be grounded in the evidence. When discrepancies come to light, as they always do when one looks hard enough, the historian almost invariably scores points by modifying the picture, not by impugning the evidence. This disposition on the part of historians is one exemplification of the general thesis that, in positive historical inquiry, truth takes precedence over intelligibility. And since I believe that the decision procedures at the his-

---

[4] *The Presuppositions of Critical History*, p. 5.
[5] *The Idea of History*, p. 247.

torian's disposal are his only means of attaining truth, I do not consider them to be impedimenta in the search for truth, as Collingwood seemed to, at least some of the time. (It is interesting to note that Collingwood's main discussion of historical truth in *The Idea of History* occurs in a section entitled "The Historical Imagination.") Unlike Collingwood, I do not feel obliged to formulate a simple criterion of historical truth by which to criticize the tortuous use of historical evidence. But perhaps the chief point of difference is that I do not share his basic philosophical prejudices. *Je ne suis pas un Idéaliste*. I have no desire to fight my philosophical battles under banners reading "Reason is the sovereign of the world" or "All history is the history of thought." I take no delight, therefore, in the particular conceptual maneuvers that idealists engage in at critical conceptual junctures. Deep philosophical positions come into play when one gets into conceptual trouble, when decision procedures fail, when criteria of intelligibility are not available, or when attempts to formulate them engender conflicting results. Think how nicely Collingwood's resolution of historical skepticism—his enjoinder to the historian to reenact the past in his own mind—dovetails with his general philosophical bias. If all history is the history of thought, then what better way to come into contact with history than by rethinking past thoughts? Not having Collingwood's particular axe to grind, however, I do not find his final solutions especially comforting or compelling.

I have my own philosophical prejudices, of course. The use I have made of the expression "decision procedure" to cover all the methods by which historians and scientists achieve objectivity of judgment provides a hint of what they are. Decision procedures, as I prefer to think of them, are essentially devices for facilitating the making of decisions. When a device fails, one is thrown back upon one's own devising. I tend to look upon the employment of decision procedures as the most important way by which man masks from himself some important realities of subjective choice. In short, my particular Saturday-night philosophical orientation is a species of voluntarism, and on Saturday nights I find congenial such gloomy figures as Augustine, Pascal, and Kierkegaard.

Professional philosophers, at least in England and America, differ from their amateur counterparts in that they are not very enthusiastic about discussing deeper issues without adequate preamble. I share the professional's distaste for parading one's philosophical convictions, but in discussing further the nature of decision procedures and some of the ways concepts get attached to them, my own bias will become quite visible.

DECISION PROCEDURES, as I have said, are devices or techniques that facilitate the making of decisions. The practical advantage in using them, accordingly, is that they save one the trouble of making decisions. When in a quandary about whether to take the left or right fork in a road, one may flip a coin. Tossing a coin, in such circumstances, is resorting to the use of a decision procedure; one is spared further effort in trying to decide which is the best route.

Compare a chef who is experimenting with a new idea for making sponge cake with a housewife who is following a sponge cake recipe, a decision procedure for making sponge cake. The chef is faced with the necessity of making a decision at each step. Six eggs or ten? Lemon? How much? By comparison, the housewife who cooks according to a recipe would seem to be more like someone who is merely carrying out orders. She need not worry about whether to add lemon or not; such questions are answered before they arise. If a recipe says lemon, then lemon it is. Now if consulting a recipe is to resort to the use of a decision procedure, and if a decision procedure is a technique that facilitates the making of decisions, then it would appear that the housewife who follows a recipe, no less than the experimenting chef, is making a number of decisions. But is she really? Is the housewife who follows a recipe doing anything quite so grand as she peers myopically at a set of instructions while absentmindedly beating the eggs?

Consulting a recipe for making sponge cake is a decision procedure because it enables one to decide, at each step in the process, how next to proceed. Yet the state of mind of the experimenting chef would seem to be entirely different from that of the obedient housewife. Pondering, cogitating and excogitating, meditating, experimenting, ruminating, weighing and resolving—our image of the decisionmaker is of a person sorely beset by difficulties that can be overcome only by strenuous mental effort. How can using a recipe be called a "decision procedure" if one who uses it apparently makes no decisions, indeed is spared the effort of having to make decisions by that very use?

One reason for the claim that consulting a recipe is resorting to the use of a decision procedure is that, should the recipe fail (perhaps the page is torn in the middle of the folded eggs), the cook will then be forced to make a decision about how to proceed. This is not a decisive consideration, however. Were my usual mode of transport to fail, I should then have to walk to the university. But this consideration of itself does not justify slighting my Ferrari by referring to it as a method of walking, as a mere "walking procedure." The expression "walking procedure" suggests some kind of regimen, perhaps the use of crutches, canes, and the like. When my recipe fails, I must make a number of culinary decisions. When my automobile fails, I must walk. Yet although driving an automobile is hardly a method of walking, or a walking procedure, I am claiming that consulting a recipe for sponge cake is resorting to the use of a decision procedure for making sponge cake. Something more certainly needs to be said.

Consider again the coin-tossing case. Let the coin decide the matter, we may say. This is a figure of speech, of course, for the coin decides nothing. It is we who have decided to employ the coin to do our thinking for us. It is we who have to decide whether to abide by the results of the toss. It is we who are responsible for what we decide. We may wish to *excuse* an inexperienced cook so foolhardy as to attempt to follow a recipe in the Alice B. Toklas cookbook. But we can never allow that following an incomplete recipe *justified* her in producing an incomplete dish. Similarly, we may wish to excuse the soldier who "only follows orders" and may desire to reduce any penalty imposed for crimes committed while acting under orders. Nonetheless, we cannot absolve the soldier of the crime, for it is no justification to say that the soldier committed the crime because he was ordered to do so. A soldier is not an automaton; he is the one ultimately responsible for his actions —a point often overlooked, though it is well recognized in common law. Absolution, on the other hand, needs no pardon.

These considerations suggest that a person who employs a decision procedure in performing a certain task is in the same position morally, though perhaps not esthetically, as a person who is actively engaged in decisionmaking, who weighs, ponders, and resolves. Although the daring chef has a much more heightened experience of the culinary art than does the housewife who cooks according to formula, I am proposing that both be considered decisionmakers. True, the housewife who follows a decision procedure is not actively making a decision at each stage of the cooking process; she made them all at once, so to speak, when she selected the recipe. She is like a chess player using a standard opening. The first n moves are preselected, run through according to ritual. It is only afterwards that the decisionmaking *Angst* begins to take hold. Is the chess player who likes to open with the Nimzo-Indian less of a decisionmaker, because he plays mechanically, than the chess player who eschews all standard openings and falls into a brown study from the outset of play? Decision procedures facilitate the making of decisions. Their use, however, does not absolve one from the necessity of choice. That the chef's state of mind differs from the housewife's does not mean that the housewife is not a decisionmaker. If this seems a puzzling thesis, it should be noted that not all decisions require strenuous mental labor; some can be arrived at quite effortlessly. Decisions can be made as easily as saying "make mine vanilla."

One tends to link decisionmaking with practical affairs, with matters of conduct. Should I take the right-hand fork? Should I add lemon? Should I disobey my superior officer? Questions of this sort can be subsumed under the schematic formula: What should I do? There are, however, certain difficulties in trying to assimilate the notions of decision and decisionmaking with matters of belief. Even so, my use of the term "decision procedure" suggests that very extension. Should I believe that Bormann existed, that the French Revolution preceded the Napoleonic Wars, that my watch loses two seconds each day? Questions of this sort can be subsumed under the schematic formula: What should I believe?

Why should it seem slightly malapropos to talk about *deciding* about matters of belief? Perhaps the explanation is that many of our beliefs are apparently forced upon us, are involuntary, beyond our control. What we believe we often cannot help believing—or so we believe. Do we really have a choice about whether or not to believe that Bormann existed? On the other hand, most of the things we *do*, activities in which we engage, are within our control, are voluntary—or so we should like to believe. Yet I am suggesting that belief and conduct are parallel notions and should be treated accordingly. If the will is free, then so is the will to believe.

Here, however, I shall not argue the complete case for voluntarism. I shall accept, without challenge, the validity of distinguishing between beliefs forced upon one and beliefs over which one has a measure of control. Examples of the latter sort? One thinks at once of beliefs adopted independently of any evidence, beliefs formed in the face of conflicting evidence, or beliefs founded on evidence insufficient to lend credibility to what one believes. Kierkegaard held that to believe in the divinity of Christ requires the believer to forge his belief in the total absence of any evidence because it is absurd to suppose that there could be any evidence for or against the divinity of Christ. Accordingly, belief in the divinity of Christ became, for Kierkegaard, the purest expression of man's freedom. Although there can be no evidence for or against the divinity of Christ, there can be evidence for or against His historical existence. A person who believes the evidence inadequate to establish that Christ existed may nonetheless believe in the historical existence of Christ. Such belief, too, would generally be regarded as belief over which the believer has complete control. It is the believer himself who is free to decide what he will believe. The evidence alone is not strong enough to command assent.

On the basis of considerations such as these, one may conclude that the difference between beliefs forced upon us and beliefs over which we have a measure of control is just the difference between beliefs founded on evidence and those which are not. According to this theory, any belief formed in the total absence of evidence will provide an unimpeachable witness to the truth of voluntarism, whereas any belief grounded on complete evidence will be an example that best supports some variant of determinism. But is this conclusion really justifiable?

True, among the beliefs that do not rest on solid evidential grounds reside the prize specimens of voluntarism—those often called "acts of faith." Yet the same class also contains, surprisingly, the best illustrations one can find of beliefs that are forced upon one, beliefs over which one has no control. Given my second-order philosophical predilections, I am naturally inclined to stretch the entire fabric of belief upon a voluntarist frame. Yet I need not advance so radical a thesis. It will suffice here to establish that beliefs formed by means of evidence—with the aid of a decision procedure—are beliefs subject to one's own control. Decision procedures, as I shall show, tend to expropriate the concepts to which they are attached. Accordingly, the first step in liberating concepts often comes through the recognition that one is never forced to believe anything upon the basis of evidence. If there are any beliefs which one is compelled to hold, such beliefs are developed in the absence of evidence. A body of evidence may oblige assent; it can never compel it.

Compare, for example, my belief that I ate eggs for breakfast with your belief that I ate eggs—your belief, we shall assume, formed through an examination of the available evidence. You were not present at my breakfast table, but you have questioned all who were. I assert that I had eggs, my wife describes how they were cooked; furthermore, there are stacked plates with egg stains on them, the garbage contains eggshells, and so on. We may imagine the evidence mounting until the case for my having eaten eggs is established beyond a reasonable doubt. You are then obliged to believe I consumed eggs, but you are not literally compelled to believe it. Unlike *your* belief that I had eggs for breakfast, which is based on evidence, *my* belief that I had eggs is not based on evidence. I simply remember that I ate eggs. A man believes what he remembers. I am compelled to believe that I had eggs in a way that you are not precisely because, in this instance, my belief—unlike yours—is not founded on evidence, was not formed by examining any evidence.

You are collecting testimony; I am providing some of it. You are examining evidence; I am not. It would surely be curious were you to ask me what evidence I had to show that I had eaten eggs after I had already told you that I did. It would be a mistake on my part to reply to such a request with the comment "I remember that I ate eggs." I should interpret your request for evidence as a sign that you did not believe me. And if you did not believe me, I should hardly be able to dispel your suspicions by asserting in forthright tones, "I remember that I ate eggs." If sufficiently provoked, I might point to the eggshells and other items of evidence in order to prove *to you* that I had eaten eggs. My own belief, however, is not based on that evidence. It is not based on evidence at all.

Suppose a third person were to ask for evidence that I had had eggs for breakfast. It is not quite right for you to reply, "H.F. remembers that he had them." My recollection is not part of the evidence; it is my statement that I had eggs which is part of the evidence. In listing the evidence upon which you rest your belief that H.F. had eggs for breakfast, you would surely include my statement. Yet think how odd it would be if I were to cite my own statement that I had eggs as evidence supporting my belief. It would make sense for me to do so, perhaps, had I forgotten that I had eggs on that particular morning. You might at that point try to convince me by pointing to my own statement, which I should then regard in much the same light as you do. If I *said* I had eggs, I probably did. What reason could I have had to lie? I am then as free as you to believe the evidence or not. Should you succeed in jogging my memory, however, my belief would at once revert to its previously unshakeable status.

To have an unshakeable belief that I did something is not the same as knowing that I did, however. Suppose I remember that I did *not* have eggs for breakfast, but all the evidence as before (excluding my statement, of course) points the other way. There are eggshells, my wife's testimony, egg stains, and so on. I may never believe that I had eggs; still, there could come a time when I might be prepared to admit that the evidence establishes that I had eggs. Perhaps the results of an examination of the contents of my stomach would show I did have eggs after all. The evidence would then oblige me to say, if asked, that I *know* I had eggs for breakfast; nonetheless, I might continue to disbelieve it. Many philosophers are convinced that believing must be a *sine qua non* of knowing, that

—to use my own jargon—a negative criterion for the intelligible application of the concept of having knowledge is that the person who knows believes what he knows. Is it really intelligible to suppose that someone could *know* he was in pain without *believing* that he was in pain? The contention seems right as long as one's thinking is tied to the epistemological model that celebrates the kind of knowledge one has when in pain. In Chapter VII, I mentioned some of the defects of this particular model when used as the sole paradigm of what it means to know something. The concept of knowledge represented by the pain model has, in fact, a very limited range of application. I would argue that there are different kinds of knowledge. A teacher who wishes to discover whether a student knows that the square root of two is an irrational number is presupposing a rather different concept of knowing than is the dentist who wishes to discover whether his patient knows that the diffuse pain he feels on the left side of his face is localized in a toothache of a lower left molar. The patient who knows that the dentist has probed a sensitive area could no more disbelieve what he knows than prevent the tears that come to his eyes. A student who lacks confidence in his abilities, on the other hand, may pass any and all conceivable tests designed to test whether someone knows that the square root of two is irrational. A lack of self-confidence may vitiate the student's belief in the irrationality of the square root of two. Should the teacher, in such circumstances, fault the student for not really knowing that the square root of two is irrational?

To have evidence that *p* is to be in possession of a decision procedure for determining whether *p*. If I have evidence that the earth is more than five minutes old, then there must exist a decision procedure for determining whether the earth is more than five minutes old. Furthermore, one is obliged to assent to those propositions for which one has conclusive evidence. A juror must pronounce a guilty verdict if there is conclusive evidence that the accused is guilty as charged, if guilt has been established beyond reasonable doubt. It is not necessary, though, that guilt be proved beyond a shadow of a doubt. A juror is not compelled to believe the accused is guilty even when finding him guilty. As long as there is any possibility of conflict between what one believes privately, perhaps perversely, and what one is obliged to affirm publicly on the basis of evidence, there may arise a challenge, at any time, to the existing decision procedure machinery.

There should be little theoretical resistance to the notion that decision procedures need occasionally to be evaluated. Even so, skeptical challenges often provoke vehement reactions. Partly this response can be attributed to sheer psychological inertia. Beliefs settle in, become integrated into one's personality, and are thus hard to dislodge. Then, too, explicit recognition of the possibility of error can weaken resolve and hamstring action. But there is another, more subtle factor at work. Decision procedures tend to capture the concepts embedded in them. Concepts have a tendency to take on the shapes of the matrices in which they are located. The schedules and scales by which concepts are applied to things mechanically and routinely come to assume a greater and greater criteriological importance. It often happens, in fact, that a decision procedure is upgraded to the point where it begins poaching on territory occupied by the criteria of intelligibility of the original concept. When that point has been reached, the original concept can be said to have changed its form; from then on, a challenge of the decision procedure threatens the intelligibility of that portion of the world whose meaning is governed by that concept. And although evaluation of a decision procedure would appear to presuppose the existence of independent criteria of intelligibility by which to determine how well the procedure applies to the concept, it is often very difficult to formulate such criteria, especially when the concept is a captive of its own decision methods.

CHAPTER XI

Decision Procedures and Conceptual Change

How are decision procedures evaluated, justified, rejected? This is a very complex question, of course, to which there is no general answer. Different branches of inquiry make different uses of decision procedures, decision procedures themselves vary, and methods of evaluating effectiveness differ. I shall start with a brief look at some decision procedures in logic and mathematics. It is appropriate to being with logic and mathematics because the expression "decision procedure" has its original home there; in borrowing it, I have deliberately stretched its meaning, though not, I hope, beyond recognition.

The phrase "decision procedure" began its career in German costume; it is a translation of a technical expression in mathematics—*Entscheidungsmethode* (or *Entscheidungverfahrens*). A decision procedure was originally a method for solving a decision problem (*Entscheidungsproblem*). Let us, accordingly, begin with an illustration of a decision problem in mathematics.

Anyone who has studied Euclidean geometry knows how difficult it can be to deduce a certain theorem from axioms, postulates, or theorems already proved. It is sometimes so difficult that one may begin to wonder whether the particular proposition in which one is interested is really a deductive consequence of the original set of postulates and axioms. If the proposition is not a deductive consequence of the original set, then one would be embarking upon a Sisyphean task in the very attempt to derive it. A decision procedure for Euclidean geometry would provide a mechanical routine or program enabling someone otherwise hopelessly inept at geometry to decide the issue. Mathematicians would require, in order for such a program to qualify as a decision procedure in Euclidean geometry, that it work for any proposition that pertained to the domain of Euclidean geometry. The mechanical routine would have to show, for any Euclidean proposition, whether it or its negation was deducible from a particular Euclidean axiom set. Furthermore, should neither the proposition nor its negation be deducible from that axiom set, a proper decision procedure would indicate that fact as well.

Suppose one began, for example, with an incomplete axiom set, one that did not contain, say, the third and fourth of Euclid's postulates. There would still exist an infinite number of propositions that could be derived from what remained. There would exist as well, however, an infinite number of propositions and their negations which could not be deduced from the abbreviated axiom set—namely, all those propositions for whose derivation the third and fourth postulates were needed. A decision procedure would reveal that fact; it would classify a proposition as *undecidable* if neither it nor its negation were deducible from a given axiom set—undecidable, that is, relative to the particular set of axioms. "Undecidable," in this usage, means "nondeducible." It should be noted that, as mathematicians and logicians employ the term, it is quite possible for decision procedures to exist side by side with undecidable theorems.

There does, in fact, exist a decision procedure for Euclidean geometry—not for *Euclid's* geometry, to be sure (Euclid's formulation is not sufficiently rigorous), but for an abstract geometry having distinct Euclidean leanings, a geometry developed by David Hilbert at the turn of the century. For many mathematical domains, however, it is known that there exists no decision procedure. A recondite branch of mathematics called "general recursive function theory" has as its focus the problem of proving or disproving the existences of decision procedures for various domains of mathematics.

In its original sense, then, a decision procedure was a mechanical method for determining whether, relative to a given axiom set, a proposition is provable (deducible), disprovable (when its negation is provable), or undecidable (neither provable nor disprovable). Mathematicians and logicians themselves have slightly extended the original meaning of the expression to refer to any mechanical procedure which provides a general method for answering an infinite number of questions of a certain kind. S. C. Kleene puts it this way:

> We know examples in mathematics of general questions, such that any particular instance of the question can be answered by a preassigned uniform method. More precisely, in such an example, there is an infinite class of particular questions, and a procedure in relation to that class, both being described in advance, such that if we thereafter select any particular question of the class, the procedure will surely apply and lead us to a definite answer, either "yes" or "no," to the particular question selected.[1]

As mathematicians now use the term, any algorithm qualifies as a decision procedure. Alfred Tarski, in his monograph *A Decision Method for Elementary Algebra and Geometry*,[2] cites as an example of a decision method Euclid's algorithm for calculating whether or not two integers are prime, relative to each other. An integer x is prime relative to an integer y if and only if the two integers have no common divisor except the number 1. Thus 12 is prime relative to 11 but not prime relative to 10. Proposition 1, Book VII, of Euclid's *Elements*

---

[1] *Introduction to Metamathematics* (Princeton: D. van Nostrand Co., 1952), p. 136.

[2] *A Decision Method for Elementary Algebra and Geometry*, Project Rand, publication R-109 (Santa Monica, Calif.: Rand Corporation, 1948), p. 1.

outlines a mechanical procedure for determining the answer to any question of the form "Is integer x a relative prime of integer y?"

My use of the expression "decision procedure" is a good deal broader than its use in mathematics and logic. There is this much in common, though: a decision procedure in mathematics or logic "must be like a recipe," according to Tarski, a recipe "which tells one what to do at each step so that no intelligence is required to follow it; and the method can be applied by anyone so long as he is able to read and follow directions."[3] An important difference, on the other hand, is that I have not required that decision procedures be complete. An incomplete recipe, as I view the matter, is still a decision procedure, albeit only a partial one. In general, it is much more difficult to lay down complete decision procedures outside the realm of mathematics and logic than within it. Recipes must often be couched in vague or general terms, leaving great leeway to individual judgment. The ideal, for anyone concerned to establish a decision procedure, is to dispense with judgment altogether; paradoxically, mathematics and logic, provinces generally held to require intelligence and thought of the highest order, are precisely those areas most amenable to the construction of complete decision procedures. Nonetheless, as I said before, many domains of logic and mathematics can be shown to be theoretically intransigent to the introduction of decision procedures, and some philosophers have thought that mathematical thought in those domains represents the triumph of human intelligence over the computing machine. Naturally enough, other philosophers have disagreed. The topic is of the greatest interest but proceeds along lines too formidably technical to pursue further.

Perhaps the greatest point of difference between the mathematical meaning of "decision procedure" and that which I accord it here arises from the nature of mathematics itself.

[3] *Ibid.*

Mathematicians establish things by deductive proof: to show that a proposed algorithm works, is a decision procedure, requires a demonstration. In other areas of inquiry, decision procedures certainly cannot be established by demonstrations; the very question of whether or not a particular decision procedure is adequate may be philosophically controversial.

In all areas of inquiry, though, decision procedures do tend to capture the concepts embedded in them. Since this process accounts for a great deal of conceptual change, it merits careful study. I shall cite two illustrations of this general thesis, one drawn from logic and the other from psychology. Although the first illustration is not difficult to grasp, it does nonetheless presuppose familiarity with notions that would take too long to explicate here—in particular, certain concepts employed in the logic of propositions. I shall, accordingly, be brief; those who do not understand the illustration should skip to the next.

THE LOGIC of propositions does admit of a decision procedure —in fact, at least two. One is based on the process of reducing all well-formed formulas to what is called "normal form." The other, more familiar procedure involves the use of truth tables. A truth table is a schedule or matrix for determining the truth value of a compound proposition, given the truth value of its basic components. One of its functions, then, is to provide a way of determining under what conditions a compound proposition is true and under what conditions it is false. That is not its only use, however. It can also be employed as a decision procedure for resolving questions of derivability. If my general thesis is correct, one should expect the concept of derivability, so neatly embedded in its truth table matrix, to be captured by its decision procedure. In fact, that is what has happened. The well-known "paradoxes of strict implication" arise precisely because there is a criteriological conflict of interest between derivability as such and "truth-functional" derivability. The paradoxes of strict implication are paradoxical only to the extent that one feels the pressure exerted by the general and more primitive concept of derivability, its inertial resistance to being reshaped in a truth-functional mode. Yet few logicians are very much bothered by the paradoxes of strict implication, for they have already accepted truth-functional derivability, defined by the truth table decision procedure, in its stead. They no longer feel the pressure, except perhaps on occasions when they teach a course on elementary logic and are forced to confront the more deep-seated and instinctive concept of derivability, a concept incarnated in the astonished stares of beginning students when told, for example, that "snow is white or not white" is deducible from "grass is green," or that the sentence "if John does not arrive on the ten o'clock plane, he will arrive on the eleven o'clock plane" is deducible from "John will arrive on the ten o'clock plane."[4]

Not all logicians have accepted truth-functional derivability as a suitable concept for the logic of propositions. A group of Dutch mathematicians and logicians, calling themselves "intuitionists," have stubbornly refused to countenance a number of principles of derivability which, from the standpoint of the truth table decision method, are considered perfectly sound. According to truth table procedure, for instance, any proposition is derivable from the double negative of itself. This principle does not accord with intuitionistic notions of derivability, however, and it is therefore rejected by intuitionists, even though its rejection blocks the use of truth tables as a decision procedure for the logic of propositions. For one trained in the use of truth tables, whose logical intuitions in the domain of the logic of propositions have been schooled by the criterion of truth-functional derivability, the cavils of

[4] The *locus classicus* of the paradoxes of strict implication is C. I. Lewis and C. H. Langford, *Symbolic Logic* (New York: The Century Co., 1932). A recent discussion of the paradoxes is to be found in Ernest Adams, "The Logic of Conditionals," *Inquiry*, VIII, 2 (1965).

the intuitionists seem to be so much unnecessary philosophical bickering. But then so do all philosophical objections with which one cannot agree.

"But God has not been so sparing to men" wrote John Locke, "to make them barely two-legged creatures, and left it to Aristotle to make them rational...."[5] Locke's point was that there was more to reasoning than what was captured by the rules of the Aristotelian syllogism. My point is in a way similar: concepts transcend the particular decision procedures in which they happen to be embedded at a given time. Locke, however, thought that the principles of correct inference were implanted, as it were, once and for all in man's faculty of reason and were constant throughout the history of mankind, remaining aloof from the various attempts to snare them in explicit rules and procedures. The same is not true of all concepts. I think that most concepts are changed by the decision procedures which capture them, that decision procedures, by poaching on criteriological territory, redefine the concepts attached to them. In short, my view is that most concepts are subject to historical erosion and transformation—that the philosophy of history, instead of being treated as a peripheral and esoteric philosophical subject, ought to be brought close to the center of the philosophical enterprise. I have touched on some of these matters earlier in this book. The following illustration of the way decision procedures modify concepts should provide further exemplification of my general thesis.

In Chapter III, I pointed out that the word "criterion" can refer to a decision procedure; it can also signify the trait or traits which serve as the point of reference for decision procedures. When school pyschologists talk about criteria of intelligence, they may be referring to their testing procedures, but they may mean the quality of performance on intelligence tests. It is interesting that the expression "criteria of intelli-

[5] *An Essay Concerning Human Understanding*, II, 391.

gence" should prove so malleable, that the word "criterion," in general, can be used to designate tests as well as traits. This linguistic phenomenon signals an important philosophical point, I believe: namely, that decision procedures tend to gain criteriological weight. They originate as "mere tests," as instruments for measuring or recording the outward or surface manifestations of a process or state of affairs whose significance seems independent of the instruments used to assess it. Exerting a conceptual Heisenberg effect, as it were, they begin to transform the nature of the concept or concepts with whose routine application they have been entrusted. They then develop criteriological resonances not anticipated when the decision procedures were initially adopted. They obtain purchase on the concepts connected with them and thereby change them. A quick look at what has happened to the concept of intelligence since the introduction of intelligence testing methods will provide an insight into this extremely significant process—a process to which little attention has been given in Anglo-American philosophical circles, perhaps because of its ahistorical bias.

An intelligence test serves as a decision procedure. Consider the interrogative schema "Is A more intelligent than B?" The formula can be employed to generate a class of indefinitely many particular questions, to which the application of an intelligence test will in every instance provide a definite "yes" or "no" answer. There are certain restrictions, of course. The particular interrogative "Was Socrates more intelligent than Plato?" cannot be decided by a Stanford-Binet testing procedure, any more than a bathroom scale can be used to resolve the question "Was Socrates heavier than Plato?" But, within certain obvious limits, intelligence tests function as decision procedures for making comparative judgments about intelligence.

Modern intelligence testing had its origin in a method designed by Alfred Binet to cull out school children too slow to be processed by the normal pedagogical techniques employed in Paris in 1905. The Binet-Simon scale, revised in 1916 by L. M. Terman of Stanford University and renamed the "Stanford-Binet scale," served as the standard test of intelligence for a quarter of a century. Insofar as it was deemed *standard* by psychologists, the test of necessity took on criteriological importance. For one thing, it became the basis for evaluating the effectiveness of other tests of intelligence. The so-called Army Alpha intelligence test developed by Terman, Thorndike, and others in 1917, for example, was designed with an eye to correlating favorably with the Stanford-Binet scale. Functioning as the standard procedure for measuring intelligence, the Stanford-Binet scale thus became the fundamental decision procedure for evaluating other intelligence testing procedures. Its relationship to other tests was precisely that of a standard clock to other clocks.

Once institutionalized, a decision procedure begins to acquire a life of its own. Practical importance creates vested interests; use gets out of hand. When decision procedures are cast adrift in the seas of historical change, the original concepts attached to them, once the special darlings of the specialists who formulated them, enter the public domain. Consider the concept of I.Q. Originally, "I.Q." was simply an abbreviation for "Intelligence Quotient," an expression coined by Terman to designate the ratio of a person's so-called mental age, as determined by intelligence test, to a person's chronological age (as determined by clocks). The concept of mental age plays a fundamental role in the design of intelligence tests; nonetheless, it is the derived concept of Intelligence Quotient, or I.Q., on which I shall concentrate, for it is the latter concept that has occupied a good deal of the ground formerly held by the older concept of intelligence.

To get a feel for the concept transformation that has really taken place, ask yourself what you would make of the following remark: "Harry is very intelligent but has a low I.Q."

The distinct air of paradox is explained by the fact that the expressions "high I. Q." and "low I. Q." have become partly synonymous with the expressions "very intelligent" and "stupid" respectively. Yet this fact by itself does not establish that a conceptual transformation has occurred. A living language is always undergoing change. New expressions are introduced, older expressions abandoned; sometimes a new phrase will partly replace an old one simply by expressing the same concept, more or less, that was expressed by the old. Furthermore, change in the parent language is often initiated by adaptations from the technical language of specialists. Consider, for example, the impact of cybernetics: "feedback," "memory tape," "storage area," "track." That "high I. Q." has come to be partly synonymous with "very intelligent" does not mean that a metamorphosis of the original concept of intelligence has taken place. Not every linguistic exchange indicates a conceptual transformation. Something more is needed to support the case that the concept of intelligence, to a certain extent, has been captured by the decision procedures designed to measure it.

The first point to establish is that not every use of the expression "high I. Q." is a simple *façon de parler*, meaning neither more nor less than what is meant by "very intelligent." Of course, for some speakers of the language, the use of the phrase "high I. Q." will be jargon—a linguistic reflex, a spasm of speech. Such speakers will certainly be able to recognize the paradoxical quality of the utterance "Harry is very intelligent but has a low I. Q." In fact, they will be paralyzed by it, for all that their innermost ear will register is "Harry has a high I. Q. but has a low I. Q." A person for whom the term "I. Q." is not simply jargon will respond differently. He will be aware of the paradoxical overtones but will nonetheless be able to respond to a request to make sense of the utterance.

What can it mean? Perhaps one of the following: (a) There was a clerical error in the administration of the intelligence test. Harry really has a high I. Q., though the recorded I. Q. score is low. (b) There was no clerical error; however, Harry had a bad day. If he had taken the same test when up to it, he would have scored well. (c) Harry is a Negro brought up on the wrong side of the tracks. He really has a high I. Q., but there are so many "culturally weighted" items on the intelligence test that no culturally deprived person could score well on it.

These resolutions of the paradoxical statement "Harry is very intelligent but has a low I. Q." will certainly be among the first to suggest themselves. But the very fact that they do come to mind immediately constitutes the strongest argument in support of the thesis that the decision procedures for applying the concept of intelligence have taken it prisoner. A person who interprets the statement to mean either (a) or (b) is in fact presupposing the criteriological use of intelligence testing methods. To say that something has gone wrong in a particular application of some test or in the recording of the results is to imply that the test itself is not at fault. Resolution (c) is somewhat different from the first two: here there is the definite suggestion that something is wrong with the test itself. However, the criticism is directed, not against the intelligence test per se, but against its scope of application. The testing method could still have criteriological force when used as an instrument in making relational judgments of intelligence of individuals not culturally deprived.

If all of the above resolutions presuppose the criteriological importance of intelligence testing procedures, then what is one to make of the following: "Harry has a low I. Q. He is an upper-middle-class, white, Anglo-Saxon Protestant who did his best when tested by a standard testing procedure; furthermore, no errors were committed in administering and scoring the test. Yet although he has a low I. Q. score, Harry is very intelligent."?

Now if Harry's I. Q. score, under the above conditions, had been 28, let us say, we might begin to wonder, when told that Harry is highly intelligent, whether he is perhaps some kind of *idiot savant*. But a dull score in the 80's when poor Harry has done his best? Highly intelligent? Nonsense!

The concept of intelligence has undergone a transformation since the introduction of intelligence testing procedures, a transformation whose occurrence and direction were quite beyond the control of psychologists. Dictionaries have responded accordingly. An entry under "intelligence" in *Webster's Third New International Dictionary* (1961) calls it "the available ability as measured by intelligence tests or by other social criteria to use one's existing knowledge to meet new situations and to solve new problems. . . ." The second edition of Webster's dictionary makes no mention of intelligence tests. *Funk & Wagnall's Standard College Dictionary* (1963), in one of its paraphrases, defines intelligence as that "quality or ability measured by an intelligence test." Not all dictionaries have bowed to the inevitable, to be sure. Those printed in England have remained politely unaware of the forces of history churning on the other side of the Atlantic; but then they record British usage only, and "the Press, together with most of the British public," according to one British psychologist, "still seem to regard intelligence tests and tests of educational attainments with a good deal of suspicion."[6]

Of course, the concept of intelligence is not a complete captive of the decision procedures to which it is presently attached. The word has more than one meaning; there is more to intelligence than that measured by intelligence tests. It was one or the other senses of the term that Binet himself was trying to snare by means of his intelligence testing procedures. For Binet, intelligence was essentially "judgment, otherwise called

[6] Philip E. Vernon, *Intelligence and Attainment Tests* (New York: The Philosophical Library, 1961), p. 9.

good sense, practical sense, initiative, the faculty of adapting oneself to circumstances. To judge well, to comprehend well, to reason well, these are the essential activities of intelligence."[7]
When Binet asked himself whether his testing procedure really measured intelligence, he was posing a matter-of-fact question; he had to presuppose that criteria for the intelligible application of the concept of intelligence existed independently of the testing procedure. He had to presuppose that it was possible for a highly intelligent child to do poorly on the test he had designed, for otherwise there would have been no way to test the testing procedure itself. But as his decision procedure and those descended from it became institutionalized, they began to take on criteriological significance. Once intelligence tests achieved the necessary status, the question "Do intelligence tests really measure intelligence?" came to have a different sound. The philosophical overtones appeared precisely because, as a matter of historical fact, one of the criteria for the intelligible application of the concept of intelligence had become performance on intelligence tests.

I must discuss one obvious objection to the above account, an objection to which, unfortunately, I cannot produce a conclusive rejoinder. I have contended that the concept of intelligence has changed since 1905 and that the change occurred because a decision procedure designed to apply the original concept became institutionalized and then took on criteriological importance. This is not the only way conceptual change can take place. The concept of time has also undergone metamorphosis since 1905, at least for physicists and the educated laity. This transformation did not come about through the institutionalization of a new decision procedure for measuring time; rather, it arose from a series of proposals, advanced by Einstein, which had the direct effect of changing some of the criteria for the intelligible application of the concept of time. Yet there is a certain resemblance between the

[7] Quoted by Vernon, *ibid.*, p. 30.

two kinds of change: both did involve shifts in criteria of intelligibility, and both were produced, in the final analysis, by historical forces little understood but certainly beyond the control of the innovators. Since, moreover, both shifts induced changes in the criteria for the intelligible application of the two concepts, both are of philosophical significance.

Now for the objection. Few will dispute the philosophical importance of Einstein's Special Theory of Relativity, though certainly some may be dissatisfied with the way I have characterized that importance. But there is sure to be special displeasure with my account of what has happened to the concept of intelligence since 1905. The tenor of the objection will be, simply, that nothing at all has happened to the concept of intelligence since 1905, for two reasons: (1) Concepts, whatever else they may be, are not the sorts of things to which anything can happen. They are not subject to historical change. (2) The concept of *intelligence* is precisely the same concept now that it always was. Intelligence is essentially what Binet said it was in 1905—namely, the capacity to judge well, to comprehend well, to reason well. . . .

The two reasons are, of course, related. Anyone who holds that concepts cannot undergo change will, if consistent, hold that the concept of intelligence has not changed. Yet since (2) does not imply (1), each must be discussed separately. As for (2), it may be true that, for some, the word "intelligence" means precisely what it would have meant to them had they never heard of intelligence tests. That, however, is a rather complex thought, and I am not sure how one would go about vindicating it. But there is majority usage to consider, reflected in recent entries in dictionaries. The entry in Webster's third edition is different from the entry in the second. Doesn't this fact have some bearing on the question of whether the concept of intelligence has changed?

At this point (1) comes into play as a position to fall back upon. Words may change their meanings without in any way affecting the concepts they express, it may be said. The word "intelligence" in 1905 had several meanings, expressed several concepts, as can be seen from the number of different entries that were listed next to the word in dictionaries of the period. What has happened since 1905 is simply that one or more entries have been added and perhaps one or more deleted. Does it matter? There is no single concept of intelligence, but at least as many concepts as there are dictionary entries. Concepts don't change, even though words do change their meanings.

I said that I could not produce a conclusive rejoinder to this objection. The reason is that differences of philosophical perception—for that is what the conflict amounts to—cannot be bridged by logical argumentation alone. Let us approach the issue by presenting a position even more extreme than that voiced by (1). It could be argued that it is impossible not only for concepts to change but also for words to change their meanings. Consider the *word* "intelligence." It can designate a source of information, as in: "He had an intelligence located in the enemy camp." It can also signify an item of information. These are just two of its meanings. Why not, then, conceptually individuate the word according to its uses? Strictly speaking, it might be said, "intelligence" functions as a generic term for a number of different words: there is "intelligence$_1$," "intelligence$_2$," and so forth. If English were an ideal language, there would be as many different words as there are differences in meaning of the generic term. Because English is not an ideal language, a language in which univocality is treated with due respect, we are misled into thinking that words can change their meanings and, in particular, that the word "intelligence" has changed its meaning. The truth of the matter, so this argument would go, is that neither *the* word nor *the* concept has changed, since there is no one word nor yet one concept of intelligence, but rather many words and many concepts neatly frozen into a permanent one-to-one relationship with each other.

It would be a mistake to think there is an easy rebuttal to this argument, even though it is quite radical. One cannot dismiss the argument by simply asserting, in the manner of Moore, that there is obviously only one word "intelligence" and not many different words. Counting words is not like counting peas. By the word "intelligence" do we mean the type or the token? If the latter, then there are many different words, instead of just one. Suppose, however, we mean the type, that is, the class of occurrences of the tokens. There are still counting problems. Is the English "vague" the same word as the French *vague*? They certainly look the same. But is "vague" as vague in English as it is in French? Is *exakt* as exact in German as it is in English?

Although words may seem, initially, to be more substantial sorts of things than concepts, the problems of the identity and individuation of words are as terrifying as similar problems with regard to concepts. Then, too, the notion that a word *expresses* a concept becomes completely amorphous when one tries to fit a pair of philosophical calipers to it. Let us resort to a powerful analogy. Suppose we compare words with tools. Just as words express concepts, so tools have uses. Just as one word can express different concepts, so one tool can have many uses. Now what would be the analogue, on the tool model, to the view that concepts do not change?

The most extreme position would be that tools do not change their use because a tool is defined by its use and the use of a tool is not the sort of thing that can change. Thus a stone that is used to open oysters is an oyster-opening tool. The stone is a different tool entirely when used to hammer coconuts. It is then a coconut-cracking tool, or perhaps simply a hammer. Hence, tools cannot change their use because a different use defines a different tool, the same use the same tool.

The position just sketched is philosophically coherent. It would be pointless, therefore, to attempt to refute it by direct assault. No matter what philosophical satisfaction it affords those inclined toward it, however, the position is an ahistorical one and thus infelicitous, to say the least, for anyone interested in history. It is not ahistorical because it denies the possibility of describing change in a certain way. It is ahistorical because it provides no conceptual room for the concepts of growth and development, concepts that play an important role in making history intelligible.

Suppose that in a certain tribe a particular kind of stone is used only to open oysters. One day someone decides to try out the stone on clams, we may imagine, never before eaten or perhaps taboo. The original function of the tool suggested a similar, but different use. The experimenter's success with clams tempts him to taste them. Perhaps he persuades others to taste them also, and as a result the tribe overcomes its initial gustatory prejudice and clam eating becomes institutionalized. Then the prototypal, oyster-opening tool may itself be modified in order to adapt it better to the task of opening clams. Its altered form, in turn, may suggest new uses for it, and so on. Contrast this story with another. We are concerned with the same oyster-eating tribe as before; this time, however, we are to imagine that the peaceful development of the oyster-opening tool is prematurely interrupted when members of a warlike tribe fall upon the oyster eaters and slit their throats with the oyster tools. The oyster tools are then gathered and used to perform human sacrifices. And yet a third story. The oyster-eating tribe suffers extinction before it has a chance to develop its tools further. Ten thousand years later a member of a different tribe discovers one of the implements and uses it to hammer coconuts.

The first two stories exhibit the basic stuff from which histories are constructed. The first episode presents a story of the peaceful growth and evolution of a certain family of tools.

The second episode provides a "dialectical" account of the development of a family of tools. The third episode presents a story of—what? The subject of the story is not a family of tools in which the members are "genetically" linked to each other. Rather, the subject of the story is a particular physical object that happens to be used one way in one tribe and another way in another tribe ten thousand years later. More stories of this kind can be told, but as history they are really quite lifeless; there is no continuity between incidents except the little provided in an external fashion by the continued existence of some physical object.

Consider the first and second stories. One feels that the development of oyster tools into clam tools, as told in the first story, is a kind of process somewhat different from the genesis from oyster tools of tools for performing sacrifices. Admittedly, it is difficult to say exactly what makes the difference. Is it that in the second story one use generates another without there being any feedback upon the original design of the tool? This much is clear, however: the first and second stories resemble each other much more than either resembles the third story. "Once upon a time clam openers were oyster openers." That is one way to begin the first story. It would be quite wrong to begin the third story in the same fashion: "Once upon a time coconut hammers were oyster openers." True, once upon a time *the particular implement* used to hammer coconuts was used to open oysters. Yet this is an entirely different kind of assertion from "Once upon a time coconut hammers were oyster openers."

In Chapter XV, I shall turn again to the concept of genesis and its bearing upon the idea of history. Notice now that discussion of the genesis of one kind of tool from another is truncated or blocked altogether by the following philosophical positions: (a) The use of a tool cannot change, because uses are not the sorts of things that can change. A given tool can change its use, to be sure, but this is not the same as saying that the *use* of a tool changes, that use generates use, and other absurdities. (b) Not only can the use of a tool not undergo change; a tool itself cannot change its use, either, for a tool is defined in terms of its use. Same use, same tool. Different use, different tool.

There are differences, one feels, between the kind of change exhibited by the first story and that exhibited by the second. But awareness of the differences will be dulled by an objection like (a) because, I am afraid, the differences are best brought out by the absurd notion that the uses of tools can change in different ways, can generate other uses in different ways. Position (b) is even more chilling to one's historical sensitivities, for, according to it, even the difference between the first and third stories vanishes. After all, if a tool is individuated by its use, we cannot say that oyster openers can become clam openers. A tool used to open oysters is an oyster opener. A tool used to open clams is a clam opener. A tool used to hammer coconuts is a coconut hammer. Since one tool cannot become another, it is absurd to look for differences in the ways that one tool becomes another.

Well, there is no conclusive rejoinder to either (a) or (b). I have labeled them "ahistorical" because either one is capable of withering historical insight. If one wishes to do philosophy of history in a proper way, one must lay aside one's ahistorical prejudices. Issues such as the ones just considered should provide incentive, for those philosophically inclined, to become involved with the philosophy of history. But when one turns to the usual topics discussed in so-called analytical philosophy of history, one finds no mention of them. Analytical philosophy of history seems to contain nothing but leftovers from the philosophy of science. Speculative philosophy of history is something else again, as we shall see.

CHAPTER XII

Speculative and Analytical Philosophy of History

THE MOST NOTABLE attempts of professional philosophers to entangle themselves with history have been roundly condemned by historians and philosophers alike. If historians, as Sir Lewis Namier once observed (going von Ranke one better), can in the end only aspire to an intuitive understanding of how historical events do *not* happen, then philosophers, on one version, are madmen who try to demonstrate how historical events *must* happen. The philosopher, said Fichte, "follows the *a priori* thread of the world-plan which is clear to him without any history; and if he makes use of history, it is not to prove anything, since his theses are already proved independently of all history."[1] Naturally, such a remark does

---

[1] Quoted in J. B. Bury, *The Idea of Progress* (New York: Dover Publications, 1955), p. 253. Although Bury did not intend to ridicule Fichte, he did manage to cite a passage that is both obscure and damaging. By his particular choice Bury expressed, perhaps inadvertently, a typical Anglo-American attitude toward philosophy of history, especially German philosophy of history. To understand that attitude, it is not really necessary to understand Fichte. The point is not what Fichte actually said, but what historians and philosophers, particularly in England and America, took him to be saying. Bury's citation is from Fichte's *Die Grundzüge des gegenwärtigen Zeitalters*, a series of lectures he delivered in Berlin in 1804-5. The German text reads: *Der Philosoph, der als Philosoph, sich mit der Geschichte befasst, geht jenem, a priori fortlaufenden Faden des Weltplans nach, der ihm klar ist, ohne alle Geschichte; und sein Gebrauch der Geschichte ist keinesweges, um durch sie etwas zu erweisen, da seine Sätze schon früher, und unabhängig von aller Geschichte, erwiesen sind: sondern dieser sein Gebrauch der Geschichte ist nur erläuternd, und in der*

not endear philosophers to historians. The Fichtean philosopher is still a laughingstock, the stereotype warning of what will happen to a philosopher who dabbles in history. Thus, a century and a half after Fichte, W. H. Walsh, in his influential *An Introduction to Philosophy of History*, found it necessary to commence with an apology: "A writer on philosophy of history, in Great Britain at least, must begin by justifying the very existence of his subject."[2]

With the Fichtean philosopher *persona non grata*, how ought a modern philosopher to concern himself with history, if at all? Walsh proposed an answer. He pointed out that "the word 'history' is itself ambiguous. It covers (a) the totality of past human actions, and (b) the narrative or account we construct of them now."[3] He went on to say that "this ambiguity is important because it opens up at once two possible fields for philosophy of history. That study might be concerned . . . with the actual course of historical events. It might, on the other hand, occupy itself with the processes of historical thinking, the means by which history in the second sense is arrived at. And clearly its content will be very different according to which of the two we choose."[4] The upshot, according to Walsh, is that the expression "philosophy of history" designates "a double group of philosophical problems; it has both a speculative and an analytic part. And even those who reject the first of these may perfectly well (and indeed should) accept the second."[5] Whether or not one agrees with Walsh's way of distinguishing between the two kinds of philosophy of history, the fact remains that the division of philosophy of history into an analytic and a speculative part is

---

Geschichte darlegend im lebendigen Leben, was auch ohne die Geschichte sich versteht. Johann Gottlieb Fichte, *Die Grundzüge des gegenwärtigen Zeitalters* (Berlin, 1806), p. 304.

[2] *An Introduction to Philosophy of History* (London: Hutchinson & Co., 1951), p. 9.

[3] *Ibid.*, p. 14.   [4] *Ibid.*   [5] *Ibid.*, p. 15.

"widely accepted and basic," to cite a recent treatise on the subject.[6]

Walsh was not the first to attempt to make philosophical capital out of the ambiguity of the word "history." Hegel also observed that "in our language the term *History* unites the objective with the subjective side, and denotes quite as much the *historia rerum gestarum* as the *res gestae* themselves; on the other hand it comprehends not less what has *happened,* than the *narration* of what has happened."[7] He went on to hint darkly that "this union of the two meanings we must regard as of a higher order than mere outward accident."[8] Hegel's point was that the idea of history did not blossom until there was a proper subject for historical narratives: "it is the State," he wrote, "which first presents subject-matter that is not only *adapted* to the prose of History, but involves the production of such history in the very progress of its own being."[9] The passage cited, from Hegel's lectures on the philosophy of history, has attracted little attention. Yet it is an absolutely crucial passage, for it provides a sorely needed Rosetta stone to the hieroglyphics of speculative philosophy of history. Speculative philosophy of history is "self-conscious" history, produced by authors who write, as it were, with one eye on a group of important philosophical problems—problems that center on the "narrative aspect" of history, on the circumstance that the historian, as Henri Pirenne remarked, constructs history by narrating it.

What are these problems? Hegel alludes to one of them in the passage I quoted. Narratives must be *about* something; a story requires a subject. For the orthodox political histories written in Hegel's day, the national state was a common subject. It still is. A common theme for orthodox political history

[6] William H. Dray, *Philosophy of History* (Englewood Cliffs, N.J., Prentice-Hall, 1964), p. 1.

[7] *Lectures on the Philosophy of History*, p. 60 (Hoffmeister, p. 164).
[8] *Ibid.*   [9] *Ibid.,* p. 61 (Hoffmeister, p. 164).

of the period was the growth of freedom. That theme is still quite popular. Can these selections of subject matter and theme be justified? I should like to suggest that Hegel can be interpreted as attempting that justification in his lectures on philosophy of history. Is justification of subject and theme required? Consider the following remarks of a philosopher who has contributed substantially to the "analytical side" of the philosophy of history, who has written an important history of philosophy, and who is himself comfortably situated within the main current of Anglo-American philosophy. "Historians write books," wrote J. A. Passmore," with what seem to me to be preposterous titles—titles like *The History of England*."[10] "The fact of the matter is that there is no such subject as *The History of England*. . . . What the historian calls 'general history' is a fraud—resting for its plausibility upon the metaphysical notion that there is something called 'the whole community' which moves in the manner of a single man."[11]

If Passmore is right, then many a work of speculative philosophy of history must be deemed fraudulent *ab initio*, for the unit of narrative reference, if I may call it that, is often broader than the national state. But in that case many standard histories would go by the board as well. Well, then, of what sorts of things can there be histories? Is it possible to write a history of England without swearing allegiance to a "whole community which moves in the manner of a single man"? Passmore's own "general history" is entitled *A Hundred Years of Philosophy*.[12] Does the title suggest that the way to avoid ontological entanglement is to choose, as one's narrative unit of reference, pure duration?

It might be wise, therefore, to stick to some neutral expression like "narrative unit of reference" in talking about the subjects or objects of narrative histories. The phrase is cum-

[10] "The Objectivity of History," in *Philosophical Analysis and History*, ed. William H. Dray (New York: Harper & Row, 1966), p. 84.
[11] *Ibid.*, pp. 84-85.   [12] (London: Duckworth & Co., 1957).

bersome, however, so I shall use terms like "subject," "object," "theme," "plot," and "story-line" interchangeably; any one of these expressions can function as a means of referring to what a story is about, as a mode of designating narrative units of reference. I should prefer, of course, to be able from the outset to draw fine distinctions between the meanings of these terms. It would have been nice had literary critics—for they are the specialists putatively in charge of such vocabulary—been in agreement about such differences. For the most part, however, literary critics are not very interested. In these matters, it seems, everyone is on his own.

The amorphous quality of the narrative unit of reference should give pause to anyone otherwise keen on deontologizing history, for he who asserts that there is no such object as the history of England is thereby denying the possibility, on one interpretation, of writing stories with certain kinds of subjects. Suppose one argued that there is no such subject as the history of the Buddenbrooks Family because there is no such object as *Das Geschlecht* and that, therefore, it is ontologically wicked to pretend that THE FAMILY hovers above the separate existences of fathers, mothers, husbands, wives, cousins, and aunts in their various relationships to each other. That one can write histories of families, however, seems obvious. To dispute this, it is not sufficient to disprove the existence of *Das Geschlecht* and objects of similar ilk. Similarly, one cannot count out the history of England as a proper historical subject by denying the existence of ENGLAND as an object.

This much is true: a collection of incidents do not add up to a story unless there is a narrative unit of reference to tie the incidents together. In order to exemplify a narrative structure, what features must a set of incidents have? To what extent does the task of narrating history impose a narrative structure or theme upon a set of incidents; to what extent is such a structure or theme discoverable in the incidents themselves? One cannot become involved with speculative philosophy of history without hunting for answers to these questions. Hegel's philosophy of history contains, *inter alia*, a defense of the historian's traditional concentration on political subjects—more specifically, on the national state and the growth of freedom. It presents both subjects as different aspects of a common theme, a theme that might be called "the progress of morality."

Moral progress, for Hegel, consists essentially, on the one hand, in the progressive development of a set of objective criteria against which to test the validity of subjective moral judgments and, on the other, in the development of a proper attitude toward such criteria in the making of moral judgments. Without criteria, there is no objectivity, and morality becomes a matter of taste. Without a proper attitude toward such criteria, the nature of morality will not be truly appreciated; moral principles will appear to be nothing but external constraints upon one's freedom of action. Hegel had a baroque intelligence—to borrow J. N. Findlay's phrase[13]— and his thinking proceeded by a marvelous, fantastic, and often exasperating association of ideas. The confrontation between the moral absolutist and the moral skeptic, an always important drama in the history of moral philosophy, became in Hegel's hands an underlying theme of history itself. History is on the side of moral absolutism, according to Hegel, because a careful reading of history reveals the development, in dialectical stages, of moral criteria. They are embedded in "political morality," in the legal framework of the state. It is the state's very existence, Hegel claimed, which makes a solution to moral skepticism possible. The law of the land is not only a decision procedure but also the source of the criteria for moral judgment. Thus the state, for Hegel, became the concrete embodiment of abstract moral principle, its laws functioning as the ultimate decision procedure for applying moral

[13] *Hegel: A Re-Examination* (London: Allen & Unwin, 1958).

concepts. Far from deploring the incarceration of moral concepts in legal decision procedures, Hegel extolled it.

It was not enough, Hegel argued, to develop moral criteria for assessing the validity of moral judgments. A moral person is one who not only does the right thing but has the proper attitude toward what he does. For the law of the land to function correctly as a moral criterion, it is necessary that men, of their own volition, accept the law as the proper decision procedure for applying the concepts of right and wrong; otherwise, the law will be viewed in its purely "external" aspect, as a restraint upon freedom of action. By a neat dialectical inversion, Hegel defined freedom as, in essence, the voluntary submission to moral authority, as the "freely doing" of what one is morally obliged to do. Awareness of the true nature of freedom, according to Hegel, had itself undergone a dialectical development, intimately associated with the evolution of various kinds of political institutions. Hence, it is right and proper that historians concentrate on political history, on the development of the national state and the growth of freedom, for these are the very lines along which history itself proceeds. Since the history of philosophy furnishes, as it were, the secret history of the world, the justification for the themes of orthodox political history is to be found there. The history of philosophy, however, must itself have a narrative unit of reference, and Hegel thought he had found one in the notion of a World-Historical Spirit whose struggles to attain self-awareness introduce a continuous, dialectical but progressive theme within which to locate the apparently radical discontinuities presented in orthodox history of philosophy. Thus all major change is, for Hegel, a form of growth; all major historical conflict has a transcendent reconciliation. Yet because the men who act in history act on the assumption that the causes they champion, the ideas they stand for, are right (for without such conviction they would have little disposition to act at all), they are often blind to the form of reconciliation that later arises from the clash of interests and passions. The resultant "synthesis" is beyond any one man's or any one group's control.

This, in outline, is Hegel's defense of the traditional concentration by orthodox historians on "national history" and the growth of freedom. It consists, in part, in a transformation of the usual story into quite another through the imparting of new significance to an old tale. Hegel's method resembles the techniques employed by psychoanalysts, whose own conceptual *raison d'être* rests on the ability to give a new dimension to incidents usually interpreted in a quite different way. More will be said on this point in Chapter XIV.

What is the connection between philosophy of history, as I have characterized it, and Hegel's view of history? If the philosophy of history is the search for and formulation of criteria for the intelligible application of concepts, of those concepts, in particular, that are useful to historians by way of making history intelligible, then what contributions did Hegel make on that score? Hegel, among other things, attempted to provide criteria of intelligibility for the concepts of state and freedom, key notions in orthodox political history. And because Hegel believed that these concepts themselves had undergone historical transformation, he felt obliged to present a historical narrative, or the outline of one, to trace those changes. For Hegel, tracing the evolution of these pivotal concepts was tantamount to setting out the main story-line of the history of mankind. His philosophy of history, accordingly, is at once an elucidation of certain concepts as well as a thematic presentation. In fact, most of the key concepts historians employ have a narrative function (for example, the Renaissance, the Frontier, the Reconstruction Period); they serve as principal elements in the organization of a historian's story-line. One cannot ignore the narrative role of the historian's concepts in providing criteria for their intelligible application. In historical narratives one does not have Counter-Reformations without Reformations that precede them.

I DO NOT EXPECT that I have yet allayed suspicions that speculative philosophy of history is a rather queer business. One cannot ignore the recent history of philosophy. Those Anglo-American philosophers who are interested in the philosophy of history seem to be concerned with a set of philosophical problems quite different from the ones that perplex historical speculators. Whereas Hegel gained ground by emphasizing some of the similarities in the uses of the word "history," analytical philosophers have been keen to point out the differences. (Dictionaries, which attempt to distinguish carefully between the various meanings of words, have apparently provided inspiration for much of recent Anglo-American philosophy: "Certainly, then, ordinary language is *not* the last word: in principle it can everywhere be supplemented and improved upon and superseded. Only remember it *is* the *first* word. . . . we may use the dictionary—quite a concise one will do, but the use must be *thorough*."[14] Continental philosophers, on the other hand, would be much better off with a thesaurus.)

It cannot be denied that the word "history," as it occurs in the phrases "analytical philosophy of history" and "speculative philosophy of history," does seem to be functioning in different ways. Although it sounds straightforward to espouse one or another *speculative* philosophy of the history of mankind, what could it mean to plump for a particular *analytical* philosophy of the history of mankind? Since analytical philosophy of history, as the name suggests, consists in conceptual analysis, such activity does appear to be completely different from speculating about the history of mankind. Should I succeed, therefore, in vindicating speculative philosophy of history as a genus, there is still the history of recent philosophy to consider. Modern Anglo-American philosophers, when they do philosophy of history at all, are quite content to stick to the analysis of a rather limited range of concepts—the concept of

[14] John Austin, "A Plea for Excuses," reprinted in *Ordinary Language*, ed. V. C. Chappell (Englewood Cliffs, N.J.: Prentice-Hall, 1964), pp. 49-50.

causal explanation, for example. To brood about the significance of history is regarded as distinctly unprofessional.

Here, displayed in outline, is what I termed in Chapter II "the second stereotype"—the view that there exists a sharp distinction between analytical (reputable) philosophy of history and speculative (disreputable) philosophy of history. I intend to shatter this stereotype. If there is any important distinction to be drawn between speculative and analytical philosophy of history, it is this: speculative philosophers of history are preoccupied with the kinds of philosophical problems that cluster around the narrative aspect of history, whereas analytical philosophers of history are primarily interested in the establishment and explanation of historical facts and have naturally approached this matter with an eye to how facts are established and explained in science. Dray is quite correct in saying that "the *raison d'être* of critical [analytical] philosophy of history is very closely bound up with the question whether historical inquiry is, or is not, 'scientific,' in a sense in which physics, biology, psychology, or even applied sciences like engineering are."[15] And this is why so much philosophy of history is a rehash of issues that spill over from the philosophy of science. Then, too, the philosophy of science was, until recently, dominated by the positivist tradition, which had its own historical roots in Comte's attempt to found a science of history. Positivism, before it became logical, embodied Comte's philosophical defense of the new science.

To show the relationship between analytical philosophy of history and speculative philosophy of history, one needs to show the connection between philosophical problems arising from the narrative aspect of history and those stemming from the descriptive-explanatory aspect. That is the burden of Chapter XV. First, though, I must provide further support for my thesis that speculative philosophy of history is essentially concerned with philosophical problems associated with the

[15] *Philosophy of History*, p. 2.

task of constructing historical narratives. As a way of preparing the ground, it is instructive to glance at some typical attempts by analytical philosophers of history to analyze speculative philosophy of history. The strategy which often directs such analysis seems to have as its aim the separation of speculative philosophy of history from orthodox history, on the one hand, and from analytical philosophy of history, on the other. This strategy, if it succeeded, would place the historical speculators in a no-man's land between philosophy and history. Is speculative philosophy of history between philosophy and history because it is *neither* philosophy *nor* history? Or is it that speculative philosophy of history lies between because it is *both* philosophy *and* history? It is the latter position I shall seek to establish.

W<small>HAT IS</small> a speculative philosophy of history? It would be convenient to have a checklist of speculative philosophies of history so that we could search for essential and common properties. Unfortunately, speculative philosophies of history are not neatly labeled, and they are produced by historians, social scientists, and theologians as well as philosophers. What is more, although there is usually agreement about the identity of hard-core speculators—Fichte, Hegel, and Spengler, for certain—there may well be differences of opinion when it comes to picking out other members of the genus. Did Marx advance a speculative philosophy of history? Most would think so. W. H. Walsh, however, suggests that "Marx's contribution to the understanding of history, in fact, was not made to philosophy of history in the proper sense at all."[16]

If speculative philosophies of history do not display a skull-and-crossbones warning device on their covers, how are we to recognize them? One feature commonly ascribed to speculative philosophies of history but presumed missing from ordinary history is elucidated by Walsh: "We may summarize

[16] *An Introduction to Philosophy of History*, p. 27.

by saying that if the philosopher can be said to have any specific concern with the course of history, it must be with that course as a whole, i.e., with the significance of the whole historical process."[17] Ordinary history differs from philosophical history because, according to Walsh, "seeing history as a whole is something of which working historians conspicuously fight shy: it is with the details of the past that they regard themselves as properly concerned."[18]

When a *philosopher* becomes interested in history as it happened rather than in "the processes of historical thinking," to cite Walsh again, he must be concerned with the entire course of history from man's earliest beginnings down to the present day. And he must be concerned about the "metaphysical significance" of the whole thing because, as Walsh puts it, a speculative philosophy of history "must be either metaphysical or non-existent."[19] Are speculative philosophies of history of use to anyone? We can learn from them in somewhat the way we learn from a portrait painter or a philosophical poet, Walsh claims.

One can now see why Walsh had trouble classifying Marx, why he at one point affirms that "Marx's contribution to the understanding of history, in fact, was not made to the philosophy of history in the proper sense at all."[20] We may represent Walsh's dilemma by means of a pair of arguments. Since, according to Walsh, speculative philosophy of history is of no interest to the professional historian, whereas Marxist theory does concern him, it follows that Marx's theory of history is not speculative philosophy of history. On the other hand, since, again according to Walsh, any theory concerned with the significance of the whole course of history is a spec-

[17] *Ibid.*, p. 27.
[18] "Meaning in History," in *Theories of History*, ed. Patrick Gardiner (Glencoe, Ill.: The Free Press, 1959), p. 301.
[19] *An Introduction to Philosophy of History*, p. 27.
[20] *Ibid.*

ulative philosophy of history and Marx's theory of history is concerned with the significance of the whole course of history, Marx's theory of history is speculative philosophy of history.

Walsh is convinced that there must exist an impenetrable wall between philosophical and ordinary concerns about history, though he has to resort, in the end, to metaphor in order to characterize the difference. The philosopher paints history, while the historian presumably photographs it. And so it is that we can learn something about history from both. Yet, although Walsh admits that professional historians often make use of Marxist principles in their work, he does not see that this very fact implies that the difference between speculative and ordinary history is not what he takes it to be.

Suppose I want to inquire into "the significance" of history as it happened from the beginning until the day before yesterday. I am not concerned about the whole of history, just history up to the day before yesterday. This somewhat arch consideration helps to show that Walsh's classification system fails to distinguish speculative philosophies of history from ordinary history. For one thing, professional or "ordinary" historians have been interested in so-called universal history. Von Ranke wrote that the final goal of the study of history "always remains the conception and composition of a history of mankind."[21] And he went on to say further: "To comprehend the whole while obeying the dictates of exact research will of course always remain an ideal goal, for it would comprise a solidly rooted understanding of the entire history of man.... Historical research will not suffer from its connection with the universal...."[22] Von Ranke was certainly not the only historian to hold such views. What, then, constitutes the difference between a philosopher's history of mankind and a his-

[21] Preface to *Histories of the Latin and Germanic Nations from 1494-1514*, in *The Varieties of History*, p. 61.
[22] *Ibid.*, p. 62.

torian's? Walsh's scheme obscures some crucial resemblances between speculative philosophy of history and ordinary history.

In the second place, "an interest in the significance of history" cannot be used to characterize the difference between philosopher and historian. No historian could produce a universal history of mankind without first deciding what he would take its significance to be—for example, what themes he would pick out as a structure for organizing his history. But then the same problem of significance is faced whenever a historian constructs any history. David Ogg's *Europe in the Seventeenth Century* is surely never included in anyone's list of speculative philosophies of history. Yet on the very first page Ogg is so bold as to outline the *significance* of European history in the seventeenth century: "The main interest of seventeenth-century continental history lies in this, that as politics became stereotyped abstract thought became more original."[23]

What features of Ogg's *Europe in the Seventeenth Century* make it "ordinary" history, rather than "philosophical" history? A different rationale for the distinction has been advanced by William H. Dray. He recognizes that both philosophers and historians have at times attempted to write universal history, that there is nothing improper in trying to see "history as a whole." What distinguishes philosopher from historian, speculative history from regular history, according to Dray, is that "such speculative accounts have generally claimed that there is in historical events a 'significance' or 'meaning' which goes beyond the understanding ordinarily sought by historians."[24]

Now it is true that speculators usually boast of their special historical insight, of their ability to give new significance to

[23] *Europe in the Seventeenth Century*, 8th edn., rev. (London: Adam and Charles Black, 1961), p. 1.
[24] *Philosophy of History*, p. 60.

old tales or to tell new tales altogether. Perhaps only Fichte, however, thought his thesis about history could be "proved independently of all history." Hegel stated in his first lecture on the philosophy of history that the only correct approach to understanding history is to assume that "the history of the world, therefore, presents us with a rational process," and he went on to say that "this conviction and intuition is a hypothesis in the domain of history as such. In that of Philosophy it is no hypothesis."[25] It does appear, then, that at least some speculators have looked for an understanding of history beyond that ordinarily sought by the historian. Hegel certainly thought that the main story-line of the history of mankind was an anagram, as it were, of the story-line of the history of philosophy and that the latter could be justified in an *a priori* fashion. Nonetheless, he was out to convince the professional historian, as well as everyone else, that his theory of history was valid. He told his lecture audience that he was "not obliged to make any such preliminary demand upon your faith."[26] Unlike Fichte, Hegel maintained that the philosopher of history "must proceed historically-empirically."[27]

Hegel's philosophy of history, in fact, was not directed just at his disciples, who were naturally gratified to see the philosophical principles of the master exhibited on the stage of world history. Rather, his aim was to convince everyone that his view of history was correct. If we reject Hegel's philosophy of history, we should do so for the right reason—neither because he was a philosopher and should have left history to the historians nor because he sought an understanding of history beyond that of his contemporaries. The only good reason for rejecting Hegel's philosophy of history is that history as it happened is not intelligible on Hegel's terms. Dray's characterization of speculative philosophy of history suggests that the kind of understanding of history sought by a specu-

---

[25] *Lectures on the Philosophy of History*, p. 9 (Hoffmeister, p. 28).
[26] *Ibid.*, p. 10 (Hoffmeister, p. 30).   [27] *Ibid.*

lator is utterly alien to that possessed by the ordinary historian. This position is somewhat plausible if we take Fichte as our model. It is less plausible if we think of Hegel and certainly untenable if applied to Marx. It is a fact that some speculative philosophies of history have affected the ordinary understanding of history.

A recent book on philosophy of history, by Arthur C. Danto, is entitled *Analytical Philosophy of History*. The title was meant to imply a contrast, a proclamation of what the book is not—namely, a speculative philosophy of history. Not surprisingly, then, Danto begins by attempting to distinguish between speculative (he calls it "*substantive* philosophy of history") and analytical philosophy of history: "Analytical philosophy of history . . . is not merely connected with philosophy: it *is* philosophy, but philosophy applied to the special conceptual problems which arise out of the practice of history as well as out of substantive philosophy of history."[28] Speculative or substantive philosophy of history, Danto claims, "is not really connected with philosophy at all, *any more than history itself is.*"[29]

I have called attention to certain words in the above citation to show the way in which Danto's philosophical orientation seems to be in conformity with the first stereotype—the view that philosophy is one thing and history something entirely different. He claims that neither history nor substantive philosophy of history has any real connection with philosophy— analytical philosophy, that is. Nonetheless, Danto's own characterization of analytical philosophy in general, and of analytical philosophy of history in particular, should have led him to be more cautious. He states, in the Preface, that "the philosophical analysis of our ways of thinking and talking about the world becomes, in the end, a general description

[28] *Analytical Philosophy of History* (Cambridge: At the University Press, 1965), 1.
[29] *Ibid.* (my italics).

of the world as we are obliged to conceive of it, given that we think and talk as we do."[30] He goes on to say that his *Analytical Philosophy of History* purports to be "an analysis of historical thought and language, presented as a systematic network of arguments and clarifications, the conclusions of which compose a descriptive metaphysic of historical existence."[31] Could anyone compose a "descriptive metaphysic of historical existence" without becoming deeply involved with history itself, history as it happened? Would Hegel, Spengler, and other speculators have objected to the phrase as a characterization of what they themselves set out to do? Could anyone contribute, in a significant way, to the analysis of historical thought and language without contributing something to making history as it happened more intelligible? (Consider, as an analogy, the position of a philosopher who wished to analyze the meaning of the word "chess," who desired to study chess thought and chess language, but who did not want to get involved with the game itself.)

Danto is interested in certain philosophical problems in the philosophy of history that stem from the task of constructing historical narratives. He is one of the few analytical philosophers to give the narrative aspect of history so much as a thought, though he does, in the end, mistakenly try to reduce narrative exegesis to causal explanation. What Danto fails to see is that speculative philosophers of history were also concerned with some of the very philosophical problems he appropriates for analytical philosophy alone, for he strives to locate speculative philosophy of history in that no-man's land between philosophy and history to which I alluded earlier. His strategy is quite simple. He argues first that substantive philosophy of history is not philosophy but history. His second move is to try to isolate "philosophical" history from ordinary history by contending that it is only pseudo-history, clearly distinguishable from the genuine article.

[30] *Ibid.*, p. vii.   [31] *Ibid.*

His thesis, roughly, is as follows. Real history resembles its counterfeit counterpart in that both kinds seek to relate historical incidents to each other by means of historical narratives. An important feature of historical narratives is that the historical significance imputed to earlier events is often a function of later events; in fact, the earlier events are often described in terms that prefigure events that come after them. "An historian might write," Danto points out, " 'The author of *Rameau's Nephew* was born in 1715.' But think how odd it would be were someone to have said, at the right moment in 1715, 'The author of *Rameau's Nephew* is just born.' "[32]

Everyone knows that the assessment of the historical significance of a given event can change from generation to generation. Such change can often be attributed to the simple circumstance that each generation knows something the preceding generation could not possibly have known—namely, those events that were shaped by the particular event in question but which had not yet occurred at the time the historians of the previous generation were writing. Danto recognizes that "philosophical" historians, like "real" historians, evaluate the significance of historical antecedents in light of their consequences. Philosophical or pseudo-history differs from real history, according to Danto, in that philosophical historians judge past events apocalyptically; they read into history the message of events which lie in the future, events which they are unjustifiably convinced must inevitably occur.

Danto's formulation of the difference between speculative philosophy of history and ordinary history does point to a salient feature of some philosophical histories and is in accord with a popular conception of the philosopher of history. Ibsen's *Hedda Gabler* contains an amusing confrontation between an ordinary historian and a "philosophical" historian. Tesman, Hedda's husband, and Løvborg, Hedda's lover, are competing for the chair of history at the University of Kris-

[32] *Ibid.*, p. 12.

tiania. Løvborg has just completed a history but advises Tesman not to waste his time reading it, for his new book, he
says, will be much better. His published work carries history
only up to the present, whereas his forthcoming work is to
be a continuation of the old. Tesman is astonished. How can
there be a continuation of a history that ends in the present?
The new volume, explains Løvborg, deals with the future.
But no one knows anything about the future, Tesman protests. That may be, Løvborg replies, but there are some things
that can be said about it anyway. Tesman, the orthodox historian, confesses that such a remarkable idea would never
have occurred to him—a point to which Hedda Gabler, his
wife, expresses her contemptuous assent.

Speculative philosophies of history, according to Danto, involve in one way or another a projection into the future, a
vantage point refused by the ordinary historian but seized by
the philosophical historian. There can be no doubt that some
philosophical historians are futuristic. One prominent philosophical historian, however, provides a counter-example to
Danto's thesis—Hegel.

A common criticism of Hegel's philosophy of history is that
it appears to bring history to an end with Prussia. Hegel quite
agreed that, for him, history did end in the present, *his* present.
He did not deny himself the pleasure of hazarding a few
guesses about the future—what would happen to the United
States when there was no longer a frontier to absorb the energies of its people, the possibility of a war between North and
South America, and so on. But, as a philosopher of history, he
did not take his own speculations about the shape of things
to come seriously. In defending himself against the possible
complaint that his history did not deal at all with "the great
Sclavonic nation," he stated that "this entire body of peoples
remains excluded from our consideration, because hitherto it
has not appeared as an independent element in the series of
phases that Reason has assumed in the World. Whether it

will do so hereafter, is a question that does not concern us here; for in History we have to do with the Past."[33]

For Hegel, both ordinary history and philosophical history (which he called "the conceptual consideration of history") had to be constructed without recourse to future possibilities. Hegel's philosophy of history, moreover, does not presuppose any projection into the future. Philosophical history cannot be isolated from ordinary history in the way Danto suggests.

Patrick Gardiner, in a perceptive essay, has noted that "the boundaries between what is known as 'philosophy of history' and other fields of speculation and inquiry are exceedingly difficult to draw: at some points it seems to shade off into sociology, at others into historical methodology, and at others again into history proper."[34] Speculative philosophies of history are elaborated for a great variety of reasons, and it is therefore idle to hunt for one or two common features of the genus: "To show how the stream of historical events forms a coherent pattern, to extend the techniques of science to new fields, to exhibit the realization in fact of certain political ideals, to justify and illustrate particular methods of investigating the past; it is aims like these that have been the principal driving-force behind theories of history, and such variety of purpose has been reflected in a corresponding variety of form."[35]

Perhaps, though, it is the presence of at least one of the aims mentioned by Gardiner that distinguishes philosophical history. May not the difference be that the ordinary historian merely tries to tell it *wie es eigentlich gewesen*, whereas the philosophical historian tries "to show how the stream of historical events forms a coherent pattern," to mention just one of his curious projects?

It has been fashionable for some modern historians, follow-

[33] *Lectures on the Philosophy of History*, p. 350.
[34] *Theories of History*, ed. Patrick Gardiner (Glencoe, Ill.: The Free Press, 1959), p. 7.
[35] *Ibid.*, pp. 7-8.

ing Beard and Becker, to interpret Ranke as having proposed a methodological ideal unrealizable in practice. It has often been maintained that writing history is irredeemably a subjective affair, so that it is impossible to tell it as it really was. In the next chapter I shall discuss the "relativity question" and the question whether constructing stories is incompatible with telling the truth. For the moment it will suffice to point out that adherence to the Rankean standard is not logically incompatible with any of the aims cited by Gardiner as motivating philosophical history. A man who believes, for example, that the "stream of historical events forms a coherent pattern," and who sets about to show what that pattern is, could truthfully describe himself as trying to tell what happened *wie es eigentlich gewesen*.

The trouble with the Rankean slogan is not that it displays a naïveté on Ranke's part, but that it is almost tautological and, to that extent, empty. It amounts to saying that the main objective of writing history is to tell the truth about the past. Few would publicly disagree, not even historians who lean toward Lewis Namier's view that "history is therefore necessarily subjective and individual, conditioned by the interest and vision of the historian."[36] Namier was once asked what he thought other historians meant when they spoke of "Namierizing" history. He is reported to have replied: "Finding out who the guys were." Namier's principal interest in later years was to construct the biography of every member of Parliament in the eighteenth century. As editor-in-chief of the projected *History of Parliament*, he came to represent an approach to history that depended upon a meticulous attention to matters of biographical detail. Could Namier, of all people, have denied that he was out to discover what really happened in the English Parliament during the eighteenth century?

It is a mistake, I think, to suppose that the difference be-

[36] "History," in *The Varieties of History*, p. 379.

tween philosophical history and ordinary history is a function of a difference in purpose in constructing the one or the other, that there is a difference between legitimate and illegitimate purposes in writing history. Any one of the aims that has informed philosophical history might also be, and most likely has been, the intent of some orthodox history or other. The difference between the two is not a difference in intent, but *in the way that intent is displayed* in the written work. This accounts for the instant recognition one sometimes has that what is before one is not an orthodox, but a peculiar kind of history. The author of an orthodox history keeps his intent submerged beneath the smooth flow of the narrative account. He spends a minimum of time discussing why he is writing his history and what he hopes to accomplish by it or giving detailed reasons for his selection of themes. Sometimes the themes are not explicitly stated at all. Methodological issues and philosophical questions are far removed from the body of the text. Thus Ranke, in the Preface to his *Histories of the Latin and Germanic Nations from 1494-1514,* wastes little space justifying by explicit argument his position that the Latin and Germanic nations form a "historical unity," though he believed the history of "racially kindred nations either of Germanic or Germanic-Latin descent" constitutes "the core of all modern history." "In the introduction," Ranke wrote, "I shall try to show—primarily *in the narrative* of foreign undertakings—how these nations developed in unity and in common enterprise."[37]

Unlike ordinary history, speculative history reveals the skull beneath the skin. Oswald Spengler begins his history with the following questions: "Is there a logic of history? Is there, beyond all the casual and incalculable elements of the separate events, something that we may call a metaphysical structure of historic humanity, something that is essentially independent of the outward forms—social, spiritual and political—which

[37] Preface to *Histories* . . . , *ibid.,* p. 56 (my italics).

we see so clearly? . . . Does world-history present to the seeing eye certain grand traits, again and again, with sufficient constancy to justify certain conclusions?"[38] Spengler's main purpose in *The Decline of the West* is to answer these questions, and he attempts to do so both by explicit argument and selected historical narration. By contrast, the ordinary historian deals with such questions in the essay, not in the narrative.

Yet there is no doubt that many orthodox historians are interested in the very same questions that generate speculative philosophies of history. Namier, for example, wrote in his essay "History" that in "all intelligent historical quest there is, underneath, a discreet, tentative search for the typical and recurrent in the psyche and actions of man (even in his unreason), and a search for a morphology of human affairs, curbed though that search be by the recognition that absent from the life of communities is the integration peculiar to living organisms."[39] The search for a "morphology of human affairs," so boldly proclaimed by the demonic Spengler, is discreetly alluded to by the orthodox Namier. Both believe that "what matters in history is the great outline and the significant detail; what must be avoided is the deadly morass of irrelevant narrative."[40] Both insist that historical narrative must be "guided by analytic selection of what to narrate" and that "the function of the historian is akin to that of the painter and not of the photographic camera."[41] Evidently, ordinary historians as well as demonic historians would rather paint than photograph.

Where Spengler and Namier differ, of course, is in what they make of the historian's search for a morphology of human affairs. Spengler, to be sure, does not agree with Namier that "absent from the life of communities is the integration peculiar to living organisms." Quite the reverse is true, in his

[38] *The Decline of the West*, I, 3.
[39] "History," in *The Varieties of History*, p. 372.
[40] *Ibid.*, p. 379.　　　　　[41] *Ibid.*

view. Namier refuses to reify the integration of the historical narrative in the events about which the narrative is written. If what matters in history is the great outline and the significant detail, it follows, according to Namier, that "history is *therefore* necessarily subjective and individual, conditioned by the interest and vision of the historian."[42] Are there, indeed, any criteria that govern the "analytic selection of what to narrate"? If demonic historians choose to discuss such questions and propose answers to them in the body of what purports to be narrative history, surely this in itself is no reason to condemn them. One may accuse them of being overly zealous and point out the obvious distortions engendered in their narrative accounts by philosophical rigidity. Or one may, contrariwise, complain that they do not adhere in the accompanying narrative text to their own revolutionary proposals to write history in a new way. Just such a charge was leveled by Lord Acton against Buckle's *History of Civilization in England*. The proper target for accusations of this sort, however, is the particular work and not the genus.

In many speculative philosophies of history, a philosophical torso is attached to a narrative body. Speculative philosophies of history are admittedly centaurs, as Jakob Burckhardt maintained, but they are not contradictions in terms, as Burckhardt also maintained.[43] As with centaurs, we can clearly recognize the torso as well as the body, even though there is no sharp line to indicate where one ends and the other begins.

In this chapter I have examined the second stereotype—the view that it is possible to distinguish, in a useful way, analytical or respectable philosophy of history from speculative or disreputable philosophy of history. I have attacked the

[42] *Ibid.*

[43] *Diese ist ein Kentaur, eine contradictio in adjecto; denn Geschichte, d.h. das Koordinieren, ist Nichtphilosophie und Philosophie, d.h. das Subordinieren, ist Nichtgeschichte.* Jakob Burckhardt, *Weltgeschichtliche Betrachtungen* (Leipzig: Alfred Kroner Verlag, n.d.), p. 4.

distinction from one side, concentrating on the popular opinion that speculative philosophy of history may be clearly differentiated from orthodox history. Accordingly, Hegel's lectures on the philosophy of history may be counted philosophical history (Danto) or speculative philosophy (Walsh). If the former, then should not historians alone pass judgment upon its purely historical merits? Is the professional historian not justified in dismissing Hegel's *Philosophy of History* as a historical oddity, as not meeting the standards of the guild? If Hegel's *Philosophy of History*, on the other hand, is not history but speculative philosophy, then philosophers of analytical temperament will be able to dismiss it as a philosophical oddity. Speculative philosophy is certainly not fashionable; even when analytical philosophers concern themselves with what they are prepared to call "metaphysics" (the term is no longer a shibboleth), they attempt to maintain respectability by characterizing themselves as *descriptive* metaphysicians, hoping by the nomenclature to distinguish themselves from such disreputable, speculative ("prescriptivist") metaphysicians as Hegel. Moreover, if one holds no brief for Hegel—and I don't—then it is very easy to say that whatever Hegel did in his lectures on the philosophy of history, or tried to do, was bad —bad history or bad philosophy (and does it matter which?).

Suppose, however, that I am right in contending that the difference between ordinary and philosophical history is primarily one of form—that if Namier, for example, had opened *England in the Age of the American Revolution* by setting down some of his thoughts about the nature of history and had then written that book keeping such thoughts explicitly in mind, endeavoring wherever possible to work them into the narrative, then we would have been justified in calling the result "A Speculative Philosophy of the History of England in the Age of the American Revolution." I certainly am not suggesting that narrative history, if it contained good philosophy, would therefore be better history. Nor am I proposing that historians try their hand at philosophical history. My contention is simply that there is no reason why a speculative philosophy of history cannot have both good philosophy and good history, though I am prepared to concede that many of those hitherto produced contain both inferior philosophy and inferior history. In fact, it may well be that, practically speaking, good philosophical reflection cannot be grafted on to good historical narration—that concentration on philosophical issues impairs historical sensitivity. All this, if true, does not vitiate my argument. There is nothing improper about a philosopher's becoming involved with history and a historian's trying to think philosophically about history. Demonic historians write history self-consciously, perhaps badly, when judged by the usual standards professional historians employ. Philosophers of history are often philosophically naive, their arguments shoddy when judged by the usual standards professional philosophers employ. Yet one cannot conclude from the shortcomings of its purveyors that speculative philosophy of history is either pseudo-history or a contradiction in terms.

CHAPTER XIII

The Whole Truth about History

P HILOSOPHICAL HISTORY is self-conscious history, produced by authors at pains to justify their particular narrative units of reference, their narrative organization of historical materials. The justification may proceed along two levels, by explicit argument and selected narration. Often the arguments appear at the beginning of the narrative text, and reference is made to them throughout. Spengler's *The Decline of the West*, Buckle's *History of Civilization in England*, and Toynbee's *A Study of History* are paradigmatic in this respect. Sometimes, though, the author's main argumentation occurs in another place, the "philosophical" history itself containing only echoes and overtones of the arguments. A good example is Karl Marx's *The 18th Brumaire of Louis Bonaparte*.

In *The 18th Brumaire* Marx set out deliberately to show how a segment of history, the French Revolution of 1848 and the subsequent *coup d'état* by Louis Bonaparte, could be organized through principles he had already worked out elsewhere. Marx's principles are of course well-known; Engels summarized them in his Preface to the third German edition of *The 18th Brumaire*:

> It was precisely Marx who had first discovered the great law of motion of history, the law according to which all historical struggles, whether they proceed in the political, religious, philosophical or some other ideological domain, are in fact only the more or less clear expression of struggles of social classes, and that the existence and thereby the collisions, too, between these classes are in turn conditioned

by the degree of development of their economic position, by the mode of their production and of their exchange determined by it.[1]

There can be no doubt that both Engels and Marx viewed the expression "law of motion of history" as more than mere metaphor. Both thought that the study of history could become a science like physics and chemistry, that there were "laws of motion" of history, and that Marx had in fact already discovered the most important among them. Since most of the leading thinkers of the nineteenth century shared the first two of these beliefs, it was only natural for Marx and Engels to deck out their novel historical insights in the fashionable scientific trappings of the time. With Newtonian mechanics no longer the popular scientific exemplar, such terminology now appears terribly dated.

Fortunately, one need not accept Marx's interpretation of his own contributions to the study of history in order to appreciate those contributions. His philosophy of history did not make historical inquiry any more scientific than it had been, if by "scientific" one means "amenable to subsumption under general law." What Marx did do, among other things, was to provide for subsequent historians—all historians, not just Marxist ones—a narrative frame of reference which made history intelligible in new and exciting ways. Moreover, one may legitimately accept the Marxist story-line and reject the Newtonian rhetoric in which it is couched if history is, in the end, intelligible when conceived as a struggle between social classes having competing economic interests, classes making their appearances in history as a result of certain fundamental changes in the means by which men produce the materials they consume in daily life. Many historians since Marx have decided that a great deal of history makes a good deal of sense

[1] Karl Marx, *The 18th Brumaire of Louis Bonaparte* (New York: International Publishers, 1963), p. 14.

when told that way, certainly more sense than when it is related as a tale of moral progress. That is why Marx's views of history has survived Hegel's.

In a letter apologizing to Weydemeyer for dispatching the fifth installment of *The 18th Brumaire* to the wrong address (Weydemeyer had suggested that Marx write about the then recent upheaval in France for publication, in serial form, in a political weekly he was trying to start), Marx offhandedly outlined what he believed to be his own contributions to the study of history:

> And now as to myself, no credit is due to me for discovering the existence of classes in modern society or the struggle between them. Long before me bourgeois historians had described the historical development of this class struggle and bourgeois economists the economic anatomy of the classes. What I did that was new was to prove: 1) that the *existence of classes* is only bound up with *particular historical phases in the development of production*, 2) that the class struggle necessarily leads to the *dictatorship of the proletariat*, 3) that this dictatorship itself only constitutes the transition to the *abolition of all classes* and to a *classless society*.[2]

Here, in one short passage, are most of the features which are anathema to critics of speculative philosophy of history. It is impossible to prove any thesis about the course of history; it is impossible to know the future; no historical event occurs inevitably—so tolls the litany of righteous criticism. If the status of the genus were dependent on the speculative philosopher of history making good on claims similar to those advanced by Marx, then the critics would indeed have the last word. Note, however, that Marx did not need such theses for *The 18th Brumaire*, nor did he mention them in that work. *The 18th Brumaire* is not an apocalyptic tract; there is no foreshadowing of the coming dictatorship of the proletariat, and the historical

[2] *Ibid.*, p. 139.

events as presented by Marx do not appear at all inevitable. On the contrary:

> The period that we have before us [1849-51] comprises the most motley mixture of crying contradictions: constitutionalists who conspire openly against the Constitution; revolutionists who are confessedly constitutional; a National Assembly that wants to be omnipotent and always remains parliamentary . . . a republic that is nothing but the combined infamy of two monarchies, the Restoration and the July Monarchy, with an imperial label—alliances whose first proviso is separation; struggles whose first law is indecision; wild, inane agitation in the name of tranquillity, most solemn preaching of tranquillity in the name of revolution; passions without truth, truths without passion; heroes without heroic deeds, history without events. . . . If any section of history has been painted grey on grey, it is this. Men and events appear as inverted Schlemihls, as shadows that have lost their bodies.[3]

Yet despite the play of chance in history—in this particular case, the confusion displayed by the French Legislative National Assembly—Marx maintained that it was possible to find order by paying attention to economic interest instead of political rhetoric. "Looked at with the eyes of democrats," Marx wrote, "the period of the Legislative National Assembly is concerned with . . . the simple struggle between republicans and royalists."[4] But, "if one looks at the situation and the parties more closely," he went on, "this superficial appearance which veils the *class struggle* and the peculiar physiognomy of this period, disappears."[5]

The Royalists of the period were divided politically into two main factions: the Legitimists, whose ostensible purpose was to restore the Bourbon monarchy, and the Orleanists, who favored restitution of the monarchy of Louis Philippe.

[3] *Ibid.*, pp. 43-44.   [4] *Ibid.*, p. 46.   [5] *Ibid.*

Much more important for understanding the actions of Royalist representatives in the National Assembly, according to Marx, was that each Royalist faction represented a different economic interest:

> Under the Bourbons, *big landed property* had governed, with its priests and lackeys; under the Orleans, high finance, large-scale industry, large-scale trade, that is, *capital,* with its retinue of lawyers, professors and smooth-tongued orators. . . . What kept the two factions apart, therefore, was not any so-called principles, it was their material conditions of existence, two different kinds of property, it was the old contrast between town and country, the rivalry between capital and landed property. That at the same time old memories, personal enmities, fears and hopes, prejudices and illusions, sympathies and antipathies, convictions, articles of faith and principles bound them to one or the other royal house, who denies this? Upon the different forms of property, upon the social conditions of existence, rises an entire superstructure of distinct and peculiarly formed sentiments, illusions, modes of thought and views of life.[6]

Marx's rhetorical style is familiar enough. Equally familiar, to those interested in the particular historical period, is Marx's story-line—not because *The 18th Brumaire* has been widely read, but because historical accounts of the period still follow guidelines laid down by Marx in *The 18th Brumaire.* That they do is all the more remarkable when one considers that the book was written, as Marx reminds us in the Preface to the second edition, under the immediate pressure of events. Marx had access to only a tiny fraction of the source material available to later historians. He had newspapers, a few official documents, and some private reports from Paris. *The 18th Brumaire* is, in fact, not a full-fledged history but a historical sketch, a narrative scaffolding with some roughly drawn details. Nonetheless,

[6] *Ibid.,* p. 47.

the Marxist scaffolding has proved sufficiently strong to support the weight of the mountain of historical research subsequently heaped upon it.

What, then, of the ultimate victory of the proletariat, of the inevitability in which Marx and Engels so fervently believed? Although Marx referred to that thesis in his letter to Weydemeyer about *The 18th Brumaire*, he gave the thesis itself no play at all in the book. Marx might have cited Laplace's reply to a different Bonaparte on another metaphysical point: *Je n'ai pas besoin de cette hypothèse là.* Assigned a very minor role in Marx's story, the proletariat makes its appearance during the June Insurrection of 1848, is put down in a bloody massacre, and "with this defeat the proletariat passes into the *background* of the revolutionary stage."[7]

A major contribution by Marx to the study of history was the provision of a new kind of story-line along with a new set of concepts for organizing historical data. One need not accept Marx's own assessment of that contribution in order to appreciate its value. Consider an analogy. One could write a "story," of sorts, concerning the successive positions of the earth as it journeys through the heavens on its annual voyage around the sun. One could praise both Copernicus and Kepler for having contributed to that story, though their contributions would have to be assessed in different ways. Kepler's laws of planetary motion presuppose the Copernican heliocentric picture; if one is to show that planets move in elliptic paths around the sun, one must first establish that they do move around the sun. Copernicus is not revered because he discovered any scientific laws. That the sun is to be taken as a fixed point in the solar system is not a law of nature; it is, rather, a presupposition for Kepler's laws, which could not be formulated without it. Copernicus provided, as it were, a new kind of story-line for organizing the data gleaned by planetary observation.

[7] *Ibid.*, p. 23.

Marx resembles Copernicus more closely than he does Kepler, though he and Engels evoked a Keplerian rather than a Copernican parallel in talking about the "laws of motion" of history. Need one believe that human history is governed by laws of motion in order to use Marxist principles of historical organization as a way of making history intelligible? Certainly, Marx neither needed nor used that hypothesis in *The 18th Brumaire*. And although there were occasions when Marx and Engels adopted a Keplerian model in characterizing historical episodic relationships, they employed other models as well. Their writings are studded with a vocabulary of growth and development, which conveys a rather different picture of the relationships they supposed important historical episodes had to each other. A growth-and-development stencil seems a particularly inept mode of tracing the relationship between the series of spatial positions assumed by the earth in its path around the sun. The successive positions reached by the earth, constituting as they do the incidents in that portion of its history governed by Keplerian law, do not "grow out of" each other. Similarly, it is infelicitous to portray the relationship between historical incidents as one would the relationship between successive positions of the earth in orbit. One is really forcing things even to characterize such spatial positions as "episodes" or "incidents" in a "story" of the earth's journey, as I have done above.

How, then, can a historian justify his use of Marxist principles of narrative organization in writing history? Marx himself did so by claiming that his principles expressed historical laws, though Engels in later years defended them in somewhat the same way that I have done here: "But our conception of history," he wrote in 1890, "is above all a guide to study, not a lever for construction. . . . Too many of the younger Germans simply make use of the phrase 'historical materialism' . . . only in order to get their own relatively scanty historical knowledge—for economic history is still in its swaddling clothes!—constructed into a neat system as quickly as possible. . . ."[8]

It is difficult to be explicit about how, on a Marxist basis, historical intelligibility is achieved. If, by using Marxist principles as presuppositions, historical "laws of motion" could be educed, then the formulation of such laws would be universally regarded as the positive proof that history had indeed been made more intelligible by Marx. Consider the Copernican analogy once more. Kepler's laws of planetary motion can be cited as justification for the presupposition of heliocentrism. An ellipsis is a simple kind of geometrical figure, easily imagined and understood. If the earth, rather than the sun, is taken to be a fixed point in the solar system, the paths traced by the planets become incredibly complex and can no longer be expressed by simple geometrical formulas. If one is asked to show that the solar system is more intelligible on a Copernican basis, one has only to point to Kepler's laws.

Suppose, however, that relatively simple laws of planetary motion could not have been formulated on a heliocentric model. Although one of Copernicus' two publishers, Andreas Osiander, in his Introduction to Copernicus' *De Revolutionibus Orbium Coelestium*, claimed that the heliocentric theory was to be taken as an interesting hypothesis only, and not necessarily as the true view of the nature of the solar system, the leading thinkers of that day had already accepted the heliocentric theory as fact. Until Kepler had fashioned his laws, however, the Copernican outlook was not of great use, since it was thought that planets moved around the sun in circles. Accordingly, there were still grave difficulties in putting together the data from observation of the planets' motions. Nonetheless, the heliocentric position seems to have been ripe for development, the universe somehow gaining in intel-

---

[8] *Karl Marx & Friedrich Engels: Basic Writings on Politics & Philosophy*, ed. Lewis S. Feuer (New York: Doubleday Anchor Books, 1959), pp. 396-397.

ligibility from its assumption. Kepler's laws of planetary motion were, in a way, simply an added gratuity. Marx's own justification of his historical principles—as expressing laws of history—is clearly unacceptable.

Does the failure to formulate historical laws vindicate the view that historical intelligibility is "subjective and individual, conditioned by the interest and vision of the historian"? And if the construction of history is conditioned by and relative to the interest and vision, the narrative frame of reference of the historian, is it necessarily an arbitrary affair? One may grant that the writing of history is *relative* in one or more of the important senses of that term. Even so, it does not follow that the writing of history must, on that account, be arbitrary. This is a bad, though pervasive, argument. It merits careful examination, especially because historical intelligibility cannot as yet be justified by its success in leading to the discovery of historical laws.

One early variant of the argument appears in Plato's *Phaedo*. In that dialogue it is claimed that to assert that Simmias is both larger than Socrates and smaller than Phaedo is tantamount to asserting that Simmias is both large and small —a rather dreadful conclusion to draw from so innocuous a premise. Are, then, the applications of the concepts of largeness and smallness, concepts whose criteria of intelligibility obviously depend upon the prior existence of frames of reference, arbitrary and subjective for that reason? If Simmias is our frame of reference and we call all objects larger than Simmias "large" and all objects equal to or smaller than Simmias "small," then there is nothing arbitrary or subjective in counting Socrates "large" and Phaedo "small." If Phaedo is the frame of reference, then both Socrates and Simmias will be considered "large." Once a frame of reference has been selected, our labels are not arbitrary. It will be argued, though, that this response simply skirts the real issue. Isn't the selection of a particular frame of reference, after all, always arbitrary and subjective? Why Simmias? Why Phaedo? Consequently, aren't judgments based upon such choices also arbitrary?

The latter objection is easily answered. Suppose Simmias is arbitrarily selected as a frame of reference, such that any object smaller than Simmias is to be described as "small." Anyone who adopts this standard, however arbitrarily chosen and accepted, is presumed committed to judge in accord with it. The size of Simmias thereby, in fact, becomes the basis of a decision procedure in which the concepts of largeness and smallness may be embedded. If a person who has accepted the standard should now call both Socrates and Phaedo "small," he would then be judging in an arbitrary, willful way. Although the selection of a frame of reference may be subjective, judgments made by reference to it may nonetheless be either subjective or objective. Whether the selection of a frame of reference is itself *always* arbitrary and subjective is another question. The answer to *that* question, again, is negative. One must not make hasty generalizations on the basis of the particular example considered. True, it would be arbitrary to choose Simmias as the standard by which to measure the largeness and smallness of every object in the universe. It would be arbitrary because there are no criteria to which one could appeal in support of that particular choice. Is it arbitrary, however, to call a beaver a *large* rodent but a *small* mammal?

Take another example: the color of an object varies in accordance with the kind of light under which it is observed. Are estimates of color arbitrary or subjective for that reason? Under green light red objects appear black. Under red light green objects appear black. Is a person who calls "black" a green object in red light behaving in a willful fashion? Is it merely an accident that white light is used as the standard condition for establishing the "normal" color of various objects? Can no reasons be given for using white light as the standard illumination?

The philosophical relativist may have the last word, but we shall not permit it to be uttered too quickly. That histories are written from different narrative frames of reference does not of itself prove that the writing of it is arbitrary, willful, or subjective. True, history is presented in story form, and different historians concentrate on different units of subject matter, employ different themes, and assess the significance of historical events in different ways. Yet none of these features of historical writing shows that it is "relative" in a pejorative sense of the term, though they may appear to make pejorative relativism more credible. The story-line favored by a historian constitutes his frame of reference, providing a source of illumination which colors the nature and relationship of the historical episodes he writes about. One would suppose that the number of story-lines applicable to any collection of historical episodes is endless. Yet, given all the possibilities, it is astonishing how few are the distinct story-lines that historians actually use. How many different kinds of accounts are there of the decline and fall of the Roman Empire? How many different interpretations does one find of the American Civil War? With remarkable regularity, the pendulum of historiographical fashion swings between some form of an irreconcilable interest theory and some variety of revisionism. Each theory suggests a different theme, a different plot, a different development of incidents—in short, a different narrative organization of historical events. One can always attribute the paucity of radically different interpretations of the Civil War to a lack of imagination on the part of historians. That paucity, however, could also be attributed to the limited number of selection criteria to which the historian can appeal in support of his choice of a particular frame of reference. All is not complete chaos, as might perhaps be the case if it were really true that the composition of history is a whimsical enterprise.

If I may offer a homely comparison, the situation is rather

like a dog show in which prizes are to be awarded for best-of-breed as well as best-of-show. The breed provides the frame of reference for judging any individual dog. Now a relativist dog fancier might attempt to argue that, since the individual dog must be evaluated in terms of a frame of reference, judgments of canine worth are necessarily subjective. And when it is pointed out to him that just the opposite is the case—that the existence of distinct breeds with determinate characteristics provides the basis for making *objective* evaluations of particular dogs within the breed—the relativist may then maintain that what he originally intended to say was that the selection of the best *kind* of dog is always arbitrary and subjective. If this claim is sound, it will be impossible to determine the relative merits of a chihuahua, say, when compared with a great dane. Thus although one might in time manage to persuade a relativist dog fancier that awarding a best-of-breed prize is not necessarily a hopelessly arbitrary affair, totally dependent upon the private whims of judges, the relativist could then turn around and scout the best-of-show award as a complete fraud. The only exit from the impasse lies in the effort to come up with criteria that permit cross-comparisons within breeds. And if no acceptable criteria can be formulated, the relativist will prevail, though he will fail to convince his philosophical opposite, the absolutist dog lover, that goodness-of-dog is a chimera.

I AM NOT CONCERNED here with the defense of, or attack on, any particular *kind* of historical story. I shall not argue, for example, that a revisionist account of the American Civil War is (or is not) a better kind of story than one based on an irreconcilable conflict theme. I am concerned, rather, with the general kinds of criteria, if there be such, which justify calling one historical theme *better* than another. I shall, in particular, examine the following questions: Is there a concept of truth which is applicable to a historical work as a whole, or is truth a concept which correctly applies only at the so-called individual fact level? When we rank story-lines as better or worse, do we commit ourselves to the view that esthetic or moral (or political) criteria alone govern the choice of story-lines? Truth as ordinarily conceived is, notoriously, a two-valued concept. Truth does not appear to admit of degrees. In sorting things out as better or worse in some respect or other, however, we are presupposing that the particular characteristic in which we are interested does admit of degrees. What could it mean, then, to maintain that one story-line is better than another in presenting *the truth*?

Consider the formula intoned by the court clerk in enjoining a witness to speak the truth, the *whole* truth, and nothing but the truth. If a witness speaks the truth and nothing but the truth, won't he sooner or later manage to speak the whole truth? Doesn't the concept of truth apply only to the particular statements that a witness makes, taken one by one? I shall argue that the phrase "the whole truth" in the courtroom formula is not a redundancy, as it would have to be if the whole truth could be arrived at by a process of adding true statements and subtracting false ones. I shall contend that the phrase "the whole truth," as it functions in this formula, is neither empty nor unintelligible, that there is a concept of truth which can be applied to a piece of narrative description taken as a unit, as well as a concept of truth which can be applied to the individual statements of which the whole description is composed. Histories are, among other things, pieces of narrative description. In comparing two histories of the same event, it is possible to appeal to something more than purely esthetic criteria in judging which is the better on the whole. We do speak of one account as being "more true" than another, of one description as presenting "a truer picture" than another. The same general idea is expressed when one speaks of one description as being better than another in getting at the *whole* truth.

It has at times been suggested that telling the whole truth about something that happened means telling *everything* that happened. Yet neither witnesses nor historians can recount everything that happened. If telling the whole truth, however, is equated with telling everything that happened (as it often is by historians who fancy some variety of historical relativism), then telling something less than everything that happened, by the same equation, becomes equivalent to telling something less than the whole truth. Since, moreover, telling less than the whole truth implies a kind of mendacity, one can understand why some historians have thought that the writing of history is, in the end, determined by a historian's biases and prejudices, that truth in history is a methodologically unattainable ideal.

If telling the whole truth is not the same as telling everything that happened, then what does it mean? Consider, for a start, the following two sentences: (a) The victim died of suffocation; (b) The victim died of carbon monoxide poisoning. Conjure up a pathologist who, upon discovering that the victim died of carbon monoxide poisoning, reports on the witness stand that the victim died of suffocation. Now carbon monoxide poisoning is a form of death by suffocation—whenever (b) is true, so is (a). A pathologist who asserts (a), when he knows that (b) is true as well, is surely telling the truth and nothing but the truth. Yet everyone will agree that he is not telling the court the *whole* truth. Why?

To be sure, the pathologist knows something more than he is telling. It is important to recognize, though, that "more than" cannot here be interpreted in any simple quantitative way. The pathologist is not required in court to report upon all the separate bits of data which collectively spell out, for him, carbon monoxide poisoning (unless that is the point at legal issue, a fact for the jury to decide). The pathologist always knows more than he is telling. One cannot fault him, on that account, for telling less than the whole truth.

A witness who babbles irrelevant details, though he may be telling the truth and nothing but the truth of what he observed, may nonetheless have his testimony stricken from the record. Such a witness certainly knows more than he is telling. The court, moreover, is interested in keeping it that way in its concern to get at the whole truth. The whole truth means the *relevant* truth. Relevancy, however, is not achieved in the law or history by piling up facts. Relevancy, I shall suggest, is achieved as the resultant of a complex interplay between fact, context, and conceptual framework.

Is there any relationship between the truth and the whole truth? Could a witness succeed in presenting the whole truth but fail, in the process, to tell the truth and nothing but the truth? I know a logician who reads every book as if it were nothing but a conjunction of individual sentences joined to each other by means of the connective "and." According to one of the basic principles of truth-functional logic, a conjunction of sentences is false if at least one of the sentences in the conjunction is false. When this logician spots the first false sentence in a book he is reading, he is disposed to call the entire book "false." Except for a few very short works on mathematics, his entire library contains only false books, though it includes some of the greatest books ever written.

The idea of calling an entire book "false" may occasion wry smiles, but orthodox historians have frequently played a similar game with histories written by demonic historians. Much of the attack against them consists in showing how wrong they so often are on points of historical detail. I do not deny the intrinsic value of this kind of criticism. It is not, however, the only kind of criticism that is relevant. Showing that Marx was wrong on points of fact in *The 18th Brumaire* does not justify dismissing the whole book as false.

Speaking the truth and nothing but the truth will not necessarily give access to the whole truth. One may succeed in presenting the whole truth and yet utter a number of falsehoods en route. Still, there is a conceptual connection between the truth and the whole truth. A witness who spoke falsehoods and nothing but falsehoods could never speak the whole truth. This bit of reflection, however, does not get one very far in the elucidation of the relationship between the truth, on the one hand, and the whole truth, on the other. It is equivalent to the not very informative proposition that anyone who manages to speak the whole truth must utter at least one true statement in the telling.

The complex relationship between the truth and the whole truth is not amenable to simple elucidation. Two analogies may prove helpful at this point. Imagine a sign with the legend "Trespassers will be prosecuted." There are at least three ways to report what is written on the sign, all of which will contain the truth and nothing but the truth. (1) On the sign is printed the sentence "Trespassers will be prosecuted." (2) On the sign is printed the sequence of words "Trespassers," "will," "be," "prosecuted." (3) On the sign is printed the sequence of letters *T, r, e, s, p, a, s, s, e, r, s, w, i, l, l, b, e, p, r, o, s, e, c, u, t, e, d.*

By hypothesis, each of the three reports contains the truth and nothing but the truth. What are we to say of someone who, though literate in English, presents the third report as a description of the facts? Such a person would be very much in the position of a pathologist who mentions one by one the separate items that collectively spell out carbon monoxide poisoning but neglects to inform the court of *that* fact. There is a conceptual organization appropriate to a person's knowledge in light of which we judge the extent to which that person is telling the whole truth. In uttering (3), a literate person is not speaking the whole truth. A foreigner learning English, who recognizes the individual words but is not able to master the grammatical structure of the sentence "Trespassers will be prosecuted," tells the whole truth by presenting (2). An illiterate who can recognize individual letters must resort to alternative (3). Finally, what are we to say of someone who knows nothing of the English alphabet? What does he see when he looks at the sign? Is it here that we approach bed-rock empirical experience, pure sensation unadorned by conceptual embellishment? Obviously, the whole truth is quite different from the naked truth.

One gets at the whole truth by arranging one's facts into a proper conceptual picture. The whole truth is the relevant truth; the facts, as reported, must fit together. We call upon concepts in order to show *how* facts fit together. Something further, though, needs to be said about how concepts make facts intelligible, how they aid in exhibiting the interrelationships among facts. I shall, for this purpose, have recourse to another analogy.

A jigsaw puzzle can be assembled in a number of ways. One can turn all the pieces picture side down and endeavor to put the puzzle together by referring only to the configurations of individual pieces. Another method is to assemble the puzzle by attempting to ascertain how the information conveyed by the colored side of a piece fits into the total picture, relating pieces to each other, not by comparing their shapes, but by noting the contribution each makes to that total picture. Correspondingly, one can describe each jigsaw bit in one of two basically different ways: a given bit can be characterized, for example, as having the form of a figure S, but also as being part of the left ear of a cow grazing in a meadow. Likewise, the relationships between bits can be presented in either of two ways: geometrically, as convexities fitting into concavities, or pictorially, as described by statements like "This bit is part of the left ear of the cow and that bit is part of a buttercup near where the cow is grazing."

The picture printed on one side of the puzzle serves a conceptual function in elucidating the relationship between "the facts," the separate bits of which the picture puzzle is composed. Of course, one normally does not assemble puzzles in either one of the two ways mentioned above to the exclusion of the other. One arranges the pieces, picture side up, and uses both spatial and pictorial-conceptual clues to put it together. The interplay of one method with the other is analogous to the manner in which historians reconstruct history, situating isolated bits of historical information in the conceptual framework of a story-line. Sometimes the facts fall into place seemingly of their own accord, the guidance of concept being almost invisible. Sometimes, though, the historian must deliberately bring into play certain concepts in order to exhibit the interrelatedness of certain "political facts," for example, to certain "economic facts."

It would be too much to expect of the picture puzzle model, or indeed of any model, that it should be a successful analogy at all points. The picture puzzle model fails, it may be argued, insofar as it presupposes a completed picture to begin with, one into which all historical facts can be fitted. Isn't a historian more like a man confronted by a number of jigsaw puzzles with the pieces all scrambled together? Perhaps not very many of the bits before him can be fitted into the frames of the pictures he is constructing.

Such an objection is sound. The picture puzzle model requires a good deal more elaboration before it can reasonably approximate the actual situation. Perhaps the historian is like a man confronted by a million jigsaw bits, no more than five of which belong to any one puzzle. Still, when on the job, historians seem to proceed on the assumption that bits they work with at any given time belong to one puzzle. They seem to act as if they really believe that Reason is the Sovereign of the World, as if puzzles have solutions, as if history makes sense.

A much more serious objection to the picture puzzle analogy, which, if sound, would shatter the model completely, runs as follows: The jigsaw puzzle analogy purported to show how concepts make intelligible the interrelatedness of facts, how concepts guide the manner in which the facts are described and presented. Yet one need not know anything about the picture printed on a jigsaw puzzle in order to put it together, nor must the individual bits be described in terms other than those of spatial configuration. Suppose, for example, that the jigsaw puzzle contained two different pictures printed on opposite sides. Wouldn't it be pointless to debate whether a given bit should be characterized as part of the cow's left ear rather than, say, part of a fireman's badge, especially when one has at one's disposal the "concept-neutral" language of spatial configuration? Describing a jigsaw bit as shaped like a figure S not only eliminates disputes arising from conceptual conflicts but also makes intelligible, in non-conceptual language, the real relationship between jigsaw puzzle "facts."

The hankering for a way to represent reality in concept-neutral language has always been a hallmark of empiricism and logical positivism. A party plank of the positivist platform was that any expression in any language could be classified into one of three categories: theoretical terms (such as "atomic number"); observation terms (for example, "red" or "hot"); and what were called "logical constants" (like "and" and "some"). Observation terms the positivists defined as those whose meanings could be grasped through simple, direct perception. Color words were often cited as paradigms of this type. One can come to know what the word "red" means, the positivists claimed, by—and only by—simple perception. The term "atomic number," on the other hand, cannot be understood without knowing a great deal of atomic theory. Logical positivists and empiricists felt they would be much more comfortable, philosophically speaking, if they could describe the world using a language containing only observation terms (plus logical constants, of course). An expression like "grey heavy bar turning red hot" seemed to them fundamentally more true to the facts than, say, the statement "An iron bar is turning red hot" and certainly better than "A metal having an atomic number of 26 and an atomic weight of 55.84 is being heated to a temperature of 600 degrees centigrade." The positivists, accordingly, launched what Rudolph Carnap called "a reduction program," which had as its goal the transformation of theoretical terms into observation terms. That there is a clear-cut division between the observational and theoretical expressions of a language and that a real understanding of the world can be achieved only by characterizing facts in observation terms are two presuppositions which, in one way or another, lie at the heart of positivism in all of its forms. Consider so-called historical positivism, which counsels the historian to lay stress on the collection of data rather than on fitting data together into unified pictures. According to historical positivism, it is better to describe Luther as nailing a paper to a church door than as ushering in the Reformation.

Even if positivists were correct in claiming that a clear partitioning between the observational and theoretical expressions of a language could be effected, there still remained the problem of actually reducing the latter to the former. Ingenious constructions were proposed, but the alleged hiatus between the two classes of terms withstood all attempts to bridge it.

The reduction program was in large measure misguided because there is no gap to be bridged between the observational and theoretical expressions of a language. No term is purely observational or purely theoretical in the first place. Consider the picture puzzle model once more. Spatial terms like "figure S" are, in an important sense, observational. Think how difficult it would be to describe a figure S curve, without actually drawing a diagram, to someone who had never seen one. Nonetheless, the expression "figure S curve" is not *purely* observational; it has a conceptual content as well. A figure S can be characterized by a mathematical equation. That the relationship between jigsaw bits can be described in terms of spatial convexities and concavities is no proof that it can be elucidated without appeal to concepts. Although I think this argument is perfectly sound as it stands, I shall not employ it as an answer to the objection raised before. There is no need to escape through a back door when one can stroll out the front. The objection can be overcome on its own terms.

That objection, to repeat, held the relationship between the parts of the jigsaw puzzle to be perfectly intelligible without appeal to pictorial conceptual clues. Why describe bit A and bit B as being, say, the top and bottom parts of a cow's left ear when relationships between bits can be characterized by reference to convexities and concavities?

True, the relationship between bit A and bit B can be exhibited without mentioning ears or cows. And the same applies to all *adjacent* bits. But how could one communicate the relationship between pieces of the puzzle five or ten bits removed from each other except in terms of the representation printed on the bits? Left ears fit together with right ears when both are parts of the same head of the same cow. A figure S bit does not fit together with a figure Y bit even though the representations upon them may be as intimately related as the left and right ears of a cow. Story-line representations, in similar fashion, enable historians to bring together historical facts which, without those representations, would seem to have little relationship to one another.

Conceptual representations dictate the modes in which one must describe facts to make their interrelationships intelligible. Consider, for example, the relationship between a set of symptoms and the disease of which they are said to be the symptoms. A high fever, loss of appetite, a certain type of rash provide "the facts" whose concurrent occurrence is made intelligible by the physician's conceptual framework. The physician fits the symptoms together as part of a disease pattern— scarlet fever, let us say. Having a disease, though, is something more than manifesting a particular set of symptoms. True, we speak of a patient as *having* a loss of appetite, as *having* a high fever, as *having* scarlet fever. Nevertheless, the expression "scarlet fever" does not designate one more symptom. Rather, the disease may be said to be "exemplified" by its symptoms, instead of equated with them. Similarly, it would be wrong to think of the presence of scarlet fever as an *event*, capable of causing the occurrence of other events, such as vomiting at a particular time. It is important to notice, moreover, as in the jigsaw puzzle analogy, that a concept does its work only if "the facts" are described in an appropriate manner. That a patient is suffering from scarlet fever accounts for his loss of appetite; it does not explain why he can only manage a bowl of chicken soup, whereas some fellow sufferer can also eat a boiled egg. If one insists upon describing a patient's loss of appetite in more specific terms, one will fail to explain its occurrence. That the patient is suffering from scarlet fever explains why he has a high fever; it does not explain why his temperature is 104.2 degrees Fahrenheit, when another patient's temperature is 103.3. Similarly, it does not explain why the length of the mercury column in the thermometer used to take both patients' temperatures is so many millimeters in one case, so many millimeters in the other.

The relationship between fact and concept is little understood, in science and certainly in history. How do narrative frames of reference, which I believe play an important theoretical role in organizing the facts of historical experience, make those facts intelligible? Intensive study of the role of theory in science has only begun to unravel the mystery there. Matters are murkier in history, where attention to the narrative aspect, to the theoretical role played by story-line and theme, has been insufficient. Historians are often disposed to treat story-lines as independent strings upon which to arrange the beads of historical fact. Just as one kind of string will usually do as well as another in making a necklace, so many historians believe that it really is the particular historical facts discovered that count, not the narrative string on which the beads of fact are arranged for public inspection. Yet it is the story-line that makes the relationship between historical facts intelligible, that dictates how facts shall be described, which facts selected as relevant and which omitted in presenting the truth, the *whole* truth about some historical event. If the role of the narrative structure in which history is laid out is not appreciated, then one can pretend that truth in history is simply an affair of getting at bare facts and that, when it comes to narrating history, it is every historian for himself.

I do not claim to have "refuted" philosophical relativism as applied to the study of history. Rather, I have tried to set forth some considerations that militate against it. In the final analysis, the relativist may be right. The themes which appeal to historians may have no more real relationship to the facts they are supposed to organize than the obsessions of a madman. A friend of mine once heard some lectures on Greek myths and became so ensnared by the myth of Sisyphus that all stories for him became as one—the myth of Sisyphus seemed to him the sole plot for all human enterprises. Marxists suffer from a similar malady. Their very excesses and exaggerations show how urgently needed is an examination of the function of historical story-lines in the apprehension, description, and explanation of historical facts. The remaining chapters will contain some exploratory moves in that general direction.

CHAPTER XIV

History as Story

STORY-LINES and themes enable a historian to tell what happened by providing a method for reducing, to a short description, events of the greatest complexity. A theme summarizes the data and thus gives the historian his plan of organization. The shifting coalitions of the French Legislative National Assembly, the betrayals, the alliances, the incredible rhetoric displayed by that body during its short existence must somehow be fitted into one picture if a narrative history of even so brief a span is to be constructed. What in the world was going on? Marx gives us an answer in a few words: "it was the old contrast between town and country, the rivalry between capital and landed property." Whether the incidents of historical interest were of great or of short duration, a narration of them presupposes a theme. And although it may at first sight seem absurd to ask "What happened?" when surveying the history of mankind, that question must be asked and answered if a narrative history of mankind is to be attempted. One may dislike various responses to that question—Hegel's, for example, of a World-Historical Spirit struggling to attain self-consciousness—and consequently decide that an effort to compose a history of mankind is as vain as trying to discover the meaning of life. Less thrilling histories may appear more tenable. The choice of a narrower temporal scope, however, does not necessarily make it easier to write a narrative history. It may be more difficult, conceptually speaking, to make narratively intelligible events of some five minutes' duration than to produce a narrative history of mankind.

During the last fifteen minutes, as I gazed out of my office window, I saw a great number of people walking in a variety of directions, each seemingly intent on his own affairs. Could I write a history of what was going on during that brief stretch of time? What did happen? Nothing? Merely a lot of people walking here and there? Those familiar with life on a university campus could immediately identify the scene as a change of classes. What was going on? A change of classes. And with that short description one is provided with the handle needed for organizing narratively the separate lives of the people who would be part of that history of fifteen minutes' duration.

Does the historian discover his story-line and theme "objectively" in the events he writes about, or does he dredge them up "subjectively" from the depths of his being to superimpose on the data? Unfortunately, there can be no simple answer because the question poses important issues in too simple-minded a way. Did I discover the theme for my fifteen-minute history *objectively*, by gazing out the window? Yes, in a way. Will I ruthlessly superimpose that theme on the data, arranging the episodes in my history with reference to it, relating separate incidents to each other by means of it, blue-penciling all events which do not fit into my chosen narrative scheme? And does this imposition make the writing of history *subjective*, conditioned by the interests and vision of the historian? Yes, in a way. A reasonable approach to a subject of such difficulty is by way of searching for criteria of intelligibility that govern the relationships which episodes must have to each other in order to be narratively intelligible, in order to be said to exemplify a common theme or story-line. I shall touch on this matter in the next chapter. It is the kind of issue that would naturally interest a philosopher, once he became concerned about the narrative aspect of history. Yet there exists another issue, related to the first, that is also connected with the narrative aspect of history, but not so visibly. The writing of history involves more than just the presentation of a story. Even if one could define the relationships events had to have to each other in order to be considered as episodes exemplifying one common theme, there would still exist the problem of how one turns a story into history.

Suppose a number of players, sitting around a table, set out to compose a story by means of a kind of parlor game. The agreed-upon procedure is this: someone will commence by writing down one sentence on a piece of paper and passing the paper to the next man, who, in turn, will write a second sentence and pass the paper to the third, and so on around the table until the story is completed. Contrary to the usual arrangements of joint authorship projects, no consultations or revisions will be permitted. Each person must continue the story as best he can from the point at which he is placed in charge of it.

Doubtless there are better ways of embarking on joint writing ventures, but stories can be produced by the sort of parlor game described. Whether good stories are producible in this "dialectical" fashion—each author striving, in turn, to bend the tale to his own will, yet being continuously frustrated and forced to yield up the story to the wills of others—does not concern me at the moment. It is more interesting, at this preliminary stage, to inquire whether one may speak, under these circumstances, of a joint authorship at all. Do we partition the responsibilities of the authors, each author being liable only for those lines he has actually written, or must we recognize an overriding collective responsibility, despite the possibility that the story as a whole may not have been anticipated or intended by any of its writers? Another question, closely connected with the first, concerns the description of actions. As each writer is presented with the unfinished story, we may state what he does in a number of ways—as putting on paper the *n*th sentence of *a* story, as continuing *a* story from where it was left off, and so on. But may we not also correctly present his act as writing *that* story, where by "that story" we mean the whole story, even though its shape is not anticipated by the writer who puts on paper its *n*th line?

Compare this situation with the usual method of story composition. We do not hesitate to describe what Tolstoy did when he wrote the *n*th line of *Anna Karenina* as "writing *Anna Karenina*." Similarly, we feel no compunctions about describing what Joseph Conrad did when he penned the *n*th line of *The Nature of a Crime* as writing that novel, though it was jointly authored by Conrad and Ford Maddox Ford. In both cases we assume a single or common purpose that informs the novel as a whole, a purpose that can be identified as Tolstoy's, in the one case, and as the joint purpose of Conrad and Ford, in the other. But to what common purpose can we appeal to support a description of each of the separate acts of the individual players of the parlor game as writing the story that is the dialectical outcome of their labors?

One might be inclined to say that there is no great difficulty in presupposing a common purpose in the parlor game situation; after all, the players did set out to compose *a* story, albeit by a peculiar method. The common purpose, however, only sanctions a description of the several acts of each writer as composing some story or other—a different one, perhaps, for each writer's turn, since the story which resulted was presumably not intended by any single writer. We are searching instead for a justification for characterizing each of the acts of the authors as writing *the* story that finally emerged. And if you grant that a story could be produced under the conditions as outlined—a real story, one that would have a recognizable theme, a clear plot, some continuity between incidents (call it the "Tale of Many Tongues")—then the problem becomes one of justifying the description of what each writer did as an occasion upon which he was composing the "Tale of Many Tongues." How may a thousand actions, once afoot, end in one purpose? What are the criteria for the intelligible application of the concept of a single action to the union of a thousand separate acts?

Admittedly, such questions appear artificial at first. Why worry about them? One may allow that a "Tale of Many Tongues" could be written in the curious manner hypothetically posed. But why the concern about whether it is correct to refer to the separate acts of each writer as occasions on which he was composing the "Tale of Many Tongues"? Such questions would be idle unless one could show in what situations they became important. One such situation would arise were one to attempt to construct *a history* of the composition of the "Tale of Many Tongues," in which the tale would become, as it were, a twice-told tale.

How would you go about writing that history? Suppose you attempted it by first discovering who contributed which sentences when and then setting down a sequence something like this: At time t_1 player A wrote "Some men are born lucky, but Albert Fox was not among them." At t_2 player B wrote "Albert's first mischance befell him at the moment of his birth." At t_3 player C wrote "The midwife had had to resort to instruments in order to assist his delivery." At t_4 player D wrote "As a result, Albert's face was elongated into the permanently mournful expression he wore until the day his undertaker transfixed him with a smile." At t_5 player E wrote. . . .

If you count chronology a species of history, then you will have written a history when you have finished, though a history of no interest at all. What does it matter who wrote what when? As history, the twice-told tale would be bloodless, the temporal ascriptions and the references to contributors mere annoyances interfering with the story within the quotation marks. How could you transform the chronology into a proper history? Surely, you would have to make use of the actual narrative structure of the "Tale of Many Tongues." The various contributions of the writers would have to be analyzed and assessed in light of that structure. Which players kept to the main plot; which of them saw what was ripe for development? Who kept the story running in the same direction? Who broke new ground? Now it is important to note that, in using the actual narrative structure of the "Tale of Many Tongues" as the basis for constructing your history, you would tend to think of the players as having been engaged in writing that tale all along, though no one knew or intended the finished product at the time he made his contribution. The "internal logic" of the story would become the logic of your history, and the description of the contribution of each player would be prefigured by the role it played in that story.

Part of one's task as historian might involve rewriting the tale, perhaps filling in gaps in the story-line, eliminating unnecessary allusions, and, in general, making the story more intelligible while at the same time preserving what could be called "the historicity" of the improved version. The relationship between the historian and the contributors to the tale would resemble that between editor and author. The editor's job is not simply to improve the story he edits by way of making it more intelligible; he must also strive to preserve as much as he can of the original version. Changes of script require the author's permission. Both editor and author must pretend they are carrying out the original intent of the author, an assumption that seems necessary in order to guarantee the historicity of the edited version. The author's story must somehow be preserved at the same time it is being improved. Even when the author cannot actually remember what his intentions were, he and the editor must suppose they can discern them in the original story. The relationship between author and editor is distinguishable from that of author and co-author.

I submit that the historian can be compared with an editor who must try to preserve an original story while seeking at the same time to increase its intelligibility. Unlike the editor who deals with a single author, however, the historian is confronted with a tale produced by many authors, often working at cross-purposes, each busy with his own activities. Since the editor may support the historicity of his edited version with an appeal to the author's original aim, how convenient it would be if the historian could follow Hegel in presupposing transcendent purpose at work, a World-Historical Spirit to whose original intent he could appeal in order to justify the historicity of his twice-told tale!

Consider the advantages. If the historian-editor assumes a transcendent purpose in the composing of the original story, one rational in intent, then he can attempt to justify his editorial clarification by claiming that he is doing nothing more than showing what really happened, what the real story was. For the real story must be an intelligible one. Hegel makes essentially the same point in saying that Reason is the Sovereign of the World, that the history of the world presents us with a rational process. Suppose the historian-editor submits his improved version of the tale to the scrutiny of its authors, and some of them complain that certain of the lines they contributed were altered beyond recognition or omitted altogether. "But don't you see," the editor will retort, "some of the lines you wrote were not integrated into the story, were ignored by the other players, and were in fact so many lost opportunities? Should the historian deal with might-have-beens or with what actually happened?" Another charge might be that, although the edited version is vastly superior to the original tale, its historicity has been impaired precisely because of the changes. This view of historicity, however, would prevent the historian from editing the tale at all; his task would be simply to record who said what when and to leave it at that. An appeal to a transcendent purpose does justify historical editing, provided that the historian can say he knows what that purpose was. Moreover, if the material with which he deals displays an intelligible story, what is to prevent him from reading purpose into the sweep of the story itself? He may even get the indignant authors to admit that the edited tale is their tale more perfectly realized.

What functions in one age as a criterion of intelligibility can, with historical erosion, be downgraded into a "presupposition" and then to a "necessary fiction," finally passing to the stage where it is regarded as a fiction pure and simple. Hegel lived at a time when the notion of transcendent purpose was intellectually acceptable, when it could derive support from commonly held theological assumptions. Hegel explicitly played upon theological similies in expounding the conceptual role of a World-Historical Spirit in the understanding of history. That recourse is, of course, no longer available. If one can maintain that a thousand actions, once afoot, did in fact end in one purpose only by assuming that an independent transcendent purpose guided those thousand actions to their resolution, then one would be forced to give up altogether the teleological framework of history, a framework many historians presuppose, though they would perhaps be embarrassed to admit it. This dilemma is particularly serious for the history of ideas, and it is interesting that Marx, in rejecting the Hegelian view of history, denied as well the possibility of writing histories of ideas.

We may suppose the historian-editor to have completed an extensive revision, eliminated unnecessary details, provided smooth transitions, and, in general, made the "Tale of Many Tongues" much more intelligible than it was when handed to him. His task, however, is not dictated solely by esthetic criteria. He is not like a writer who borrows a tale from another and reworks it to his own devising. Somehow he must manage to justify the historicity of his revisions, without appealing to transcendent purpose; he is not the author of the tale, but only its historian-editor.

Let us shift ground by asking whether we are prepared

to accept the editor's version of the "Tale of Many Tongues" as a history in the first place. If a history, what kind is it? One must remember that the historian-editor is not an editor *simpliciter*; he is also a historian. He has not been asked merely to edit the "Tale of Many Tongues"; he has been invited to write a history of its composition. I have suggested that these two tasks overlap. To write a history of the tale's composition, he must first get straight in his own mind what that tale was—he must sort out the important elements from the irrelevant details. He must try, wherever possible, to make his version more intelligible than the original. Nevertheless, the story itself must appear within quotation marks. The historical interest must center in the story's composition and not in the story as such; the story of how it was composed is not the same as the story itself. The Hegelian view of history in fact conflates the two stories. Yet if the "logic" of the "Tale of Many Tongues" itself provides the structure for a narrative account of how the tale was composed, does the latter differ from the former in any substantial fashion? To put it another way, the story of the composition of the "Tale of Many Tongues" has to be interesting in its own right and not be merely a tedious repetition of the tale itself, the writers appearing as marionettes, duped by the cunning of the logic of the story into contributing the right lines when taking their turns. But how can it be made intrinsically interesting when the structure of the original story is itself being used for writing the narrative of its composition?

I must emphasize at this point that, although I have presented the problem with the aid of a simple model, the model does have application. The problem, or rather its analogue, confronts everyone who has ever tried seriously to write intellectual history. Consider, for example, the task of writing a history of mathematics. The historian-mathematician is comparable to the historian-editor of the model. Just as the historian-editor must understand the real structure of the "Tale of Many Tongues" in order to write a narrative history of its composition, so the historian-mathematician must first comprehend the structure of the story of mathematics before he can write his history. There is a complication here, however, one which does not arise with the model. In the model situation, there was no question about whether history actually presents us with a story because it was presupposed that the players were indeed writing a story. The problem was how to transform story into history. In the real situation, however, one cannot simply assume that history presents us with a story. The men who made mathemathical history were not writing stories, but doing mathematics. Separate arguments are needed to show that the result of their individual labors does reveal a narrative structure. No doubt historians of mathematics do presuppose that there is a story to be told; in fact, the greater part of their efforts goes into writing that story. Accordingly, a crucial task for the philosopher of history is to attempt to formulate the criteria which must be fulfilled in order that the concept of a story can be intelligibly applied to a set of incidents, a task I shall examine more carefully in the next chapter.

The historian-mathematician, then, differs from the historian-editor of the model because he is in charge of the story of mathematics, his role being closer to that of author than to that of editor. Nonetheless, the historian of mathematics does assume that he is retelling a story which has already been told, as it were, by mathematical deeds and discoveries. As in the model situation, there is a distinction to be drawn between two kinds of stories: the story of mathematics and the story of its composition, that is, the story of how mathematicians came to have the ideas that provide the incidents and episodes which comprise the story of mathematics. Yet, again, if the historian concentrates solely on the story of mathematics, his history will tend to give mathematical ideas a life of their own, and references to the places, dates, and individual mathematicians will seem a tiresome, almost unnecessary, interruption of the story of mathematics. What does it matter, one may think, which mathematicians discovered negative numbers if such a discovery can be made to appear the inevitable consequence of a certain algebraic symmetry? Who cares whether Fermat was French?

The danger which threatens any historian of ideas is that he will set out to write history but instead produce what I call "Hegelian history," history in which one idea leads to another of its own momentum, independent of the men who had the ideas and of the world in which they lived. The problem is brought out by our model, where it can be seen clearly that there is a difference between rewriting the original "Tale of Many Tongues" and writing a history of its composition. If a historian of ideas is interested solely in the story of mathematics or the story of philosophy, rather than in the history of mathematics or the history of philosophy, he will never succeed in finding a place for the men who make history. Historians are fond of condemning Hegel, particularly for his view that historical events are inevitable—that men do not make history but are instead seized by ideas which have their own inner dialectic. Hegel's mistake, apparently, was to proclaim as doctrine what historians of ideas often do in fact, namely, regard the story of mathematics or philosophy as primary and the history of mathematics or philosophy as secondary (where the term "history" is taken to mean the account of how the individual developments in the story of mathematics or philosophy were brought about by the work of individual mathematicians or philosophers). The difficulty, I have contended, arises from the necessity that the historian use the narrative structure of the story of mathematics as the basis for writing a history of that story's composition—that is, a history of mathematics. The problem, then, is how to write a history of mathematics or of philosophy in such a way that the story of mathematics or philosophy remains firmly within quotation marks, the center of historical interest being fixed upon that story's composition, so that references to the biographies of the individual contributors are something more than bothersome footnotes.

Perhaps, for the history of ideas at any rate, this problem can never be adequately resolved; perhaps the most that can be expected from a history of ideas is a good story in which lip service is paid to certain historical demands by including anecdotes about the lives of the contributors. But then would it not be more honest to avoid placing the original story within quotation marks in the first place and to reduce to the vanishing point attention to the role of the individual contributors—in a word, to write Hegelian history pure and simple?[1]

[1] When one compares the caricature I have called "Hegelian history" with Hegel's history proper, certain contrasts are notable. Hegel's major historical work, his *Lectures on the History of Philosophy*, contains the best general history of philosophy written up to his time. Now the heroes of Hegelian history, according to the caricature, are supposed to be "faceless," yet Hegel's treatment of the most famous personality in the history of philosophy—Socrates—occupies 64 pages of the Haldane translation (*Hegel's Lectures on the History of Philosophy*, 3 vols. [New York: Humanities Press, 1955]). This lengthy discussion of Socrates is all the more curious in view of Hegel's warning to his audience in the Introduction that "the events and actions of this history are . . . such that personality and individual character do not enter to any large degree into its content and matter" (I, 1). Moreover, Hegel's portrait of Socrates is not entirely abstract art. The likeness is there: the robust Socrates, the soldier, the boon companion, the deadly marksman drawing a bead on the pretensions of mankind. How, then, did Hegel square his historiographical prejudices with his history? Hegel evidently felt the need for some kind of justification, for he remarks at several points that he has gone into the details of Socrates' life at somewhat greater length than one might have expected. "I have been more detailed here," Hegel concludes the section on Socrates, "because all the features of the case have been so completely in harmony, and he constitutes a great historic turning point" (I, 448). In Hegel's story of philosophy, Socrates represents the subjec-

In writing Hegelian history, one is neither restricted by time and place nor tied down by considerations of cause and effect. One can begin with certain ideas entertained in ancient China, skip over to Greece and Rome, pick up the tale in Peru, and wind up wherever one pleases. Suppose one discovered that, if all the works of literature ever written were arranged in the temporal order of their composition, it would be possible to select certain sentences from each which, when assembled in the temporal sequence in which they were produced, collectively formed an intelligible, albeit transcendental, literary work. This would be a most surprising discovery, but I doubt if we would call the genius who made it a historian,

---

tivization of abstract moral principle: "As regards the Socratic principle, the first determination is the great determination which is, however, still merely formal, that consciousness creates and has to create out of itself what is the true. This principle of subjective freedom was present to the consciousness of Socrates himself so vividly that he despised the other sciences as being empty learning and useless to mankind; he has to concern himself with his moral nature only in order to do what is best—a one-sidedness which is very characteristic of Socrates" (I, 407). All of the features of Socrates' life, as Hegel saw them, exemplified the role Socrates was given to play in Hegel's story: "He lived amongst his fellow-citizens, and stands before us as one of those great plastic natures consistent through and through, such as we often see in those times—resembling a perfect classical work of art which has brought itself to this height of perfection" (I, 393). Hegel, in sum, was interested in Socrates as a work of art—*Hegel's* art. Thus are the personages of Hegelian history faceless. They seem, in Hegelian history, more like actors behind masks, speaking the lines *the historian* has assigned them rather than seen as having somehow originated those lines from their own fleshly substance: "In a real work of art the distinguishing point is that some idea is brought forth, a character is presented in which every trait is determined by the idea, and, because this is so, the work of art is, on the one hand, living, and, on the other, beautiful, for the highest beauty is just the most carrying out of all sides of the individuality in accordance with the one inward principle. Such works of art are also seen in the great men of every time" (I, 393).

even a historian of ideas. Something more would be needed. This problem is closely related to the one of how to write a history of a story's composition, for it would be virtually impossible to write a history of the composition of a "transcendental story." What, for example, did some ancient Chinese author have to do with Shakespeare, though we may imagine that both unwittingly contributed a few sentences to the transcendental story?

Let us once more consider the problem in reference to the model situation. Remember that using the structure of the "Tale of Many Tongues" as the basis for writing a history of its composition means, in general, analyzing and assessing the contributions of the players in light of the structure of the whole story that emerged. This method may require one to ignore certain brilliant contributions which were marginal to the development of the main story and to concentrate on others which were of no great stylistic worth yet which, as a matter of "historical fact," provided key elements of the story that eventuated. It would surely be a mistake to confuse historical importance with esthetic worth, rather like the error Hegel committed when trying to clothe morality in the garments of historical necessity.

The historical significance of a contribution to a historical story is evaluated by reference to the structure of the story as a whole, a story over which no man has control. Seen from the vantage point of the total story, the individual contributors seem like pawns, their contributions controlled by the story rather than the other way around. Yet if the historian is to be interested mainly in the composition of the story rather than in the story itself, he must somehow provide a place in his history for the men who make it. How can this be done?

An important suggestion is contained in R. G. Collingwood's principle that the historian must aim at reenacting past experience.

Suppose, for example, [the historian] is reading the Theodosian Code, and has before him a certain edict of an emperor. Merely reading the words and being able to translate them does not amount to knowing their *historical significance*. In order to do that he must envisage the situation with which the emperor was trying to deal, and he must envisage it as that emperor envisaged it. Then he must see for himself, just as if the emperor's situation were his own, how such a situation might be dealt with; he must see the possible alternatives, and the reasons for choosing one rather than another; and thus he must go through the process which the emperor went through in deciding on this particular course. Thus he is re-enacting in his own mind the experience of the emperor....[2]

Consider now the bearing of Collingwood's principle upon the task of writing a history of the "Tale of Many Tongues." One way, and a most important one, of shifting attention from the story itself to the story of its composition consists in interrupting the smooth narrative flow of the original story by considering each separate contribution, in turn, as a solution to a problem, a problem posed by the earlier contributions of the other players. This procedure, if it can be successfully applied, will accomplish a number of objectives at once. It will encourage the historian to pay heed to the composition of the story as well as to the story itself. References to the individual contributors and their situations, accordingly, will amount to something more than a ritualistic display of erudition. Assessing the various alternatives open to the individual contributor at any given stage of the story's development in light of the particular one selected will provide the historian with insight into the mind of the individual contributor. The historian will thus be in on the composition of the story, will see it from "the inside," to use Collingwood's phrase, from the standpoint of

[2] *The Idea of History*, p. 283 (my italics).

those who contributed to it. And since each selection of alternatives by individual contributors is presumed to be based upon a free decision, the story itself will seem to be under some measure of control by its authors, rather than the reverse.

There are, however, serious difficulties with the Collingwoodean resolution of the dilemma. It forces the historian to represent decisions and actions in far too rationalistic a fashion. Are the men who make history consciously solving problems, carefully noting the alternatives open to them and then selecting the one that appears to be the best solution? Don't solutions and resolutions often pop into one's head, unbidden and seemingly undetermined? Can the historian really know *all* the alternatives, if indeed there were any, actually entertained by the persons about whom he writes? Finally, aren't the alternatives the historian imagines to be those considered by his historical characters often, in fact, suggested to the historian by "the logic" of the whole story, the end of which is not yet in sight for those who are writing it?

There is a logical tension between Collingwoodean history and Hegelian history, though both Hegel and Collingwood belong to the same philosophical tradition. Notice, for example, that Collingwood, in the passage about Theodosius, equates the evaluation of the *historical significance* of the Theodosian Code with the discovery of *the reasons* Theodosius had for issuing it. Yet surely there is a difference between the one and the other. The evaluation of the historical significance of an action is a function of the narrative structure of the story in which the account of that action plays a part. And if the historian should successfully fathom an agent's conscious reasons for doing something, what then? He would see nothing more than what the agent himself saw. Hegelian history is concerned, primarily, with evaluating the historical significance of actions. Collingwoodean history is centered almost exclusively on discovering a historical agent's conscious reasons for acting the way he did. For Hegel, to understand the historical significance of an action, to understand what eventuated as a result of a historical deed, is to grasp the reasons why it was done, to see how it fits into the plan of the World-Historical Spirit. Collingwood, too, believed that understanding the historical significance of an action means grasping the reasons why it was done. He differed from Hegel by equating the reason for a deed with the agent's conscious intention in perpetrating it.

The historian who writes narrative history has at the minimum two tasks. He must construct a story of what happened, a story whose incidents were originally told by deeds as well as words. But a story, even a true one, is not history. The historian must in addition write an account of the composition of the original story. For a history of ideas, the incidents of the original story will consist of descriptions of what ideas were entertained on particular occasions. The story-line will be revealed in the logical development of one idea from another, a development that must also preserve the temporal sequence in which the ideas occurred. Using that story-line as the structural basis for preparing a history, the historian then has to construct the account of how the men who had the ideas came to have them. It is the latter account, I have argued, that is the *history* of the ideas in question. Thus there is a difference between a history of philosophical thought and a story of philosophy, between a history of scientific thought and a story of the rise of science. To write a history of ideas, the historian must somehow cope with both tasks. If the historian concentrates solely on the story of mathematics or philosophy, he will produce what I have termed "Hegelian history," an account in which ideas will seem to develop one into the other by their own agency and what men think will appear to be predestined by the pattern revealed in the story of what they thought. On the other hand, if the ideas of which the historian writes do not fall into some narrative scheme, there will be no story-line with which to bind them together, no foundation upon

which to construct their narrative history. Suppose, for example, that the players of the parlor game do not produce an
intelligible story, that there is no development of incidents,
no story-line or plot, that what finally emerges looks like a
random collection of sentences. It may of course still be possible to explain, in Collingwoodean fashion, why each player
wrote what he wrote, picturing each line as a reasonable solution to a problem which confronted the player at the particular time. But if there is no narrative line of development
from one problem to the next, it will be impossible to produce
a narrative history of the composition of a story, for the simple reason that there is no story to begin with; all that one has
is a collection of incidents together with their particular
explanations.

I spoke before of a tension between Hegelian and Collingwoodean history, a tension rooted in the fact that the ways in
which men evaluate and understand their own actions often
differ from the ways in which historians evaluate and understand those same actions. The historian, in working out the
story-line of his history, views the incidents about which he
writes with reference to that story-line. But the men whose
activities or ideas provide the incidents of the story are not
privy to *that* story. The historical significance of their own
activities or ideas remains hidden to them. Must the historian
describe those incidents in the terms in which the agents
themselves understood and described them? It would seem he
must, according to Collingwood, for otherwise the historian
will never be able to explain why agents did what they did.

Consider an example. In most histories of the Second
World War, Hitler's decision to invade the Soviet Union is
regarded as a crucial turning point in the story of that war, an
incident portrayed by historians as having led directly to Germany's defeat. Hitler, to be sure, guessed correctly that his decision was historically significant, that the world would, as
he said, "hold its breath" while awaiting the outcome. What

Hitler did not know, of course, was its particular significance —that it would bring about his own demise. If one describes Hitler's decision as that which brought about his own downfall, then how could one explain it on Collingwoodean terms? Certainly, Hitler did not consciously select, from all the possible courses of action of which he was aware, that alternative which would cause his defeat. Thus if the decision is described, with reference to the story-line, as that which led to Germany's defeat, it is impossible to explain that decision by examining Hitler's situation as he envisioned it. Yet if we ask "Who made the decision which led to Germany's defeat?," the correct answer is "Hitler."

With this difficulty in mind, it is illuminating to reconsider Hegel's contention that great men are duped by the "cunning of Reason" into engaging in projects the outcomes of which are hidden to them. We may all assent to the seemingly innocuous formula that understanding an action or a decision depends on understanding the reason why that action took place or that decision was made. There is, nevertheless, an ambiguity in the expression "the reason why." It might be used to refer to an agent's conscious reasons, those of which he is explicitly aware and in terms of which he will describe, explain, or justify his actions and decisions. This is the way Collingwood understood the expression "the reason why an action takes place." For Hegel, however, understanding "the reason why" an action takes place meant, in part, to understand the significance of that action in light of the logic of the story in which it played a part. Did Hitler make the decision which led to the defeat of Germany? Hegel would have answered affirmatively: Hitler made that decision, though he was duped by the cunning of Reason into making it.

The Hegelian solution resembles one resorted to in psychoanalytic theory. By postulating the existence of unconscious reasons, the analyst manages to graft his own assessment of the significance of a patient's action on to that action itself. The psychologist Else Frenkel-Brunswik once described, in a lecture, the case of an intelligent student who was failing examinations, though he could not understand the reason why. The student studied hard for the examinations, reading the many books that were on the suggested reading lists for his courses. It seemed, however, that he unwittingly neglected to read the definitely assigned texts; as a result, he could not answer specific questions on the examinations. In Mrs. Frenkel-Brunswik's interpretation, the student, far from desiring to pass, as he consciously thought, actually had the will to fail—for a number of reasons familiar in the annals of psychoanalytic literature. She refused to accept the student's own general description of what he was doing—namely, studying to get good grades. She redescribed those same actions in light of the consequences that eventuated. The student's consistent failures put a different cast upon his actions; he was studying in such a way as to flunk the examinations. Hence, the reason why he studied was not his reason for studying, according to his analyst. He was quite unaware of what he was really doing, but *what he was really doing could not be assessed until after the consequences of his actions figured in the redescription of them.*

How does the psychoanalyst attempt to justify his own redescription of a patient's actions? Here we see the role played by the concept of an unconscious reason. If we are prepared to accept the notion that the student *unconsciously* wished to fail, then there is nothing odd about the describing what he did as studying to fail his examinations, though the student himself would initially resist that interpretation since, by hypothesis, he was unaware that that was what he was really doing. In schematic form, the case may be represented as follows: A performs an action X, which he would himself describe as "doing X." By doing X, A unwittingly brings about a situation S. Suppose one wanted to describe A's action as "bringing about S." A, of course, would not at the time he is bringing about S describe his action in that way, for the simple reason that he is not consciously aware that, by doing X, he is bringing about S. Now if we are really prepared to accept the idea that it is possible for a man to be unaware of his own reasons for doing something, and if, in this case, A's unconscious reason for doing X was to bring about S, then we have a way of justfying describing what A did as "bringing about S."

The historian's problem resembles that of the analyst to a certain extent. Both are often in the position of having to describe deeds in ways different from the ways in which they would be described by those who did them. Hegel saw the conceptual difficulties and talked, too, about unconscious reasons and impulses which lie in back of actions. Thus he said of Julius Caesar that "it was not . . . his private gain merely, but an unconscious impulse that occasioned the accomplishment of that for which the time was ripe. Such are all great historical men—whose own particular aims involve those large issues which are the will of the World-Spirit."[3] And again: "Such individuals had no consciousness of the general Idea they were unfolding, while prosecuting those aims of theirs; on the contrary, they were practical, political men. . . ."[4]

It is not sufficient, of course, to point to a parallel between the Hegelian and psychoanalytic resolutions of a similar conceptual difficulty. No one is really very happy with the psychoanalytic concept of an unconscious reason, so that showing its resemblance to some of Hegel's ideas does not exactly throw bursts of light upon the latter. It does, however, help make Hegel's ideas more palatable by providing a sympathetic interpretation of some of the more notorious features of Hegel's philosophy of history.

[3] *Lectures on the Philosophy of History*, p. 30 (Hoffmeister, pp. 89-90).
[4] *Ibid.* (Hoffmeister, pp. 97-98).

CHAPTER XV

History as Science

THE PHILOSOPHICAL penumbra that surrounds what I have termed "the narrative aspect" of history is worth exploring. Those features of speculative philosophies of history which critics find objectionable do not appear quite so outlandish when projected as resolutions of important problems—problems not even apparent unless one is initially sensitive to the narrative dimension of history. Hegel's notion of a World-Historical Spirit which dupes great men, through the cunning of Reason, into performing those deeds which are linked with their names—in particular, those deeds for which the world is ripe—may seem quaint to some, bizarre to many. Yet think of that notion against the background problem of attempting to justify a narrative unity of action composed of the separate historical deeds of actors who not only work at cross-purposes but are often unaware of each other's existence. The diverse activities of assembly-line workers are no longer disparate when properly seen as episodes in one enterprise—the assembly of an automobile. Workers need not know each other or what it is they are fashioning. Just as one may try to justify the ascription of one action, one purpose, to the thousand separate acts of assembly-line workers by referring to the blueprints, so Hegel tried to justify the unities of action presupposed in the narrative histories of his day. Hegel's particular resolution, of course, need not be accepted.

Should one take seriously the question of justifying the various narrative unities of action which are chosen by historians? It might be argued that the model described as the "Tale of Many Tongues" is particularly misleading—that the unity of action theme is blown up disproportionately by a

277

malicious sidestepping of the real issue. The real issue facing the historian is not that of justifying the redescription of disparate historical acts and purposes in light of the narrative unity of which they seem a part. Rather, so this argument goes, it is whether there are narrative unities in history beyond those provided in obvious fashion by the single purposes of men who act alone or the joint purposes of men who cooperate in common enterprises. The model situation presupposed that *some* story or other was being written by the players, and the problem posed was whether and in what sense one could justify the statement that all players were engaged in writing *the* story which inadvertently emerged. In the model situation, the historian was portrayed as an editor. It might be protested that such characterization begs the entire question of whether history initially presents the historian with a story. Is not the historian really the *author* of his tale? And does not this observation suggest that the narrative aspect of history is only peripheral to the main historical enterprise?

Natural history, too, can be presented in story form. Important facts of the titmouse life cycle can be arranged as a tale of Tilly the Titmouse. Although naturalists may make up such instructional stories for children, no serious student of natural history would take them seriously. Perhaps the time has come for serious students of human history to put away childish things. F. J. Teggart suggested some years ago that historians "in adopting the [narrative] mode of presentation for their results . . . have cut themselves off from any possibility of the attainment of scientific results" because "with whatever care the facts are sifted, with whatever sincerity they are subsequently presented, narrative statement remains art, and, as such, not science."[1] Not content just to grumble, Teggart went about the study of history in what he took to be a new and different way. His book *Rome and China* had as its sole target

---

[1] *Theory of History* (1925), republished in *Theory and Processes of History* (Berkeley: University of California Press, 1960), p. 39.

the explanation of certain barbarian uprisings against Rome. After a long and incredibly painstaking (all the more painful for having been undertaken before the advent of computers) study of all available Chinese and Roman records dating from the period, Teggart managed to elicit the following generalizations:

Within these decades [58 B.C.–A.D. 107] every barbarian uprising in Europe followed the outbreak of war either on the eastern frontiers of the Roman empire or in the 'Western Regions' of the Chinese. Moreover, the correspondence in events was discovered to be so precise that, whereas wars in the Roman East were followed uniformly and always by outbreaks on the lower Danube and the Rhine, wars in the eastern T'ien Shan were followed uniformly and always by outbreaks on the Danube between Vienna and Budapest.[2]

Teggart based his generalizations on forty cases of barbarian uprisings. He hoped that historians would, by formulating generalizations, at last be able to explain the occurrences of historical events. He advised historians to cease trying to make sense of history by narrating stories and to get down to the business of explaining particular events in a scientific manner:

. . . it became clear that the possibility of obtaining verifiable knowledge from historical data turned upon the acceptance of three requirements: first, that the aim of the historian should be, not the composition of a narrative, but the investigation of a problem; second, that the problem to be investigated should have reference to a class of events; third, that the procedure of the investigation should be based upon the comparison of events in different parts of the world or different areas.[3]

[2] *Rome and China* (Berkeley: University of California Press, 1939), p. vii.
[3] *Ibid.*, p. vi.

Teggart's approach, plainly enough, was motivated by the methodological ideals of positivism, by an orientation according to which "all scientific explanation"—to cite a very recent reaffirmation of that methodological ideal—"involves, explicitly or by implication, a subsumption of its subject matter under general regularities; that it seeks to provide a systematic understanding of empirical phenomena by showing that they fit into a nomic nexus."[4]

Those familiar with recent Anglo-American philosophical debate are aware of the extent of the controversy provoked by the positivist conception of explanation. Some Anglo-American philosophers, in fact, seem to identify all of the philosophy of history with the task of attacking or defending the positivist conception of explanation as it bears on historical explanation. Despite the popularity of this debate among professional philosophers, I do not think it of paramount importance for the philosophy of history. Indeed, I would argue that concentration on that debate obscures much more serious problems. Of more moment, so far as the philosophy of history is concerned, is the alleged contrast between history and science brought out by Teggart's remarks, a suggestion reinforced by the entire positivist tradition. Has the historian cut himself off from science by his persistence in presenting history in narrative form? Is narrative exegesis something entirely apart from scientific explanation?

The questions I have just raised are related to one another in rather complicated ways. Before proceeding to unravel the complications, it may be helpful if I outline my answers to the various questions considered separately:

(1) Are there narrative unities in history beyond those exhibited in the single or joint purposes of historical agents? I take the affirmative position. The basic problem is how to

---

[4] Carl G. Hempel, *Aspects of Scientific Explanation* (New York: The Free Press, 1965), p. 488.

decide under what circumstances a collection of incidents should be deemed episodes in one and the same story.

(2) Is the historian the author of his tale? This query is more provocative than penetrating. The implication is that the historian, as author of his tale, has made it up, that the tale itself has no more intimate application to the study of history than a tale of Tilly the Titmouse has to the study of the titmouse life cycle. Note, though, that the historian rarely authors his tale. Historical stories are for the most part traditional, handed down from historian to historian like folk tales. In the literal sense of "making up," historians seldom make up the stories they use. And even in those instances when a historian or demonic historian suggests a new story-line, he does not fashion his story from whole cloth. Story-lines can be read *from* the facts as well as *into* the facts. The achievements of the men who developed mathematics may fall into a story-line, though the mathematicians themselves did not intend to act out stories but to do mathematics. A monkey may, by hitting typewriter keys at random, succeed in producing an absolutely exquisite story. That the monkey did not mean to write the story he produced is irrelevant in deciding whether a story emerged as the outcome of his labors. (Whether one could proceed to write a history of the composition of a monkey's tale is an important but different issue.)

(3) Has the historian cut himself off from science by his persistence in the use of narrative form? Although the more philosophically profound features of the positivist tradition can be traced to David Hume, those which have had the most impact on the outside world are the work of Auguste Comte. Comte dreamed of a science of history, a method of historical analysis which would eliminate narrative exegesis in favor of scientific explanation. The positivist tradition, right down to its most recent adherents, has changed little in this regard: either narration is an affair of tracing causal relationships and

thus must be a kind of causal explanation, or else it provides no explanatory insight at all.

If, whenever one used the word "science," one thought of physics, and if, whenever one used the word "history," one thought of standard political history (that dreary succession of princes and principalities), then the narration-explanation polarity might seem as good a way as any to characterize, in general terms, the difference between history and science. Suppose, however, that by "science" one referred to geology and that by "history" one also referred to geology. Isn't geology a historical science? And isn't it one of the geologist's tasks to produce a narrative history of the earth, just as a cosmologist must write a narrative history of the universe and an evolutionary biologist must construct a narrative history of the origin of species? The relationship between history and the social sciences is perhaps best drawn by using as exemplar the relationship between historical geology and the so-called earth sciences—geophysics, petrology, sedimentology, tectonics, and the like. Why should one accede to the Comtean tradition, which harps upon a dichotomy between history and the social sciences? There is still the problem, though, of the correct response to Teggart's enjoinder to historians to eschew the narrative in favor of a search for causes.

(4) Is narrative exegesis entirely different from causal explanation? I shall argue that, although narrative exegesis is one thing and causal explanation usually something else, the two activities are not competitive. The barbarian uprisings against Rome between 58 B.C. and A.D. 107 are episodes that form part of the history of Rome. They have a dramatic role to play, foreshadowing as they do later episodes in the history of Rome. That they were singled out for special study by Teggart, that their causal explanation posed a special problem for historians, can be partially accounted for in terms of their narrative function. True, if certain incidents which traditionally constitute part of the history of Rome could

be causally linked with incidents normally considered part of the history of China, then one would possess a new basis for writing a new narrative history, one in which the history of ancient China would have a more important function than merely that of foreshadowing the later developments of Roman history. The incidents of a story *may* have a cause-and-effect relationship, but not all narrative connections are so reducible. Many philosophers will find this statement surprising, for an Anglo-American philosophical disposition, since Hume, prompts the claim that events can be brought into an intelligible framework only by being shown to be causally related to each other.

LET US TACKLE the concept of narrative intelligibility by attempting to determine what it is that makes a group of episodes part of one and the same story. There can be little doubt that everyone is equipped with certain intuitions about narrative coherence. Look, for example, at a problem in a fourth-grade workbook currently being used in English schools:

More Mixed Stories. Write the sentences of each group in the right order. Begin each sentence in turn with *first, next, then, finally.*

He started up the engine.
Mr. Smith opened the garage doors.
He got out and closed the doors behind him.
He drove out of the garage.[5]

The fourth-grade problem of sorting out the episodes of a mixed story demands for its solution a fourth-grade ability to recognize narrative coherence, to see a collection of episodes as being part of one and the same story. Are there any criteria to which one can appeal in support of the claim that a collection of episodes is narratively coherent? Such criteria, should

[5] Ronald Ridout, *Second English Workbook* (London: Ginn & Co., 1963).

they exist, would have to have a common reference in certain relationships assumed by the incidents described in the episodes of the story. Accordingly, I shall pose the criteriological question by seeking the relationship or relationships a number of incidents must have to one another in order to exhibit narrative coherence, to be part of one and the same story. Reflection upon how one unscrambles a mixed story supplies a good approach to the criteriological issue because one here confronts the problem of seeking narrative intelligibility in a collection of incidents whose relationship seems unintelligible, as those incidents are initially juxtaposed.

Mixed story problems, furthermore, are not confined to the fourth grade. In his short story *Three Phases*, the German writer Alfred Andersch writes:

> Some beer had been spilled; it was forming a stain on the dark-brown table top. I took care that the *Rote Fahne* I was reading should not get wet. 'Paulenerbräu,' it said on the walls./ Now the second barbed-wire stockade was almost finished too, and tomorrow the striped prison outfits would be issued./ Some had been working as much as two weeks in the war cemetery; by some bad luck they had not been assigned for transfer to other camps./ The comrades were sitting on the pub chairs, talking to each other in hushed tones. They were straining for sounds from the street./ ...[6]

Despite the surface unintelligibility of Andersch's story, sense can be made of it with the aid of the same principle that works with the fourth-grade story. The instruction "Begin each story in turn with *first, next, then, finally*" provides a broad hint of what the principle is. In the fourth-grade problem, each sentence describes an incident of a story that emerges when the sentences are arranged in the sequential order corresponding to the temporal order of the incidents referred to by the

[6] "Three Phases," *The Night of the Giraffe and Other Stories*, tr. Christa Armstrong (New York: Pantheon, 1964), p. 60.

sentences. Application of the same principles gives narrative coherence to Andersch's *Three Phases*. Each strophe contains a partial description of an incident in the narrator's life. Three incidents or phases are being described, and they can be sorted out and properly arranged by putting together the first, fourth, and seventh strophes, the second, fifth, and eighth strophes, and so on.

"And now the story can be defined," wrote E. M. Forster in *Aspects of the Novel*: "It is a narrative of events arranged in their time sequence—dinner coming after breakfast, Tuesday after Monday, decay after death, and so on."[7] Forster's definition of a story suggests at least a negative criterion for deciding whether a collection of episodes forms part of one and the same story: if a collection of episodes is part of one and the same story, then there exists a principle for determining the correct chronological ordering of incidents.

Suppose, for example, that you were presented with the following group of sentences: One cat sat upon a mat. Two cats sat upon a mat. Three cats sat upon a mat. And so on. Each episode describes an incident. Are all the episodes part of one and the same story? Perhaps one muses in this way: Before there could be n cats upon that mat, there must have been $n - i$ cats sitting on it. At once a story jumps before the mind. First one cat, lonely and mewing piteously, eased herself upon the mat. Then the striped lordly Tom joined the first. After that. . . . Not much of a story, to be sure—an incipient story at best. Or so one might think until realizing that the above sentences had not been read with care. There is no logical reason for assuming that one and only one mat is being referred to in each and every sentence. One day one cat sat upon a mat in Clapham Junction. Many moons ago two Putney cats sat upon a mat. Once upon a time three cats sat upon a mat, in a latitude and clime unknown. It seems reasonable to

[7] *Aspects of the Novel* (New York: Harcourt, Brace and Co., 1927), p. 47.

admit, in this case, that there is no principle by which one can determine the correct chronological ordering of the cat-mat-incidents. And with that admission we have destroyed all possibility of writing one story containing all the cat-mat episodes as components. The negative criterion is sound: if a collection of episodes is part of one and the same story, then there exists a principle for determining the correct chronological ordering of incidents. No principle, no story—just a mixed bag of episodes. Forster asserts:

> But it is never possible for a novelist to deny time inside the fabric of his novel: he must cling however lightly to the thread of his story, he must touch the interminable tapeworm, otherwise he becomes unintelligible. . . .[8]

To Forster's authority, let us add that of another novelist— Günter Grass:

> You can begin a story in the middle and create confusion by striking out boldly, backward and forward. You can be modern, put aside all mention of time and distance and, when the whole thing is done, proclaim, or let someone else proclaim, that you have finally, at the last moment, solved the space-time problem.[9]

If the principle works as a negative criterion, perhaps it can function as a positive criterion as well: if there exists a principle for determining the correct chronological ordering of incidents, then all the episodes describing those incidents are part of one and the same story. A moment's reflection will show that the positive criterion is unsound. Take the following episodes: On October 10, 1643, a goldfish swallowed a sweetmeat. On July 3, 1859, an astronomer observed three of the moons of Jupiter. On March 5, 1737, there was a snow slide in Antarctica. If each sentence is true, we have a principle

---

[8] *Ibid.*, p. 50.
[9] *The Tin Drum* (New York: Random House, n.d.), p. 17.

for arranging the incidents into their chronological order of occurrence. All the same, there is no reason to think that the episodes describing those incidents are part of one and the same story. The principle of chronology is not a positive criterion, but a negative one only. Although it is churlish of me to point the icicle of criticism at so delightful a book, Forster's definition of a story in *Aspects of a Novel* is not a true definition—not every arrangement of events in their temporal sequence has a narrative coherence. Forster recognizes as much by distinguishing later on between higher and lower stories: higher stories have plots, and there is more to them than chronological ordering of incidents.

The negative criterion, which tells us what a story is not, is itself not particularly penetrating. Are there other criteria, positive or negative, which are more felicitous for getting at the heart of the matter? Consider the fourth-grade "mixed story" problem once more. Notice that a grammatical principle can be used to determine which is the first sentence of the story. Other things being equal (though they never are), it is better to begin a story with a sentence containing a proper name than with a sentence containing an unidentified third-person pronoun. Now if metaphysical principles are nothing but grammatical principles in disguise, then perhaps the unidentified pronoun rule contains the kernel of the story: a collection of episodes is part of one and the same story if and only if each episode describes an incident in the career of one and the same entity (object, person, thing, subject). Our recognition of the four one-sentence episodes as all part of the same, though mixed, story perhaps presupposes our accepting all four episodes as descriptions of incidents in the career of Mr. Smith, who is an entity, object, person, thing, subject. Similarly, we cannot arrange the episodes of Andersch's *Three Phases,* perhaps, unless we presuppose that we are presented with three phases in the life of the same person, the narrator. The one entity–one story (two entities–two stories) criterion, if I may call it that, is persuasive and pervasive. What is more, we have here a criterion at once positive and negative: if the criterion works, we not only know what a story is, but what a story is not. The one entity–one story criterion would, in fact, short-circuit the chronological criterion proposed earlier because, according to the one entity–one story criterion, if we know that a number of episodes all describe incidents in the career of one entity, we need not bother to sort them chronologically to determine that all the episodes are part of one and the same story. Indeed, there may not even exist a principle for determining the correct chronological ordering of incidents, in which case, according to the chronological criterion, the episodes describing those incidents are not all part of one and the same story. There is, in short, a conflict of interest between the two criteria that requires further examination. For this purpose I shall partition the one entity–one story criterion into its positive and negative components and take up each separately:

(1) If a number of incidents are all part of the career of one and the same entity, then each of the episodes describing one or more of the incidents is part of one and the same story.

(2) If a number of episodes are all part of one and the same story, then each describes one or more incidents in the career of one and the same entity.

The plausibility of sentence (1), which embodies the positive side of the one entity–one story criterion, probably accounts for the widely held opinion that biography is the easiest kind of history to write. The biographer can sink his teeth into something tangible. His subject is concrete, and the incidents about which he writes, therefore, cohere of their own accord in one and the same story. Or so it seems to those who have not attempted biography. Anyone who has tried, however, knows that not all the incidents which happen to a biographical subject can be worked into one and the same biography. Although a biographer may grant that a particular incident ought to be treated, in theory, in *some* biography of the subject, he is aware that he need not mention that incident in *his* biography merely because he knows it to be an incident in the career of the subject. And there is sound reason for this attitude: it simply is not the case that all the incidents in the career of one and the same entity must be treated in one and the same story. The one entity–one story principle fails as a positive criterion. Does it work as a negative criterion? Does sentence (2) hold true? It is easy to show that the one entity–one story principle fails also as a negative criterion. A story of Tristram Shandy need not begin with episodes in the career of Tristram Shandy; in fact, one might almost go so far as to say that a story of Tristram Shandy does not have to contain any episodes from Tristram Shandy's life. Well, almost. Is a biographer of Domenico Scarlatti to be denied the recital of certain incidents in the life of Alessandro Scarlatti? Could not narration of such incidents form part of a biography of Domenico, though they are incidents in the career of a person not identical with the subject of the biography?

The one entity–one story principle, I claim, works neither as a positive nor as a negative criterion in determining whether or not a collection of episodes forms part of one and the same story. A great quantity of bad metaphysics and bad history has been written on that assumption, however. Take Oswald Spengler's contention that the history of early Christianity has nothing at all to do with Christianity from the eleventh century on. Now many theologians, to be sure, are acutely aware of a spiritual gulf separating contemporary from early Christianity. They differ from Spengler in supposing that the history of early Christianity is nonetheless relevant to the history of contemporary Christianity, however disparate they appear, and it is an assumption that accounts for much anguish. Spengler argued that the events making up the life of Christ and the spreading of the Gospel are incidents in the career of an entity he labeled "Magian culture," whereas events we normally associate with the history of contemporary Christianity are incidents in the career of an entirely different culture he termed "Faustian":

> But the Faustian Culture, again, when it awoke and needed a symbol whereby to express its primary feeling for Infinity in time and to manifest its sense of the succession of generations, *set up the 'Mater Dolorosa' and not the suffering Redeemer* as the pivot of German-Catholic Christianity of the Gothic age; and for whole centuries of bright fruitful inwardness this woman-figure was the very synthesis of Faustian world-feeling and the object of all art, poetry, and piety. Even to-day in the ritual and the prayers of the Roman Catholic Church, and above all in the thoughts of its people, Jesus takes second place after the Madonna.[10]

Having convinced himself that the incidents making up the history of early Christianity formed part of the career of one entity and the incidents making up the history of contemporary Christianity formed part of the career of an entirely different entity, Spengler supposed he had a crushing argument against those who began histories of Christianity with the life of Christ. The same principle he called upon to prove that there is no such thing as world history.

Spengler's general views of the nature of history offer one of the best available illustrations of the one entity–one story principle in action. His artistic sensibilities were offended by the radical discontinuities exhibited in those general historical tales that began with Greece and ended with contemporary Europe. If episodes do not narratively cohere, Spengler seems to have concluded, then not all the incidents described by those episodes can be part of the career of the same entity. These reflections led him to search for entities whose existences would provide the principles for a more successful nar-

---

[10] *The Decline of the West,* II, 224.

rative integration of historical episodes. Unfortunately, even if one's ontological nose were not put out of joint by having to countenance the smell of Culture-Things, their thinghood would not supply the principles of narrative coherence sought by Spengler. Father is distinct from son, but an incident in the life of the father may very well cohere narratively with an incident in the life of the son, may form part of a common history embracing both father and son.

No one is surprised, I suppose, to discover a speculative philosopher of history being duped by the cunning of a bogus piece of philosophical reasoning. Analytical philosophers of history have also succumbed, however. In Chapter XII I mentioned Passmore's claim that there is no such historical subject as the the history of England because there is no entity whose career is studded with the deeds of Englishmen. Passmore's argument makes use of the one entity–one story criterion on its negative side, as a reason for rejecting the possibility of fitting together a collection of historical episodes into one and the same story. Perhaps it is true that no story-line could ever be formulated that would show all the historical episodes English historians have found important to be part of one and the same story. If one could produce a conclusive reason to that effect, one would then be justified in maintaining that there is no such historical subject as the history of England. The one entity–one story principle will not turn the trick, though. Aristotle, one of the first to look into this matter, came to a similar conclusion: "The unity of a Plot does not consist, as some suppose, in its having one man as its subject. An infinity of things befall that one man, some of which it is impossible to reduce to unity; and in like manner there are many actions of one man which cannot be made to form one action."[11]

[11] Aristotle, *De Poetica*, tr. Ingram Bywater, in *The Works of Aristotle*, ed. W. D. Ross (London: Oxford University Press, 1928), 1451ᵃ.

Narrative coherence, "the unity of a plot," Aristotle maintained, is achieved when the incidents described by its episodes
have a "necessary or probable connexion with one another":

> In writing an *Odyssey*, he [Homer] did not make the poem
> cover all that ever befell his hero—it befell him, for instance,
> to get wounded on Parnassus and also to feign madness at
> the time of the call to arms, but the two incidents had *no
> necessary or probable connexion with one another*—instead
> of doing that, he took as the subject of the *Odyssey*, as also
> of the *Iliad*, an action with a Unity of the kind we are
> describing.[12]

The italicized phrase in the above citation embodies Aristotle's
criterion of narrative coherence: a collection of episodes are
part of one and the same story if and only if the episodes of
which the story is composed describe a set of incidents that
have a necessary or probable connection with each other. An
understanding of Aristotle's criterion is difficult, however, for
it involves coming to grips with the Aristotelian concept of
necessity, no mean task. It must be remembered, though, that
Aristotle doubted that the concept would be useful in making
history intelligible:

> The construction [of narrative poetry] should clearly be like
> that in a drama; [its stories] should be based on a single
> action, one that is a complete whole in itself, with a begin-
> ning, middle, and end, so as to enable the work to produce
> its own proper pleasure with all the organic unity of a liv-
> ing creature. Nor should one suppose that there is anything
> like them in our usual histories. A history has to deal not
> with one action, but with one period and all that happened
> in that to one or more persons, however disconnected the
> several events may have been. Just as two events may take
> place at the same time, e.g., the sea-fight off Salamis and

[12] *Ibid.*, 1451[a] (my italics).

the battle with the Carthaginians in Sicily, without converging to the same end, so too of two consecutive events one may sometimes come after the other with no one end as their common issue.[13]

In order for a number of incidents to have a necessary or probable connection with each other in the Aristotelian sense, they have to begin somewhere and then converge, lead to a point, have a final upshot. The incidents with which the historian deals, however, have neither natural beginnings nor natural endings. History cannot be turned into narrative poetry merely by putting the works of Herodotus into verse, as Aristotle cautions us. Consequently, according to Aristotle, most of history, being devoid of plot, remains in outer philosophic darkness.

There may be difficulties in understanding exactly what Aristotle meant by necessary connection, but at least this much is clear: a number of incidents have no necessary connection with one another, in the Aristotelian sense, unless they contain a natural beginning as well as a natural ending, with all of the intermediary events leading up to the final incident or outcome which serves as the natural ending. Yet the incidents with which history deals, as Aristotle observes, do not converge toward one end as their common issue. Consequently, the Aristotelian concept of necessary connection, tied as it is to notions of natural beginnings and endings, is of no use to historians. Aristotle himself tells us so.

Is it fruitless to inquire whether a collection of episodes forms part of one and the same story when we are unaware of the nature of the initial and final episodes of the story itself? Indeed, must we assume that *all* stories have beginnings and endings? It was the study of history that demanded the concept of a story without beginning and without end, and necessity proved to be the mother of invention. Attempting to con-

[13] *Ibid.*, 1459ᵃ.

struct a geological history of the earth, James Hutton came to the conclusion that the formation and destruction of continents require an indefinite length of time for the completion of the process. Therefore, Hutton argued, the history of the earth presents us with a vista in which "we find no vestige of a beginning,—no prospect of an end."[14] The incidents making up the geological history of the earth—the formation of mountains, the erosion of continents, the growth and diminution of glaciers—are not related to each other by necessary connection in the Aristotelian sense. They have neither a culmination nor a natural beginning. Still, the incidents of geological history—at least some of them—can be accounted for causally. Perhaps here is to be found the criterion for narrative coherence and intelligibility which we sought: a collection of episodes are all part of one and the same story if and only if the incidents described by the episodes are related to each other as cause and effect.

The modern concept of causality differs from the Aristotelian concept of necessary connection in a number of important respects, one of the more noteworthy being that the modern concept requires no fixed *terminus a quo* or *terminus ad quem* for its intelligible application. Consider, as a model, a string of railroad cars being pulled along a track. According to the modern concept of cause, the motion of the last car is completely explained, causally, by the force exerted by the car pulling it; the fact that the car pulling the last car is itself pulled —that its motion, in turn, can be explained by the force exerted by the car immediately preceding it—does not diminish the cogency of the original explanatory account. On the Aristotelian view, however, we have not explained the motion of the last car by the motion of the car which pulls it if the latter itself needs explaining. The Aristotelian concept of necessary

---

[14] "Theory of the Earth; or an investigation of the laws observable in the composition, dissolution, and the restoration of land upon the globe," *Royal Society of Edinburgh Transactions*, 1 (1788), 304.

connection cannot be applied to a set of incidents whose beginning and end points are unknown. In contrast, the modern concept of causal connection applies to intermediaries even in cases where one finds no vestige of a beginning, no prospect of an end.

Is it true that narrative coherence is achieved, and *only* achieved, when the incidents related by the narrative are causally related to each other? Here is E. M. Forster's opinion:

> Let us define a plot. We have defined a story as a narrative of events arranged in their time sequence. A plot is also a narrative of events, the emphasis falling on causality. "The king died and then the queen died," is a story. "The king died, and then the queen died of grief," is a plot. The time-sequence is preserved, but the sense of causality overshadows it. . . . Consider the death of the queen. If it is in a story we say "and then?" If it is in a plot we ask "Why?" That is the fundamental difference between these two aspects of the novel. A plot cannot be told to a gaping audience of cave men or to a tyrannical sultan or to their modern descendant the movie-public. They can only be kept awake by "and then —and then—" They can only supply curiosity. But a plot demands intelligence and memory also.[15]

It is only through plot, according to Forster, that the incidents related by a story make sense relative to each other. Not all stories, however, have plots, on Forster's view. In primitive stories, for example, one incident merely follows another, and our interest in the incidents lies only in seeing what will come next. Remember, though, that Forster did not succeed in formulating a positive criterion for the concept of a story— not every chronological ordering of incidents yields a story, not even a primitive story. Nor is our curiosity to see what comes next aroused by any random assortment of incidents

[15] *Aspects of the Novel*, pp. 130-131.

narrated in their correct temporal sequence. Having over-looked that point, Forster began with a concept of a story that was much too weak and ended with a concept of a plot that was much too strong. I shall argue presently that the incidents described by the episodes of a narrative can be shown to lead one to the other without supposing that they are related to each other as cause to effect. The causal criterion will not do. A narrative need not purport to explain causally the incidents related by the story.

Consider, in illustration, the task of constructing a geological history of the earth. Such a history would surely contain an account of those glacial episodes known as the "ice ages." The relationship between the successive ice ages is certainly not that of cause and effect: one ice age is not the *cause* of another. Notice, too, that geologists cannot causally explain the coming of any particular ice age, though there are any number of theories floating about from which to choose. Still, despite the lack of adequate causal explanations of particular ice ages, a geological history of the earth would be incomplete if it failed to contain a chapter on them. The ice age episodes are all part of one and the same geological story, even though the incidents described by these episodes are not related by means of cause and effect. An incident cannot be excluded from a story merely because it cannot be causally explained.

If the ice ages are not related to each other as cause to effect, we may be told, their relationship to each other can be nothing but that of temporal succession. "There is a great dif-ference," Aristotle reminds us, "between a thing happening *propter hoc* and *post hoc*."[16] An event is not explained by a mere temporal bracketing of it between the occurrence of any earlier and any later event. If we wish more insight into his-tory, we must arrange historical events into *causal* narra-tives. What are causal narratives? Apparently, narratives in which each episode describes an event which is the cause, or

---

[16] *De Poetica*, 1452ᵃ.

the effect, of at least one other event described by some other episode in the same story. Once one begins to think of narrative coherence in terms of some relationship between *events,* though, one will be conceptually pilloried between the relationship of cause and effect, on the one hand, and temporal predecessor and successor, on the other. The concept of event, it so happens, has been expropriated by professional philosophers and refashioned to suit certain philosophical theories. One is not *supposed* to see other relational possibilities. And that is why I have used the term "incident" all along, rather than the term "event." The concept of incident has not yet been honed down on any philosopher's grindstone, and it is therefore useful for taking a fresh philosophical look at some very familiar relationships.

Events, unlike incidents, do not give birth to one another, do not evolve from each other, do not grow out of each other. Events *cause* one another. Why can't events give birth to one another? Perhaps because one thing cannot give birth to another by remote control—there must be a point of contact between them. Events, however, in order to be distinguishable, must be separable. This latter feature, in turn, supports the positivistic analysis of causality, an analysis first proposed by David Hume:

> In a word, then, every effect is a distinct event from its cause. It could not, therefore, be discovered in the cause, and the first invention or conception of it, *a priori*, must be entirely arbitrary. . . . In vain, therefore, should we pretend to determine any single event, or infer any cause or effect, without the assistance of observation and experience.[17]

One can witness the birth of a calf from a cow. One cannot witness the production of one event by another. There is a

---

[17] *Enquiries Concerning the Human Understanding and Concerning the Principles of Morals,* ed. L. A. Selby-Bigge, 2nd edn. (London: Oxford University Press, 1902), p. 30.

hiatus between events even when they are causally related—a hiatus that can only be bridged, according to Hume, by assuming that, whenever events of the first kind happen, events of the second kind will follow hard upon. One cannot observe the causal connection between two events, but only one event coming after the other. One can witness temporal succession, but not causal connection.

Were someone to gather evidence that B was the offspring of A, he would certainly include in his evidence anyone's claim to have seen the birth of B from A. No such evidence, for the reasons given above, can support the claim that one event caused another. Supporting a claim of causal connection between an event A and an event B requires, according to the Humean analysis, the additional and general claim that events of the second kind invariably follow events of the first kind. Hume's brilliant analysis of causation has remained a cornerstone of logical positivism. The positivistic conception of science itself became tied to that analysis of causation: without generalization, all positivists have maintained, there can be no scientific explanation.

Narrative coherence between episodes depends, at bottom, upon showing how one episode leads to another, how one incident generates another. Once one has taken on the positivistic philosophical style, though, one will strive to ensnare the concepts of growth, development, evolution in a "nomic nexus," to treat genesis as nothing but an archaic form of causal production. Since, moreover, the main purpose of narrative history is to trace genetic relationships between historical incidents, it is no surprise that positivists have failed to give an adequate account of history. One impulse, prompted by the Humean tradition, bids the positivist to construe genetic relationships as being expressible, in essence, by means of universal (or statistical) laws. Another impulse, traceable to Comte, urges the positivist to dismiss historical narratives as little better than chronologies, containing nothing but a collection of episodes with no more significant relationship to each other than that of temporal predecessor to temporal successor.

A good recent example of the collision of both tendencies can be found in Carl Hempel's *Aspects of Scientific Explanation*. "One explanatory procedure, which is widely used in history, though not in history alone," Hempel writes, "is that of genetic explanation; it presents the phenomenon under study as the final stage of a developmental sequence, and accordingly accounts for the phenomenon by describing the successive stages of that sequence."[18] Note the expression "genetic *explanation*." Hempel does not doubt that tracing a developmental sequence of incidents "can enhance our understanding of a historical phenomenon."[19] Nevertheless, Hempel is philosophically committed to the view that "all scientific explanation involves, explicitly or by implication, a subsumption of its subject matter under general regularities; that it seeks to provide a systematic understanding of empirical phenomena by showing that they fit into a nomic nexus."[20] Enhancing our understanding of a historical phenomenon is equated, by Hempel, with giving a scientific explanation of its occurrence; giving a scientific explanation of its occurrence, in turn, means showing by means of general regularities how that particular historical phenomenon is causally or statistically connected with previous incidents in its genetic chain.

In a genetic explanation each stage must be shown to "lead to" the next, and thus to be linked to its successor by virtue of some general principles which make the occurrence of the latter at least reasonably probable, given the former. But in this sense, even successive stages in a physical phenomenon such as the free fall of a stone may be regarded as forming a genetic sequence whose different stages—characterized,

[18] *Aspects of Scientific Explanation*, p. 447.
[19] *Ibid.*, p. 448.   [20] *Ibid.*, p. 488.

let us say, by the position and the velocity of the stone at different times—are interconnected by strictly universal laws; and the successive stages in the movement of a steel ball bouncing its zigzaggy way down a Galton Board may be regarded as forming a genetic sequence with probabilistic connections.[21]

It is philosophically instructive to pay attention to the kinds of models a philosopher picks to make a point. Hempel sees nothing wrong in using, as a model of a genetic relationship, the successive spatial positions of a stone in free flight. Surely, though, it is stretching things a bit to talk of spatial positions "leading to" spatial positions. It is much worse to picture one spatial position as *evolving* or *growing into* or *giving birth to*—in a word, *generating*—another spatial position. Instead of the successive positions of a stone in flight or the successive positions of a steel ball on a Galton Board, it would be far better to choose, for one's genetic model, a cow giving birth to a calf. One is concerned, after all, with *genetic* understanding.

Consider a family tree. The relationship between parents and children is not that of causes to effects. Naturally, generative acts must be performed by parents in order to produce offspring. Certain "events" must transpire. But parents are not events and children are not events, though parents cause the birth of their children. If one is on the trail of cause and effect, of course, one will focus upon the relationship between reproductive causes and parturitive effects. But the relationship between parents and child is not that of cause and effect, though an act of the father and mother causes the birth of their child. The relationship between parents and child is *genetic,* not causal.

Genetic relationships must somehow be reduced to causal ones, we may be told, or else we cannot really grasp what is genetically related to what. The child is genetically related to

[21] *Ibid.,* pp. 448-449.

his parents because his birth is caused by the generative act of the parents. Without some comprehension of a causal process, we would have no understanding of the true nature of a genetic relationship. Although an argument of this kind has a surface plausibility, it reduces to sheer confusion when scrutinized closely. Genetic relationships are perfectly intelligible on their own terms, quite independently of the fact that in *some* cases, not all, the final proof of a genetic relationship depends upon the establishment of a causal claim. The number three can be generated from the number one by the so-called successor operation. It is perfectly intelligible to call the number one "the ancestor" of number three, to portray the relationship between one and three as a genetic one. It would be absurd, however, to characterize the relationship between one and three as causal.

Genetic relationships are not reducible to causal relationships, even though, admittedly, the determination of genetic relationship often depends upon proving or disproving a causal claim. A man who proves that he never had an affair with a particular woman disproves a genetic relationship with her children. Sometimes, though, the situation is the other way around: establishment of a causal claim depends upon the prior establishment of a genetic relationship. The brindle markings on a particular calf can be shown to be causally linked to the brindle markings of a particular cow (and not the one in the next field) by proving that the particular calf is genetically related to the particular cow. The genetic relationship may be established without presuming upon nomic nexuses, but simply by seeing the calf born from the cow.

The arguments I have just presented will fail to convince those for whom the positivistic view of science, scientific explanation, and, I should add, history has not begun to cloy. A determined opponent can point out that causal terminology is often tightly linked to genetic terminology—the relationship between the brindle marks on one cow and those on another, for example, could just as well have been called "genetic" as "causal." That we often do use causal and genetic terminology interchangeably suggests a conceptual identity. And although genetic terminology—not causal terminology—is used by mathematicians to express certain relationships between numbers, one can always retort that such usage is metaphorical only. I think a reply of this kind is fundamentally mistaken, but demonstrating that it is would require a debate over what is and what is not metaphorical usage and, rather than peer into *that* bottomless well, I shall try another line of argument.

Consider, once again, the fourth-grade "mixed story" problem. After Mr. Smith of the story opened the garage doors, he started up the engine. It is perfectly plain that the relationship between those two incidents in the story is not that of cause and effect. Opening garage doors did not, causally speaking, start the engine (though it could have startled the dog). Incidents of a story *may* be causally related, but narrative coherence between episodes can be achieved in the absence of causal connection between incidents. The critic has a position to fall back upon, though. He may grant that the incidents of a narratively coherent story need not be causally related. Why deny what is so obviously true, especially when an escape route looms? If opening garage doors does not "startle" engines, it must at least make those latter incidents more *probable*. The positivistic critic assumes, of course, that probabilistic relationships cannot be expressed without covert reference to general regularities of statistical form. If his view of the nature of probability is sound, he does not yield on an essential element of his philosophical position by settling for the reduction of genetic relationships to probabilistic rather than causal connections.

Let us allow the positivist, without challenge, his analysis of probabilistic connection. Can genetic relationships be reduced to those of probability? Opening the garage doors *occasions* the starting of the engine, it *leads up to* the starting of the engine, the first incident of the story *generates* the second. But it also makes the second incident *more probable*, though it does not cause it. Put the point in a slightly different way: one assumes that the sequence "open garage doors, start engine" is more probable than the sequence "start engine, open garage doors"; otherwise, one would have no real basis for gauging which incident in the mixed story is supposed to come first and which second. Our perception of which incident generates which, apparently, relies upon a tacit estimate of which sequence is more probable. A member of a society of carbon monoxide addicts would have different perceptions of genetic succession. Has the critic, then, won the last round? Is tracing genetic connections between incidents nothing but an affair of estimating causal or probabilistic connections between them?

HISTORY, even to the casual observer, seems to consist of one improbability piled upon another. Still, narrative coherence seems to be maintained despite the play of chance; one episode can be shown to lead up to, one incident to generate, a second even if the second incident may be extremely improbable given the occurrence of the first. Consider an analogy: The probability that a particular sperm cell will unite with a particular egg cell is minute. That Adam and Eve should have generated Seth was extremely improbable, yet one understands very well what it means to say that Seth was genetically descended from Adam and Eve. The relationship of Adam and Eve to Seth was not that of cause and effect, though the birth of Seth was the effect of an antecedent act of his parents. Moreover, the occurrence of the particular sperm-egg combination that eventuated in Seth was extremely improbable. Or, to put it another way, that Seth should have been born instead of someone else was highly unlikely, given the combinatorial possibilities. Narrating the story of Genesis depends, nevertheless, upon an ability to trace lines of genetic descent, an ability in no way compromised by those combinatorial possibilities.

True, in exhibiting a genetic relationship between two incidents, one often shows the second incident to have been more probable relative to the first—more probable, presumably, than it would have been had the first incident not occurred. When Mr. Smith opens his garage doors, the odds are increased that he will start his engine. Suppose, though, that his automobile is a vintage Rolls in mint condition which he rarely drives. Taking into account the great number of occasions when Mr. Smith opens his garage doors in order to fuss with his car without starting the engine, the conditional probability of his starting the engine, given his opening the doors, is extremely minute. And although the odds that Mr. Smith will drive his car, given that his garage doors are open, may be better than the odds that Smith will drive his car, given that his garage doors are closed, the difference between the two may be very small—so small that the increase in the one over the other is negligible. Still, opening the garage doors does provide the opportunity to drive the Rolls, even though it does not increase very much the probability that the Rolls will in fact be driven. By so providing that opportunity, moreover, one particular occasion of opening the garage doors, one bright morning, will become one of the incidents in a genetic chain which culminates in Mr. Smith's backing down the driveway in his Rolls. Our understanding of the relationship between opening a garage door and driving a car out of a garage is surely something different from our assessment of the conditional probability relationship between the one kind of incident and the other. Genetic relationships are not reducible to causal or probabilistic relationships. This is not to say that causal relationships are *not* genetic; a causal relationship, in fact, provides *one kind of example* of a genetic relationship, and incidents related by means of cause and effect do form a genetic sequence. Not all genetic sequences of incidents, however, are causal in nature.

There seems to be no way to mitigate the force of this argument except by denigrating the kind of understanding of history that one has when one has succeeded in tracing noncausal genetic relationships. The critic may, in the end, reluctantly acknowledge that the concept of genetic connection is not reducible to that of causal or probabilistic connection. He may also grant that placing A in a genetic relationship to B is something quite distinct from merely determining their chronological relationship to each other. Without causal or probabilistic understanding, the critic will then say, what is the narrative of Genesis except the bare genetic succession of one damned thing after another: Seth was a hundred and five years old when he begot Enos and lived to be nine hundred and twelve; Enos was ninety years old when he begot Cainan and lived to be nine hundred and five; Cainan was seventy years old when he begot Malaleel . . . begot Jared . . . begot Henoch . . . begot Methuselah . . . begot . . . begot . . . begot . . . ?

I spoke before of a dual tendency in positivism, a Janus-faced impulse either to portray narrative history as an affair of establishing causal or probabilistic connections between historical events or else to dismiss the historian as a mere narrator whose stories provide no real nourishment for the understanding. We have seen, in partial illustration, how Hempel attempts in his *Aspects of Scientific Explanation* to reduce narrative exegesis to causal or statistical explanation. Let us complete the illustration by noting how Hempel deals with "the story of evolution" in that same essay.

Let me distinguish what might be called the *story* of evolution from the *theory* of the underlying mechanisms of mutation and natural selection. The story of evolution, as a hypothesis about the gradual development of various types of organisms, and about the subsequent extinction of many of these, has the character of a hypothetical historical narrative *describing* the putative stages of the evolutionary process; it is the associated theory which provides what *explanatory insight* we have into this process. The story of evolution might tell us, for example, that at a certain stage in the process dinosaurs made their appearance and that, so much later, they died out. Such a narrative account does not, of course, explain why the various kinds of dinosaurs with their distinctive characteristics came into existence, nor does it explain why they became extinct. Indeed even the associated theory of mutation and natural selection does not answer the first of these questions, though it might be held to shed some light on the latter. Yet even to account for the extinction of the dinosaurs, we need a vast array of additional hypotheses about their physical and biological environment and about the species with which they had to compete for survival. But if we have hypotheses of this kind that are specific enough to provide, in combination with the theory of natural selection, at least a probabilistic explanation for the extinction of the dinosaurs, then clearly the explanans adduced is also qualified as a basis for a potential probabilistic prediction.[22]

The story of evolution, as Hempel portrays it, contains basically uninformative descriptions of one species begetting another. The dinosaur episode is a particularly exciting chapter for children, and it is interesting that Hempel should use it as an illustration of his thesis that the story of evolution provides no "explanatory insight," to use his expression. Children and historians are content with stories; scientists, however, seek insight. The trouble with the Hempelian scheme is that the importance of the story of evolution in the development of

[22] *Ibid.*, p. 370.

the theory of evolution is completely overlooked, and there-fore Darwin's contribution to the history of science cannot be appreciated. Darwin would never have searched for a mechan-ism to account for evolution if he had not been convinced that species evolved from one another, that the evolutionary story of genesis was correct in outline. To characterize that story as containing nothing but descriptions of dinosaurs and other curious creatures does the story of evolution a great disservice. It also misses the point about the nature of explanatory in-sight itself. True, Hempel is correct in saying that the mechan-isms of mutation and natural selection cannot, without further specification, be used to calculate the appearance and dis-appearance of species. Mutation and natural selection do explain, however, how one species *can* evolve into another by suggesting a plausible mechanism for evolutionary accomplish-ment. Without the explanatory hypotheses, there is no con-clusive reason to accept the genetic, historical account, despite the fossil records. Without the fossil records, there is no reason to accept *the very idea* that species are genetically related to each other. A conceptual symbiosis exists between the story of evolution and the theory of evolutionary mechanisms, a symbiosis responsible for any explanatory insight one has into the nature of evolution.

The *story* of evolution traces the descent of man and other contemporary species from their ancestral species. The *history* of evolution includes an appraisal of how that story was "com-posed"; it contains an account of how, by mutation and natural selection, profound changes were wrought in the structure and form of living organisms. Writing a story of evolution presupposes that the elements of the story are genet-ically related to one another. Writing a history of evolution presupposes, in turn, a story of evolution. The kernel of the history lies in the story, and it is for that reason I have identi-fied the locus of the historian's special mission as the task of narrating the story of mankind, the story of chess, the story of philosophy, the story of evolution. There is more to doing history than writing stories, however, and that is why I have tried to distinguish the story of evolution from the history of evolution, the story of philosophy from the history of philosophy. To compose a story of evolution or philosophy requires genetic insight, an ability to arrange one's historical material into ancestral patterns. To transform a story into a history, however, the historian must seek for the mechanisms that underlie the genetic relationships he perceives between historical incidents. The Marxist history of mankind differs from the Hegelian history of mankind not only in its story-line but also in its judgment of the kind of mechanism there is underlying historical change.

Although it is legitimate, for analytical purposes, to separate the story of ＿＿＿＿ from the history of ＿＿＿＿, in historical practice the one quickly merges into the other. Just as the story requires the mechanism, so the mechanism can suggest modifications in the story. One expects the historian to be sensitive to the different kinds of historical stories that might be written by focusing on the various mechanisms of historical change discovered and studied by the social scientists. One also expects social scientists not to put themselves in competition with historians but to be aware that, at least some of the time, their task is ancillary to the historians'. The history of mankind need not be the story of the price of grain, the story of population growth and decline, the story of the use of gold as a medium of exchange, though the mechanisms underlying these phenomena have been carefully studied by social scientists. What story-line should a history of mankind adopt? That is the sort of question for historians and philosophers of history to debate. A history without the right story is blind. The right story without a history is empty.

CHAPTER XVI

Epilogue:
The Covering Law Model of
Historical Explanation

IN THE LAST CHAPTER I remarked, without attempting any defense at all, that the covering law model of historical explanation ought not to be of central concern in the philosophy of history. It would, accordingly, be somewhat remarkable were I now to launch, by way of justification, into a full-scale discussion of the covering law model of explanation in a work whose central concern is the philosophy of history. Perhaps, though, I can get away with presenting a brief sketch of such a defense.

We all possess very strong causal beliefs, beliefs which serve to order events into etiological relationships or to rule out such relationships as not obtaining. Informed that a certain man had swallowed one hundred grains of arsenic and subsequently died, we would show little hesitation in attributing the cause of the man's death to the ingestion of the arsenic. Should we be further informed that the unfortunate man had enjoyed a cucumber sandwich prior to the arsenic, we would regard such intelligence as extraneous to the causal diagnosis of his death. Why? Our causal beliefs about the matter could be summarized by saying: arsenic will kill you, but cucumbers won't.

The covering law model of explanation, a historical descendent of Hume's analysis of the concept of cause, is in the first instance an attempt to analyze the nature of causal relationships. According to that model, all causal relationships must be expressible by means of sentences of universal conditional form. If the consumption of arsenic is causally connected to the advent of death, if arsenic kills, then that causal relationship must be expressible, on the covering law model, by means of a sentence of universal conditional form: if *anyone* swallows arsenic, then he will die. The word "anyone" signals the universality of the generalization. The expression "if . . . then . . ." signals the conditionality of the generalization. A causal explanation of the death of a man poisoned by arsenic will consist of two parts: first, a sentence is required which states that the man whose death we are trying to explain did in fact consume arsenic; and, second, a sentence of universal conditional form is needed from which, together with the first sentence, the sentence which states that the man did in fact die is deducible.

From the sentence "Harry consumed one hundred grains of arsenic" and the sentence "If anyone consumes a hundred grains of arsenic, then he will die," one can deduce the sentence "Harry will die." If Harry is already dead and we are informed that prior to his death he consumed one hundred grains of arsenic, then deducing "Harry died" from "Harry consumed one hundred grains of arsenic" and "If anyone consumes one hundred grains of arsenic, then he dies" amounts, according to the covering law model, to giving a causal explanation of his death. If, however, Harry has just swallowed the arsenic but has not yet expired, deducing "Harry dies" ("Harry will die") from the requisite two sentences amounts to *predicting* that Harry will die. Enthusiasts of the covering law model in its original formulation maintained that explanation and prediction are "structurally identical."

What are the advantages of the covering law model? Perhaps the most succinct rehearsal of its philosophical appeal was tendered by one of its strongest critics:

If it is supposed that an explanation need not logically entail what it explains, but may be consistent with several other possibilities, then it will fail to explain why one or other of those possibilities was not realized, *i.e.* it will fail to explain why what it purports to explain should have happened rather than something else. Now, it may be contended, no statement that a certain individual happening took place can be logically derived from other statements about individual happenings except by way of general laws.[1]

There is yet another satisfaction provided by the covering law model, one that has passed unnoticed but which, I think, has contributed much to its allure. The covering law model seems to offer a powerful and uniform method for examining all causal claims, from the most recondite of the sciences to the most mundane of workaday technologies. We can reject, apparently, the claim that a certain woman caused, by stroking a broomstick, a cow to run dry simply by inquiring whether, whenever broomsticks are stroked, cows' udders dry up. Did the imbibing of one hundred grains of arsenic cause Harry's death? According to the covering law model, if swallowing one hundred grains caused Harry's death, then it must be true that, whenever anyone swallows one hundred grains of arsenic, he dies. For many of its adherents, the covering law model seemed to provide not only a correct analysis of the concept of cause but a decision procedure for both accepting and rejecting causal claims as well. Superstition could become instant science, it almost seemed, simply by convincing witches to try to cast their spells in sentences of universal conditional form.

Let us take a closer look at the covering law model by asking first whether it really presents us with a method for *reject-*

[1] Alan Donagan, "Explanation in History," in *Theories of History*, p. 430.

ing causal claims. Should we base our entire argument against witchcraft on our inability to formulate true generalizations such as "Whenever broomsticks are stroked, cows' udders dry up"? Those whose view of science has the covering law model of explanation as a focal point will be disposed to reduce the argument against witchcraft to just such simple terms. Did Judy, the witching woman, cause Harry's cow to run dry by rubbing her broomstick? Just let her try the same trick with Sam's "25,000 pounder" Holstein. Should the witch fail to bring it off with the Holstein, then it is false that, whenever broomsticks are stroked, cows' udders dry up. Hence, the witch didn't cause Harry's cow to run dry in the first place. Farewell to witchcraft, on with science.

Matters are not quite so simple, however. Judy could have had a bad day with Sam's Holstein or used the wrong spell—any number of things might have gone wrong. If she caused Harry's cow to run dry, must it be the case that, whenever broomsticks are rubbed, cows' udders *invariably* dry up? Note that we are not so exacting in the arsenic situation. Is it really true that anyone who swallowed one hundred grains of arsenic would die on the spot? Are there no antidotes, stomach pumps, differences in individual tolerances, and so on? To save the covering law model as a rejection procedure, one must be able to crib a generalization with enough qualifications to make it true universally. I am not sure that this cribbing can be done for any generalization of the kind being considered. Those generalizations that *do* hold universally, such as the second law of thermodynamics, are quite remote from the causal pushes and pulls of everyday experience. The covering law model of explanation cannot be used as a simple rejection procedure for causal claims. One surely would not reject the causal diagnosis that Harry was killed by the arsenic because one could not set down the exact qualifications under which the generalization would become true.

Suppose, though, that science could, in all circumstances,

be carried to the *n*th decimal point. Suppose we could precisely type individuals according to their poison tolerances and could formulate the very conditions—without using blanket expressions such as "unless a suitable antidote is taken"—which permitted filling in universal conditional schemata in a way that would produce a true generalization that really *covered* all the contingencies of the individual cases under its scope. Imagine it were possible to do this for all instances of genuine causal attribution. Could the covering law model of explanation then serve either as an acceptance procedure or as a positive criterion of intelligibility for the concept of cause? Unfortunately, as far as the covering law model is concerned, the answer is negative. Consider poor Harry once more. Harry was unlucky, everyone will agree, because he swallowed arsenic. No one but a cucumberphobe would have the slightest inclination to blame Harry's death on Harry's last cucumber sandwich. Nonetheless, the following generalization is true: if anyone eats a cucumber sandwich, then he will die. It is true because everyone, sooner or later, dies. And if *everyone* sooner or later dies, then everyone with red hair sooner or later dies. And the same thing goes for cucumberphiles (as well as cucumberphobes). Hence, if *anyone* eats a cucumber sandwich, then he will die. From the sentence "If anyone eats a cucumber sandwich, then he will die" and the sentence "Harry ate a cucumber sandwich," one can deduce that Harry will die. Still, no one supposes that Harry's death is explained by his consumption of a cucumber sandwich. Although the universal conditional generalization is true, cucumbers did not *kill* Harry. The covering law model of explanation, which purports to be an analysis of the concept of cause, simply fails to capture the essence of any causal relation expressed by the schema "x kills y." It fails both as a positive and as a negative criterion of the concept of cause.

Covering law enthusiasts, to be sure, were well aware that a great deal of further clarification of their model was necessary before one could demonstrate its adequacy as a criterion for the concept of causal explanation. No one supposed that every true sentence of universal conditional form expresses a causal law of nature. Thus, to use an example similar to those cited by covering law enthusiasts, imagine that in a little park situated in Stavanger there exists a bench upon which black-haired Norwegians, but only black-haired Norwegians, sit. One does not explain why Tordenskjold has black hair by pointing out that every Norwegian who sits on that particular bench (which is Tordenskjold's favorite bench) has black hair. Why not? Carl Hempel, in a famous essay entitled "Studies in the Logic of Explanation," suggested that the trouble stems from the reference to a particular object (the park bench) and a particular space-time region (present-day Stavanger) which prevents the generalization from being purely universal in outlook:

> More specifically, the idea suggests itself of permitting a predicate in a fundamental lawlike sentence only if it is purely universal, or, as we shall say, purely qualitative, in character; in other words, if a statement of its meaning does not require reference to any one particular object or spatio-temporal location. Thus, the terms "soft," "green," "warmer than," "as long as," "liquid," "electrically charged," "female," "father of," are purely qualitative predicates, while "taller than the Eiffel Tower," "medieval," "lunar," "arctic," "Ming," are not.[2]

The restriction proposed by Hempel would accomplish its objective: it would rule the argument which purports to account for Tordenskjold's black hair as nonexplanatory. One may, of course, disagree with Hempel's reasons for excluding that argument, but I shall not debate that issue here. Note, though, that Hempel's restriction would block any spe-

[2] "Studies in the Logic of Explanation," reprinted in *Aspects of Scientific Explanation*, pp. 268-269.

cific attempt on the part of historians to account for the occurrences of particular historical events by means of limited historical generalizations. F. J. Teggart's study of the barbarian invasions of Rome between 58 B.C. and A.D. 107 is a case in point. Given the kinds of tasks historians set for themselves, it seems almost inevitable that any generalization formulated by them would involve temporal and spatial restrictions from the outset. How could historians heed a model of explanation which deems limited historical generalizations to be useless for explaining the occurrences of particular historical events? The covering law model of explanation, in one of its most important modifications, presents a utopian ideal so far as the study of history goes. And that in itself is a reason to seek to dislodge discussion of its merits and demerits from center stage in the philosophy of history.[3]

There is an even better reason for playing down the covering law issue in the philosophy of history, however. The search for causes, on the covering law model, is portrayed as a search for universal laws, as an attempt to elicit laws of nature, such as the second law of thermodynamics, which hold unconditionally for all space-time regions. Although scientific glory is often measured by the range and scope of the laws of nature discovered, not all scientific activity is directed to so lofty a goal. In particular, it is a serious error to identify the search for causes with the attempt to formulate laws of nature. Searching for causes, one seeks what can be called "causal mechanisms," which are presumed to underlie the phenomenon that wants explaining. "What makes the hands of a clock go round?" That is the sort of query that makes one reach for a screwdriver, not a table of logarithms. It is a causal question—practical in scope, mechanistic in outlook, the very reverse of recondite. The search for causes, on the covering

---

[3] See the author's article "Some Problems of Causal Explanation," *Mind*, LXXII (1963), 519-532, for a more extended discussion of some of the above points.

law model of explanation, seems more an affair of attempting to formulate the second law of thermodynamics than a matter of examining the interplay of gears and springs. Historians, when hunting for causes, are looking for social, political, or economic mechanisms. And just as one can discover and understand the mechanism of a clock without knowing anything about the laws of mechanics, so it is possible for historians to discover and understand the mechanisms underlying historical events without knowing anything about laws of history.

One should not really be surprised that the covering law model of explanation should, on closer inspection, be found to fit the study of history so poorly. The positivist view of science which fathered the model placed history on the lowest rung of the epistemological ladder. Nor is it surprising, I suppose, that so astute a philosopher as Carl Hempel should have completely missed the significance of Darwin's theory of evolution. Darwinian theory, at bottom, suggests a causal mechanism underlying a series of historical changes. The theory nourishes the understanding of how those changes came about, though it does not provide a table for precisely calculating the appearance and disappearance of species. The covering law model, in contrast, equates the causal understanding of how events happen with the calculation (prediction) of their occurrences. (It is interesting to note that Hempel's discussion of Darwinian theory occurs in a passage defending the position that every adequate explanation is potentially a prediction.) The covering law model does a disservice not only to the study of history but to many other branches of science as well.

It is fitting, in a way, that the main defects of the covering law model of explanation should show up so glaringly when one attempts to apply the model to Darwinian theory. A theory of evolution, after all, is basically a theory about history, and positivistically inclined philosophers were never much inclined in a historical direction. Positivistic philosophy of science is ahistorical in outlook and remote from the history of science it-self. The reasons for this ahistoricism are complex. The expla-nation is not so much that philosophers of science who flew the banners of positivism had little to do with historians of science, professionally speaking. Nor is it that positivistic philosophers of science did not have a working knowledge of science. Some of them had advanced degrees in one or the other of the natural sciences. The trouble lay in the fact that logical positivists had nothing special to say about the *history* of science; they accepted uncritically the usual story-lines upon which most orthodox history of science is constructed. But then the positivist tradition contained, as an integral part, a rather shallow story-line of its own—Comte's story-line, ac-cording to which the direction of science is toward the aban-donment of metaphysics in favor of the calculation of appear-ances and disappearances of phenomena which, like colored lights flashing upon a dark board, reveal nothing of a deeper structure underlying them.

True, modern positivists have paid little attention to Comte. Nonetheless, it seems as if modern positivism has been a victim of its own historical tradition. What positivism lacked, I con-tend, was a penetrating speculative philosophy of the history of science, the encouragement to fashion story-lines upon which better histories of science could be constructed. Just as there is more to history than orthodox political history, so is there more to speculative philosophy of history than Hegel's philosophy of history, which is, essentially, a speculative phi-losophy of *political* history. Each kind of history requires its own kind of speculative philosophy of history. Until that point is fully appreciated by professional analytical philos-ophers, analytical philosophy of history will consist largely of hand-me-downs from analytical philosophy of science, a sub-ject itself in urgent need of nourishment from the history of science.

SUGGESTIONS FOR FURTHER READING

A series entitled "Bibliography of Works in the Philosophy of History" may be found in the journal *History and Theory*: 1945-57 compiled by John C. Rule, Beiheft 1 (1961), 1958-61 by M. Nowicki, Beiheft 3 (1964), and 1962-65 by Lewis P. Wurgaft, Beiheft 7 (1967). For a list of articles and books published prior to 1945, see R. Thompson's "Selective Reading List on History and the Philosophy of History" in the Social Science Research Council's *Theory and Practice in Historical Study: Report of the Committee on Historiography* (New York, 1946). A forthcoming book by Paul K. Conkin and Roland Stromberg, to be published by Dodd, Mead and Company, tentatively entitled *History: Its History and Its Theory*, contains an excellent bibliography on historiographical subjects.

There are two excellent anthologies on philosophy of history, one edited by a philosopher and the other by a historian: Patrick Gardiner, *Theories of History* (Glencoe, Ill.: The Free Press, 1959), and Fritz Stern, *The Varieties of History* (New York: Meridian Books, 1956). Another collection of readings may be found in Hans Meyerhoff, ed., *The Philosophy of History In Our Time: An Anthology* (Garden City, N.Y.: Doubleday Anchor Books, 1959). The Gardiner and Meyerhoff volumes contain useful bibliographies.

I have stressed the importance of the concept of the narrative in the writing of history. Those who wish to pursue that topic should read F. J. Teggart, *Theory and Processes of History* (Berkeley: University of California Press, 1960), W. B. Gallie, *Philosophy and the Historical Understanding* (New York: Schocken Books, 1964), and Arthur C. Danto, *Analytical Philosophy of History* (Cambridge: At the University Press, 1965). Two articles on the subject are William H. Dray, "Explanatory Narrative in History," *Philosophical Quarterly*, IV (1954), 15-28, and W. H. Walsh, " 'Plain' and 'Significant'

Narrative in History," *Journal of Philosophy*, LXV (1958), 479-484. A symposium on the logic of historical narration is contained in Sidney Hook, ed., *Philosophy and History* (New York: New York University Press, 1963). Another discussion may be found in Maurice Mandelbaum, "A Note on History as Narrative," *History and Theory*, VI (1967), 413-419, with replies by Richard Ely, William H. Dray, and Rolf Grumer, *History and Theory*, VIII (1969), 275-294. See also A. R. Louch, "History as Narrative," *History and Theory*, VIII (1969), 54-70. Many important books are structured on the problem of historical objectivity: R. Aron, *Introduction to the Philosophy of History* (London: Weidenfeld and Nicolson, 1938), Maurice Mandelbaum, *The Problem of Historical Knowledge* (New York: Liveright, 1938), and W. H. Walsh, *Introduction to Philosophy of History* (New York: Hutchinson, 1951). Morton White's *Foundations of Historical Knowledge* (New York: Harper & Row, 1965) is of special interest because it relates problems of objectivity to problems of narration. See also Sidney Hook, "Objectivity and Reconstruction in History," Maurice Mandelbaum, "Objectivity in History," and Ernest Nagel, "Relativism and Some Problems of Working Historians," all in Sidney Hook, ed., *Philosophy and History*. Two important articles on objectivity are Christopher Blake, "Can History Be Objective?" *Mind*, LXIV (1955), 61-78, reprinted in Gardiner's *Theories of History*, and J. A. Passmore, "The Objectivity of History," *Philosophy*, XXXIII (1958), 97-111, reprinted in William H. Dray, ed., *Philosophical Analysis and History* (New York: Harper & Row, 1966).

Questions concerning the objectivity of history are tightly linked with attitudes toward historical skepticism and the possibility of obtaining historical knowledge. J. W. Meiland, *Scepticism and Historical Knowledge* (New York: Random House, 1965), presents a viewpoint different from my own. A. J. Ayer, *The Problem of Knowledge* (London: Macmillan & Co., 1958), contains relevant discussion of skepticism. On

the concept of the past and the meaning of historical state-
ments, two topics closely connected with historical skepticism,
see C. I. Lewis, *An Analysis of Knowledge and Valuation*
(La Salle, Ill.: Open Court Publishing Co., 1946), E. Masi,
"A Note on Lewis' Analysis of the Meaning of Historical
Statements," *Journal of Philosophy*, XLVI (1949), 670-674,
I. Scheffler, "Verifiability in History: A Reply to Miss Masi,"
Journal of Philosophy, XLVII (1950), 158-166, and A. J. Ayer,
"Statements About the Past," in his *Philosophical Essays* (Lon-
don: Macmillan & Co., 1959). Other articles in this area include
G.E.M. Anscombe, "The Reality of the Past," in Max Black,
ed., *Philosophical Analysis* (Ithaca, N.Y.: Cornell University
Press, 1950), E. J. Bond, "The Conception of the Past," *Mind*,
LXXII (1963), 533-544, and J. Nelson, "The Validation of
Memory and Our Conception of a Past," *Philosophical Review*,
LXXII (1963), 35-47.

Although I have treated the topic of historical explanation
in a cursory way, it has traditionally been of the greatest interest in the philosophy of history. Perhaps the best single volume
presenting and defending the covering law model of explanation is Carl Hempel, *Aspects of Scientific Explanation* (New
York: The Free Press, 1965), which also contains an excellent
bibliography. For works somewhat critical of the covering law
model, see Patrick Gardiner, *The Nature of Historical Explanation* (London: Oxford University Press, 1952), William H.
Dray, *Laws and Explanation in History* (London: Oxford
University Press, 1957), and H.L.A. Hart and A. M. Honoré,
Causation in the Law (Oxford: Clarendon Press, 1959). My
comments on the Hart and Honoré work appear in *Inquiry*,
IX (1966), 322-338. Some philosophers, in partial reaction to
the positivistic account of the nature of explanation, have
explored the concept of action and its bearing on the explana-
tion of human conduct. See G.E.M. Anscombe, *Intention*
(Ithaca, N.Y.: Cornell University Press, 1957), R. S. Peters,
The Concept of Motivation (London: Routledge & Kegan

Paul, 1958), and also A. I. Melden, *Free Action* (London: Routledge & Kegan Paul, 1961), Jonathan Bennett, *Rationality* (New York: Humanities Press, 1964), and D. G. Brown, *Action* (Toronto: University of Toronto Press, 1968). *Readings in the Theory of Action*, ed. Norman S. Care and Charles Landesman (Bloomington: Indiana University Press, 1968), contains a number of interesting essays on this topic.

Many writers take Collingwood's position that history is quite different from science or that, insofar as history is a social science, social science is totally distinct from natural science. See, for example, Isaiah Berlin, "The Concept of Scientific History," *History and Theory*, 1 (1960), 1-31, reprinted in Dray, *Philosophical Analysis and History*, and also Berlin's *Historical Inevitability* (London: Oxford University Press, 1954). A critique of Berlin's thesis is contained in Ernest Nagel, "Determinism in History," *Philosophy and Phenomenological Research*, xx (1959-60), 291-317. An orientation similar to Berlin's is expressed in W. Rotenstreich, *Between Past and Present: An Essay on History* (New Haven: Yale University Press, 1958). The case for the autonomy of social science is made in Peter Winch, *The Idea of a Social Science* (London: Routledge & Kegan Paul, 1958).

Among American historians it has become unfashionable to pick quarrels with social science. Since the fifties a number of attempts have been made to integrate methodological practices. See, for example, the Social Science Research Council's *The Social Sciences in Historical Study*, Bulletin 64 (1954), Louis Gottshalk, *Generalization in the Writing of History* (Chicago: University of Chicago Press, 1963), R. Hofstadter, ed., *Sociology and History: Methods* (New York: Basic Books, 1968), and "Studies in the Quantitative History and the Logic of the Social Sciences," *History and Theory*, Beiheft 9 (1969).

Historians often prefer to approach the philosophy of history via the historiographical route. See, for example, Louis Gottschalk, *Understanding History* (New York: Alfred A. Knopf,

1950). Two interesting exceptions are E. H. Carr, *What Is History?* (London: Macmillan & Co., 1961), and John Lukas, *Historical Consciousness* (New York: Harper & Row, 1968). See also P. Geyl, P. Sorokin, and A. J. Toynbee, *The Pattern of the Past: Can We Determine It?* (Boston: Beacon Press, 1949). G. Iggers, in his *The German Conception of History* (Middletown, Conn.: Wesleyan University Press, 1968), explores some of the relationships between philosophy of history and historiography. A stimulating attack on analytical philosophy of history by a professional historian is J. H. Hexter's "The One That Got Away," *New York Review of Books*, Feb. 9, 1967, pp. 24-28. Hexter's article is a review of Danto's *Analytical Philosophy of History* and White's *Foundations of Historical Knowledge*. An exchange of letters between White and Hexter appears in the *New York Review of Books*, March 23, 1967, pp. 28-31.

Speculative philosophers of history, in the classical sense, were concerned with drawing the outlines of general histories of mankind. An excellent bibliography of primary and secondary sources on Bossuet, Vico, Montesquieu, Voltaire, Turgot, Kant, Herder, Condorcet, Hegel, Comte, Buckle, Feuerbach, Marx, Toynbee, Spengler, and others is included in Gardiner's *Theories of History.* See also Gardiner's essay "Metaphysics and History" in D. F. Pears, ed., *The Nature of Metaphysics* (London: Macmillan & Co., 1957). For a recent appraisal of the speculators, see Bruce Mazlish, *The Riddle of History* (New York: Harper & Row, 1966). Two interesting attempts by historians at tackling the history of mankind in a speculative fashion are Geoffrey Barraclough, *History in a Changing World* (Oxford: Basil Blackwell, 1955), and F. Manuel, *Shapes of Philosophical History* (Stanford: Stanford University Press, 1965). Speculative philosophies of history that have received the widest attention recently are either Marxist or Freudian in orientation, or a bit of both: for example, Norman O. Brown, *Life Against Death* (Middletown, Conn.:

Wesleyan University Press, 1959), and Herbert Marcuse, *Eros and Civilization* (Boston: Beacon Press, 1955).

Each kind of history requires its own speculative approach. For professional philosophers, history of philosophy and history of science have been the most relevant kinds of history. Speculative philosophy of the history of philosophy tends to shade into historiographical discussions, on the one hand, and inquiries into the relationship between history of ideas and history of philosophy, on the other. The following list contains specimens of both types of discussion: G. Boas, "Bias and the History of Ideas," *Journal of the History of Ideas*, xxv (1964), 451-457, "The Role of Protophilosophies in Intellectual History," *Journal of Philosophy*, xlv (1948), 673-684, "Some Problems of Intellectual History," in *Studies in Intellectual History* (Baltimore: Johns Hopkins University Press, 1953); Harold Cherniss, "The History of Ideas and Ancient Greek Philosophy," in Boas, *Studies in Intellectual History*; R. Ingarden, "Reflections on the Subject Matter of History and Philosophy," *Diogenes*, xxix (1960), 111-121; Eugene Kamenka, "Marxism and the History of Philosophy," *History and Theory*, Beiheft 5 (1965), 83-104; P. O. Kristeller, "History of Philosophy and History of Ideas," *Journal of the History of Philosophy*, ii (1964), 1-14; Arthur O. Lovejoy, *The Great Chain of Being* (New York: Harper & Row, 1960), "Reflections on the History of Ideas," *Journal of the History of Ideas*, i (1940), 3-23; Maurice Mandelbaum, "A. O. Lovejoy and the Theory of Historiography," *Journal of the History of Ideas*, ix (1948), 412-423, "Concerning Recent Trends in the Theory of Historiography," *Journal of the History of Ideas*, xvi (1955), 506-517, "The History of Ideas, Intellectual History, and the History of Philosophy," *History and Theory*, Beiheft 5 (1965), 33-66; John Passmore, "A Critique of a Recent History of Philosophy" (review of J. H. Randall's *The Career of Philosophy*), *Scientific American*, 208 (May 1963), 177-182, "The Idea of a History of Philosophy," *History and Theory*, Beiheft 5

(1965), 1-32; John H. Randall, "Arthur O. Lovejoy and the History of Ideas," *Philosophy and Phenomenological Research*, XXIII (1962-63), 475-479; Harold R. Smart, *Philosophy and Its History* (La Salle, Ill.: Open Court Publishing Co., 1962); W. H. Walsh, "Hegel on the History of Philosophy," *History and Theory*, Beiheft 5 (1965), 67-82; P. Wiener, "The Central Role of Time in Lovejoy's Philosophy," *Philosophy and Phenomenological Research*, XXIII (1962-63), 480-492, "The Logical Significance of the History of Thought," *Journal of the History of Ideas*, VII (1946), 366-373, "Some Problems and Methods in the History of Ideas," *Journal of the History of Ideas*, XXII (1961), 531-548.

Philosophy of science has been an important branch of Anglo-American philosophy since the 1930s. Until quite recently, however, philosophers paid little attention to the actual history of science, being content to develop what was called "a rational reconstruction" of science. A new awareness of the history of science has led to the development of a historical school among philosophers of science, and it is here that one must look for speculations about the meaning and significance of the history of science. The discussion has recently been joined by professional historians of science. See Peter Achinstein, "On the Meaning of Scientific Terms," *Journal of Philosophy*, LXI (1964), 497-509; Joseph Agassi, "Towards an Historiography of Science," *History and Theory*, Beiheft 2 (1963); M. Bunge, *Causality: The Place of the Causal Principle in Modern Science* (Cambridge, Mass.: Harvard University Press, 1959); Joseph T. Clark, "The Philosophy of Science and the History of Science," in Marshall Claggett, ed., *Critical Problems in the History of Science* (Madison: University of Wisconsin Press, 1959); I. E. Drabkin, "Commentary on the Papers of A. C. Crombie and Joseph T. Clark," in Claggett, *Critical Problems in the History of Science*; P. K. Feyerabend, "How to Be a Good Empiricist: A Plea For Tolerance in Matters Epistemological," in *The Delaware Seminar in Philosophy of Science*, II (New York: Interscience, 1963); Arthur Fine, "Consistency, Derivability, and Scientific Change," *Journal of Philosophy*, LXIV (1967), 231-240; A. Grünbaum, "The Relevance of Philosophy to the History of the Special Theory of Relativity," *Journal of Philosophy*, LIX (1962), 561-573; R. Hahn, "Reflections on the History of Science," *Journal of the History of Philosophy*, III (1965), 235-242; N. R. Hanson, "The Irrelevance of History of Science to the Philosophy of Science," *Journal of Philosophy*, LIX (1962), 574-585, *Patterns of Discovery* (Cambridge: At the University Press, 1958); H. R. Harré, *The Principles of Scientific Thinking* (Chicago: University of Chicago Press, 1970); Thomas Kuhn, *The Structure of Scientific Revolutions* (Chicago: University of Chicago Press, 1962); a second edition of *The Structure of Scientific Revolutions* that will contain a long postscript is in press; a forthcoming volume containing papers on topics in the history and philosophy of science by T. S. Kuhn, J.W.N. Watkins, and others is *Criticism and the Growth of Knowledge*, ed. I. Lakatos and A. Musgrave (Cambridge: At the University Press, 1970); Louis Mink, "Comment on Stephen Toulmin's 'Conceptual Revolutions in Science,'" *Synthesis*, XVII (1967), 92-99; Ernest Nagel, "Commentary on the Papers of A. C. Crombie and Joseph T. Clark," in Claggett, *Critical Problems in the History of Science*; Karl Popper, "The Nature of Philosophical Problems and Their Roots in Science," and "Science: Conjectures and Refutations," in his *Conjectures and Refutations* (New York: Basic Books, 1962); Stephen Toulmin, "Conceptual Revolutions in Science," *Synthesis*, XVII (1967), 75-92, and *Foresight and Understanding* (Bloomington: Indiana University Press, 1961).

INDEX

327